A Course In Miracles In Sight

A Guide For The Visual Learner

Christopher R Scott

ACKNOWLEDGEMENTS

With deep appreciation and gratitude to Robert Scott, without whose great artwork contributions this book would be far less. And thank you Jesus and everyone for *A Course In Miracles*.

"Does not the Lord go out before you?"

Deborah, Judges 4:14

"Face to the reality."

J S Bach

Table of Contents

PREFACE

About *A Course in Miracles* and this book

As you read the teachings of the Apostles, remember that I told them myself that there was much they would understand later, because they were not wholly ready to follow me at the time. ...I do not call for martyrs but for teachers.

A Course In Miracles is a challenging, epic masterpiece of spiritual ontology and psychological architecture, gracefully interwoven with the practical application of its principles. It is also a beautiful poetic tome well ahead of its time, versed in biblical language, and written in a voice spoken with authority and without fear. The Course's teachings are radically divergent from those of the world, which, according to the Course, is itself the effect of an aberrant thought system, the ego,–*an evil flower with no roots at all,*–that was caused by a wish of the mind. Many such concepts are difficult to accept until understood, which can take much persistence and commitment.

This book, as its title suggests, offers a pictoral vantage of the course's realm, although its intent is not to simplify it nor to dumb it down. While the Course presents itself in a non-linear, somewhat homogenized format, this book consists of three sections, showing:

1. The one reality of Self in Heaven in which God created One.
2. The fancied and the unreal separated ego self.
3. The process of forgiveness, wherein one realizes that one never left 1.

There is reiteration of essential concepts, depicted in varied form. The human unconscious communicates, in part, in a language of sight (*My thoughts are images that I have made*); therefore this book's emphasis on visual aids may help quicken the reader's grasp of topics that are often parried with profound ego resistance.

Most of the included commentary is taken directly from the Course so as to avoid ambiguity, although there are many examples within *A Course In Miracles* that appear to be inconsistent in language, but not in meaning. Some Course students, inevitably, however, may not agree with this book's interpretations and or may find them perplexing.

All type in italics is quotation taken from *A Course In Miracles*, as is all exo-diagram type, and some sections conclude with many related Course quotes.

T 6 I 16.1,3   T 24 II 3.3   W 15   [**T**ext/**W**orkbook/**M**anual_chapter_section_paragraph.sentence]

A brief overview of *A Course In Miracles*

A Course In Miracles was scribed by Helen Schucman, a Columbia University academic, via an inner voice,–*the Voice*, Jesus,–in a process that she described as inner dictation. A colleague of hers, William Thetford, collaborated with her in the course's manifestation[1].

This is a course in miracles. A miracle is of the Christ Mind and is simply an awareness of the reunion of effect to cause, or the bringing back of ideas to their source. By this, it recognizes that every occurrence of unhappiness is an irrevocable portent and memory from: One's wish to banish Heaven; to maintain the mind's delusion of separation from its Creator; to become the god of oneself. Yet through this, the miracle also awakens one to see beyond wishes to one's only true Cause: *I am forever an effect of God.* It restores Christ's vision to the dissonant mind that tried to hide from its Self, and it is the correction of purpose from the fragmenting fear of the ego-mind to the unifying Joy of the Spirit-Mind. Through miracles, the mind is purified such that healing by the Holy Spirit be allowed, and that this healing be extended by Him through one to everyone, always. *This is a course in mind training.* It petitions the mind to singularly value its One True Self by contrasting the folly of valuing its false splintered self.

The Course does not aim to evince or attract self-determined manifestations of a more appealing life in this world, nor is it an instruction manual for walking on water. It is rather about healing the only error–one's wish to make oneself self-determined, unlike and apart from God–and by this is a joyous existence in the world a predestined inevitability.

A Course In Miracles appeals to motivate one to rise above the mind's and the world's conflicts that are accepted as normality, and that are called home. *Beyond this world there is a world I want.* While often it glamours otherwise, the separated person-body-world germinates from a thought system of attack, murder and fear; it is the expression of the belief in the separation from, and the opposition to, Oneness. The Course is all but mealymouthed in examining this, and in that sense, in its penetration of the tantruming rampage by which the ego so ingeniously obfuscates its modus, its wordage can be viewed as stern and dark. Yet of the Course's stylizations of non-ego, however, a gentle light rarely glimpsed in this existence is offered.

There is only one teacher of *A Course In Miracles* to the student. This teacher is the student's largely unconscious yet perfectly and eternally retained thought of its oneness with God, which the Course refers to as the Holy Spirit. All others, including "acknowledged teachers", study groups, this and other books, and indeed the *A Course In Miracles* book itself, can only point the student to the connection with this internal Teacher.

A dying world asks only that you rest an instant from attack upon yourself, that it be healed.

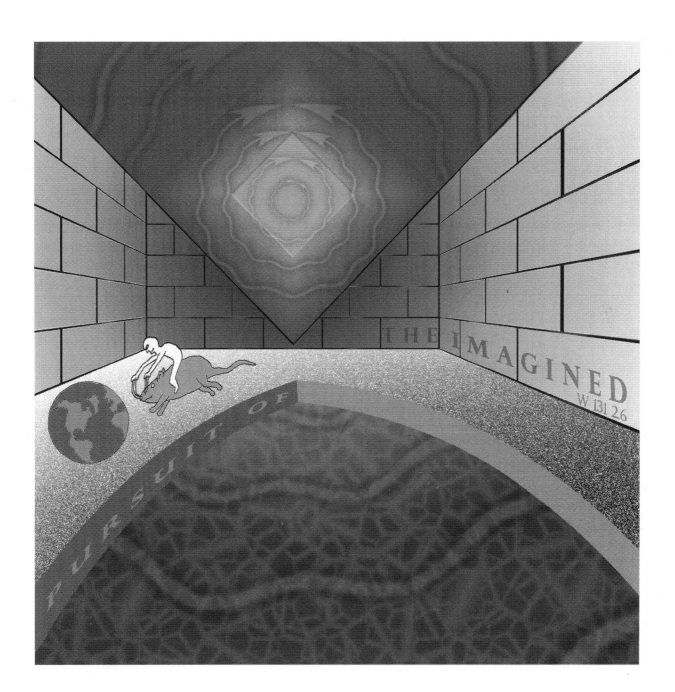

x

1. PREFACE p.vii-viii   T 26 VII 1.1   W 236   T 1 VII 4.1   W 129   T 27 V 5.5

INTRODUCTION

Attack, defence; defence, attack, become the circles of the hours and the days that bind the mind in heavy bands of steel with iron overlaid, returning but to start again. There seems to be no break nor ending in the ever-tightening grip of the imprisonment upon the mind.

W 153 3.2

Do you really want to be in hell? Do you really want to weep and suffer and die?

Tolerance for pain may be high, but it is not without limit. Eventually everyone begins to recognize, however dimly, that there must *be a better way.*

W 73 5.7   T 2 III 3.5-6

Now you are being shown you can escape.

An ancient miracle has come to bless and to replace an ancient enmity that came to kill.

...this course was sent to open up the path of light to us, and teach us, step by step, how to return to the eternal Self we thought we lost.

T 27 VI 2.1   T 26 IX 8.5   W Review V 5.4

o   o   o

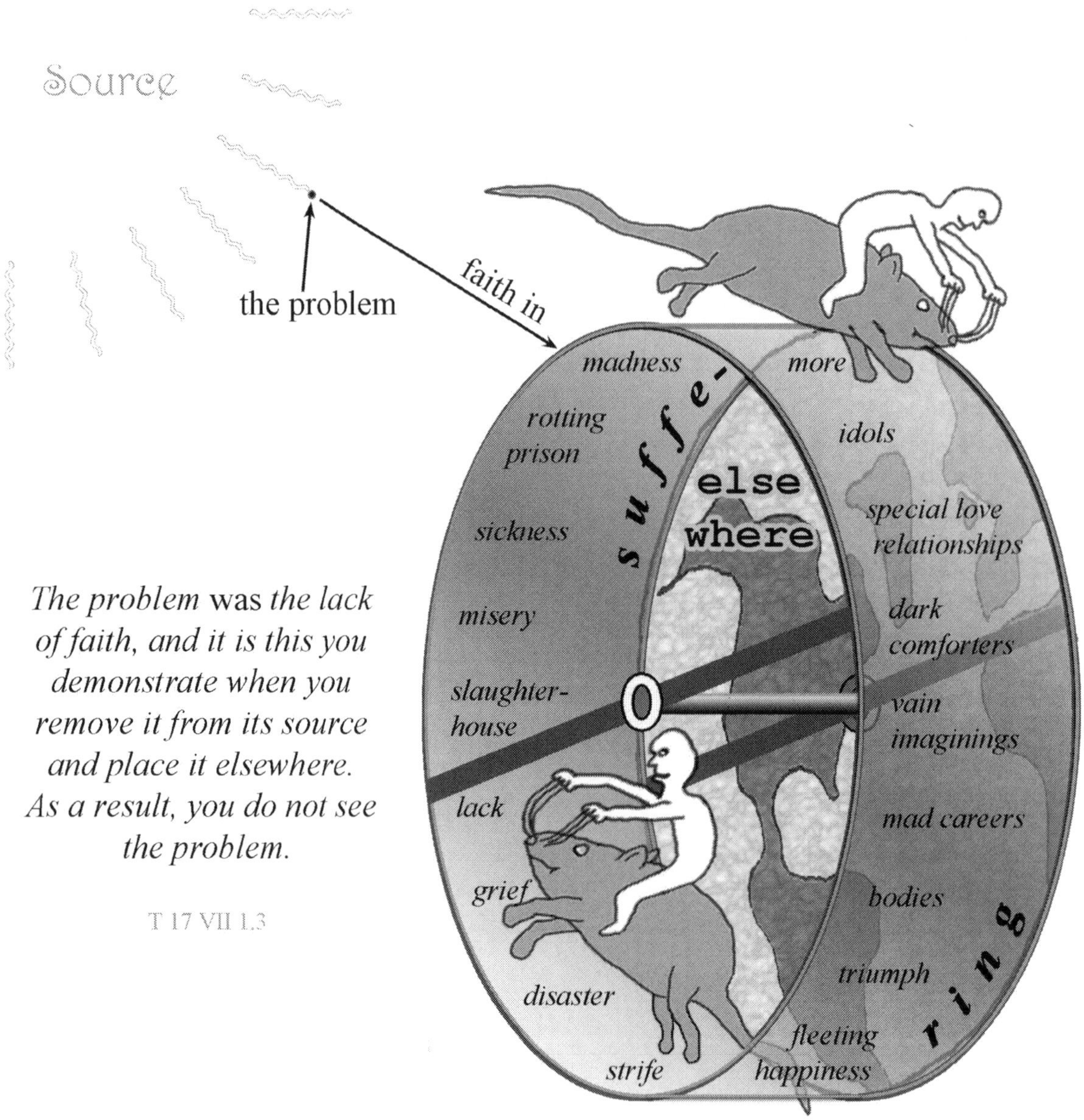

14

Source

the problem

faith in

madness   more

rotting prison   *idols*

s u f f e-   **else where**

sickness   *special love relationships*

misery   *dark comforters*

slaughter-house   *vain imaginings*

lack   *mad careers*

grief   *bodies*

triumph

r i n g

disaster   *fleeting happiness*

strife

The problem was the lack of faith, and it is this you demonstrate when you remove it from its source and place it elsewhere. As a result, you do not see the problem.

T 17 VII 1.3

Who would lay bloody hands on Heaven itself, and hope to find its peace?

And dwell not on the suffering and sin, for they are but reflections of their cause.

T 27 VII 5.8   T 29 V 6.5

This is a course in cause and not effect.   T 21 VII 8.4

o o o

What if you recognized this world is an hallucination? What if you really understood you made it up?

T 20 VIII 7.3-4

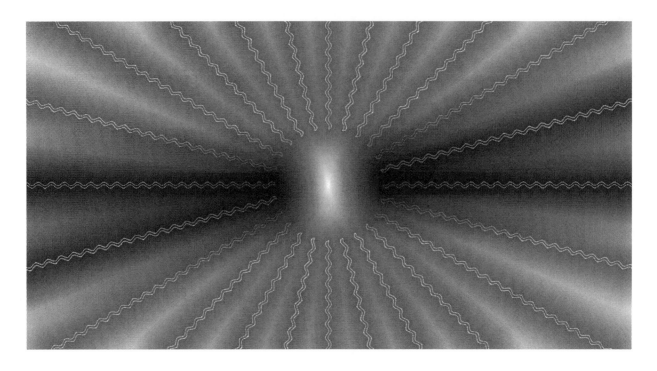

...you have removed part of your mind from God's Will. This means it is out of control.

T 10 IV 3 4-5

For you have gone from waking to sleeping, and on and on to a yet deeper sleep. Each dream has led to other dreams, and every fantasy that seemed to bring a light into the darkness but made the darkness deeper. Your goal was darkness, in which no ray of light could enter.

T 18 III 1.2-4

Home

away

You did this to yourself.

This is your chosen self, the one
you made as a replacement for reality.

T 21 II 5.4   T 18 II 5.10

...the journey into darkness has been long and cruel, and you have gone deep into it.

T 18 III 3.3

In your madness, you overlook reality completely…

You have taught yourself to believe that you are not what you are.

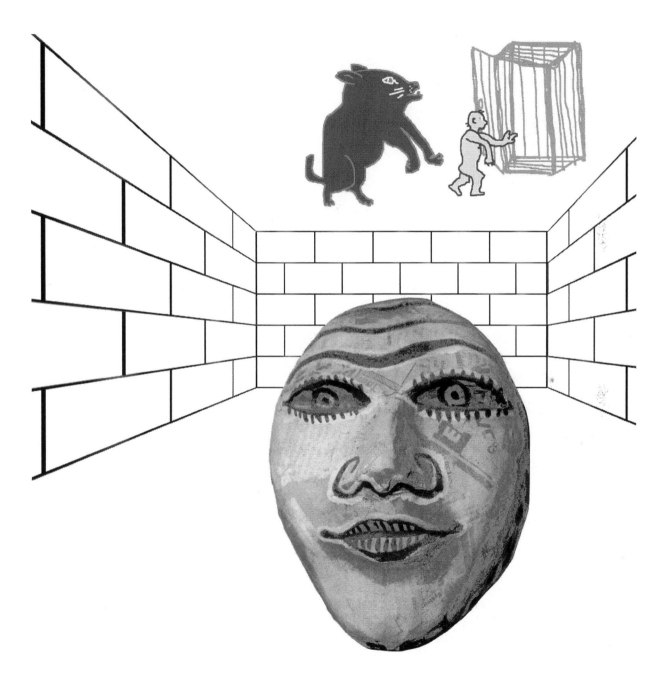

…you have taught yourself that imprisonment is freedom.

T 13 V 6.5   T 6 III 1.8   T 8 II 5.3

This sense of limitation is where all errors arise.

The mind can miscreate only when it believes it is not free.

T 9 IV 2.6   T 3 II 4.2

o   o   o

The miracle returns the cause of fear to you who made it.

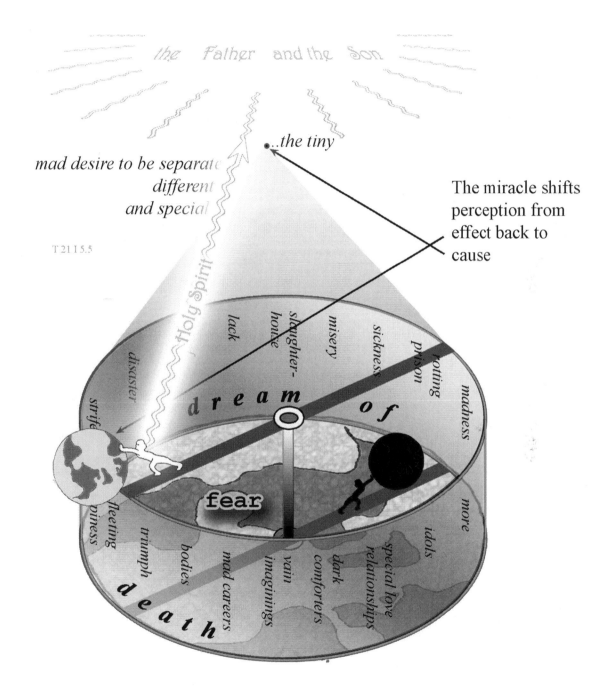

the Father and the Son

...the tiny

mad desire to be separate different and special

T 21 I 5.5

The miracle shifts perception from effect back to cause

Holy Spirit

lack

slaughter-house

misery

sickness

rotting prison

madness

disaster

strife

dream

of

fear

more

fleeting happiness

triumph

bodies

mad careers

vain imaginings

dark comforters

special love relationships

idols

death

A miracle inverts perception that was upside down before...

T 28 II 11.1   W II 13 2.3

A Course in Miracles teaches:

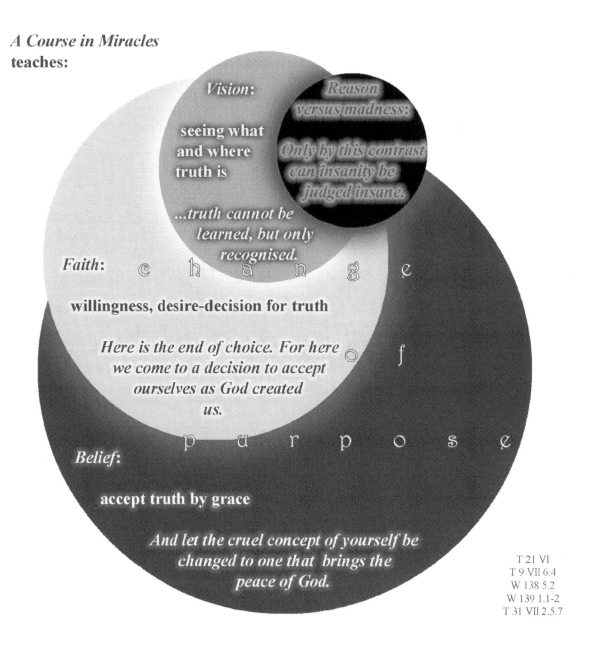

Vision:

seeing what and where truth is

...truth cannot be learned, but only recognised.

Reason versus madness:

Only by this contrast can insanity be judged insane.

Faith: change

willingness, desire-decision for truth

Here is the end of choice. For here we come to a decision to accept ourselves as God created us.

of purpose

Belief:

accept truth by grace

And let the cruel concept of yourself be changed to one that brings the peace of God.

T 21 VI
T 9 VII 6.4
W 138 5.2
W 139 1.1-2
T 31 VII 2.5.7

This course has explicitly stated that its goal for you is happiness and peace.

The decision whether or not to listen to this course and follow it is but the choice between truth and illusion. For here is truth, separated from illusion and not confused with it at all.

T 13 III 7.1   T 16 V 16.1-2

When you have learned that you belong to truth, it will flow lightly over you without a difference of any kind.

T 13 XI 6.6

Your new born purpose is nursed by angels,
cherished by the Holy Spirit and
protected by God Himself.

T 19 IV Ci 9.4

Chapter 1 ONE

1 I: Heaven

...past the gate
where
Oneness is.

T 26 III 3.5

Heaven is... an awareness of perfect oneness...

T 18 VI 1.5-6

*...the First in eternity is
God the Father, Who is both
First and
One.
Beyond the First there is no other,
for there is no order, no second
or third, and nothing
but the First.*

T 14 IV 1.7-8

*He is first in the sense that He is the First in the Holy Trinity Itself. He is the Prime Creator,
because He created His co-creators.*

*...The Will of God is without limit, and all power and glory lie within it. It is boundless in strength
and in love and in peace.*

The circle of creation has no end.

T 7 I 7.5-6   T 8 II 7.1-2   T 28 II 1.6

Nothing that God knows not exists. And what He knows exists forever, changelessly. For thoughts endure as long as does the mind that thought of them.

...God is   an idea...

...like   your Father,
you are   an idea...

Everything   is an idea.

T 15 VI 4.4   T 16 VI 4.5   T 5 I 2.4

The function of thought comes from God and is in God. As part of His Thought, you cannot *think apart from Him.*

And in the Mind of God there is no ending, nor a time in which His Thoughts were absent or could suffer change. Thoughts are not born and cannot die. They share the attributes of their creator, nor have they a separate life apart from his.

...you are the Son of God.

...The Son of God is you.

W 99 12.5   W 64 3.4

Because your Creator creates only like Himself, you are like Him. You are part of Him Who is all power and glory, and therefore as unlimited as He is.

God is not in you in a literal sense; you are part of Him.

Oneness is simply the idea God is. And in His Being, He encompasses all things.

The mind of Heaven's Son in Heaven is, for there the Mind of Father and of Son joined in creation which can have no end.

God has lit your mind Himself, and keeps your mind lit by His Light because His Light is what your mind is.

The Thought God holds of you is like a star, unchangeable in an eternal sky. So High in Heaven is it set that those outside of Heaven know not it is there.

The Son of God is one...

Every child of God is one in Christ...

T 30 III 6.1-3, 4-6   T 5 V 6.15-16   T 8 II 7.6-7   T 2 V 5.5   W 169 5.1-2   T 30 III 11.4   T 28 II 1.6   T 7 III 5
T 30 III 8.3-4   W II 9 5.6   T 12 VI 6.1

1 II: Laws of Creation

Cause and effect are one, not separate. God wills you learn what always has been true: That He created you as part of Him, and this must still be true because ideas leave not their source. Such is creation's law; that each idea the mind conceives but adds to its abundance, never takes away.

The law of creation Is that you love your creations [here: perceptions] *as yourself, because they are part of you.*

T 26 VII 13   T 10 I 1.3

A: *Cause and effect are one*

...cause and effect; the most fundamental law there is.

The cause
produces the effects,
which then
bear witness
to the cause,
and not themselves.

T 27 VII 5.5

Effects do not create their cause, but they establish its causation. Thus, the Son gives Fatherhood to his Creator, and receives the gift that he has given Him.

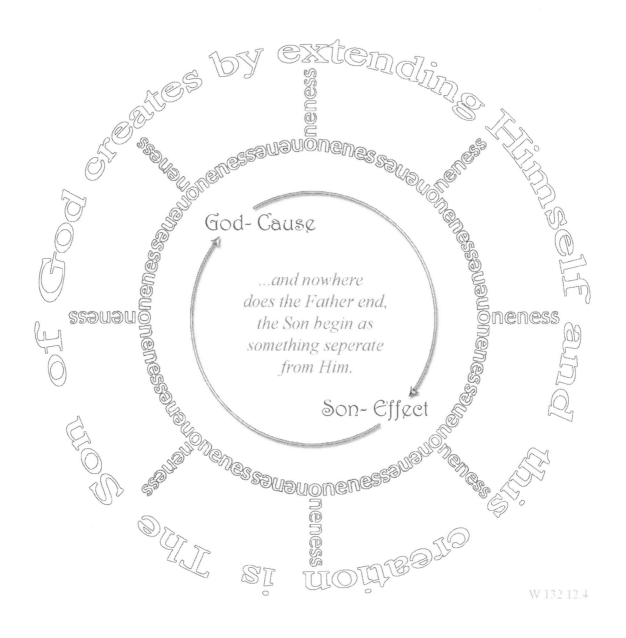

God creates by extending Himself and this creation is The Son of God

God- Cause

...and nowhere does the Father end, the Son begin as something seperate from Him.

Son- Effect

oneness

W 132 12.4

...God created you by extending Himself as you...

T 26 VII 13.1   T 26 VII 13.1   T 2 VII 1.4   T 28 II 1.3-4   T 7 I 5.2

Cause and effect but replicate creation.

Without a cause there can be no effects,

and yet without effects there is no cause.

no gravity

no attraction

no attraction

no gravity

...what has no effect does not exist...

Actually, "Cause" is a term properly belonging to God, and His "Effect" is His Son. This entails a set of Cause and Effect relationships totally different from those you introduce into miscreation.

Thus, cause and effect in Truth is not fathomable here, as:
No one on earth can grasp what Heaven is, or what one Creator really means.

T 28 II 1.1   T 11 V 2.5   T 2 VII 3.11-12   M 23 6.1

God is a Means as well as End. In Heaven, means and end are one, and one with Him. This is the state of true creation, found not within time, but in eternity. To no one here is this describable.

M 5 II 4.10   T 24 VII 6.5-8

B: *Ideas leave not their source*

Ideas leave not their source... It is the reason you can heal. It is the cause of healing. It is why you cannot die. Its truth established you as one with God.

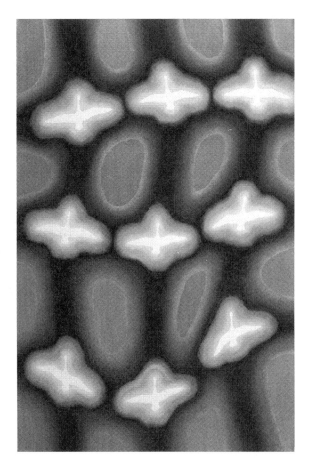

Ideas remain united to their source. They can extend all that their source contains. In that, they can go far beyond themselves. But they can not give birth to what was never given them. ...And where they come from, there will they return.

T 26 VII 4.7   W 167 3,5

The result of an idea is never separate from its source.

The thoughts you think are in your mind, as you are in the Mind Which thought of you. And so there are no separate parts in what exists within God's Mind. It is forever one, eternally united and at peace.

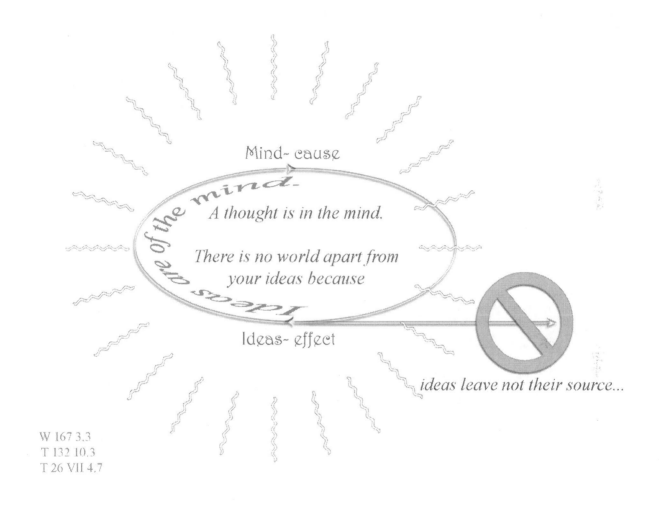

Mind- cause

Ideas are of the mind.

A thought is in the mind.

There is no world apart from your ideas because

Ideas- effect

ideas leave not their source...

W 167 3.3
T 132 10.3
T 26 VII 4.7

If this be true, how can you be apart from God? How could you walk the world alone and separate from your Source?

T 19 I 7.6   T 30 III 6.7-9   W 156 1.4-5

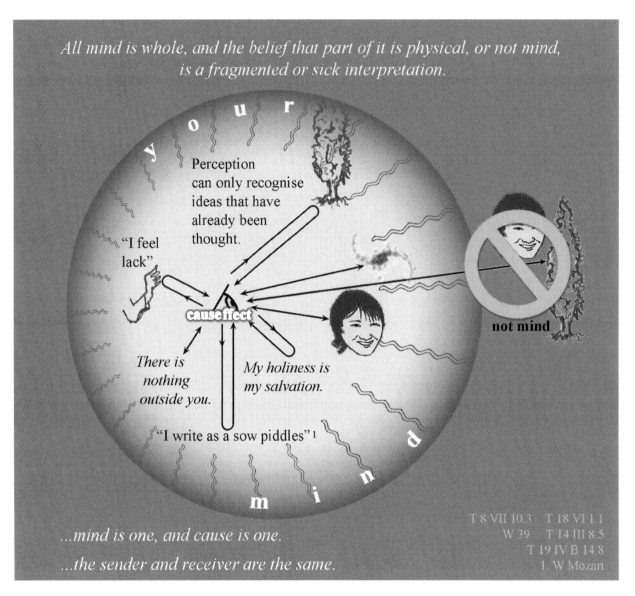

All mind is whole, and the belief that part of it is physical, or not mind, is a fragmented or sick interpretation.

Perception can only recognise ideas that have already been thought.

"I feel lack"

cause effect

There is nothing outside you.

My holiness is my salvation.

"I write as a sow piddles" 1

not mind

...mind is one, and cause is one.

...the sender and receiver are the same.

T 8 VII 10.3　T 18 VI 1.1
W 39　T 14 III 8.5
T 19 IV B 14.8
J. W Mozart

There is no giver and receiver in the sense the world conceives of them.

W 187 5.4

C: *God creates by extension*

...each shining thought of love extends its being and creates more of itself.

Forever unopposed by opposites of any kind, the Thoughts of God remain forever changeless, with the power to extend forever changelessly, but yet within themselves, for they are everywhere.

You cannot walk the world apart from God, because you could not be without Him. He is what your life is. Where you are He is. There is one life. That life you share with Him. Nothing can be apart from Him and live.

What lives is holy as Himself, because what shares His life is part of Holiness, and could no more be sinful than the sun could choose to be of ice...

Thoughts extend as they are shared, for they can not be lost.

T 11 intro 3.1   T 22 VI 14.8   W 167 8.3   W 156 2, 3.2   W 187 5.4

...love must be forever like itself, changeless forever, and forever without alternative. And so it is.

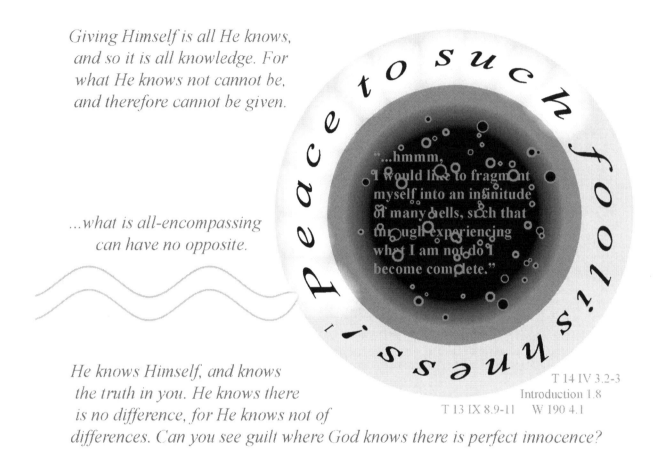

Giving Himself is all He knows, and so it is all knowledge. For what He knows not cannot be, and therefore cannot be given.

...what is all-encompassing can have no opposite.

Peace to such foolishness[1]

"...hmmm, I would like to fragment myself into an infinitude of many hells, such that through experiencing what I am not do I become complete."

He knows Himself, and knows the truth in you. He knows there is no difference, for He knows not of differences. Can you see guilt where God knows there is perfect innocence?

T 14 IV 3.2-3
Introduction 1.8
T 13 IX 8.9-11   W 190 4.1

1. The course loosely applies such terms as "foolish" and "meaningless" to all forms of egoic thought, and in this sence here is this quote used in context.

The extension of truth... rests only only on the knowledge of what truth is. This is your inheritance and requires no learning at all, but when you disinherited yourself you became a learner of necessity.

T 18 VI 9.8-9   T 7 II 5.6-7

One...ness
...the Father
and
the Son
are one.
Joined as
Joined

W 188 7.3   T 25 I 7.1

God created nothing beside you and nothing beside you exists, for you are part of Him.

Creation is the natural extension of perfect purity.

T 10 intro 2.1   T 14 V 3.4

D: *giving will increase what you possess*

Such is creation's law; that each idea the mind conceives but adds to its abundance, never takes away.

You cannot give to someone else, but only to yourself, and this you learn through teaching.

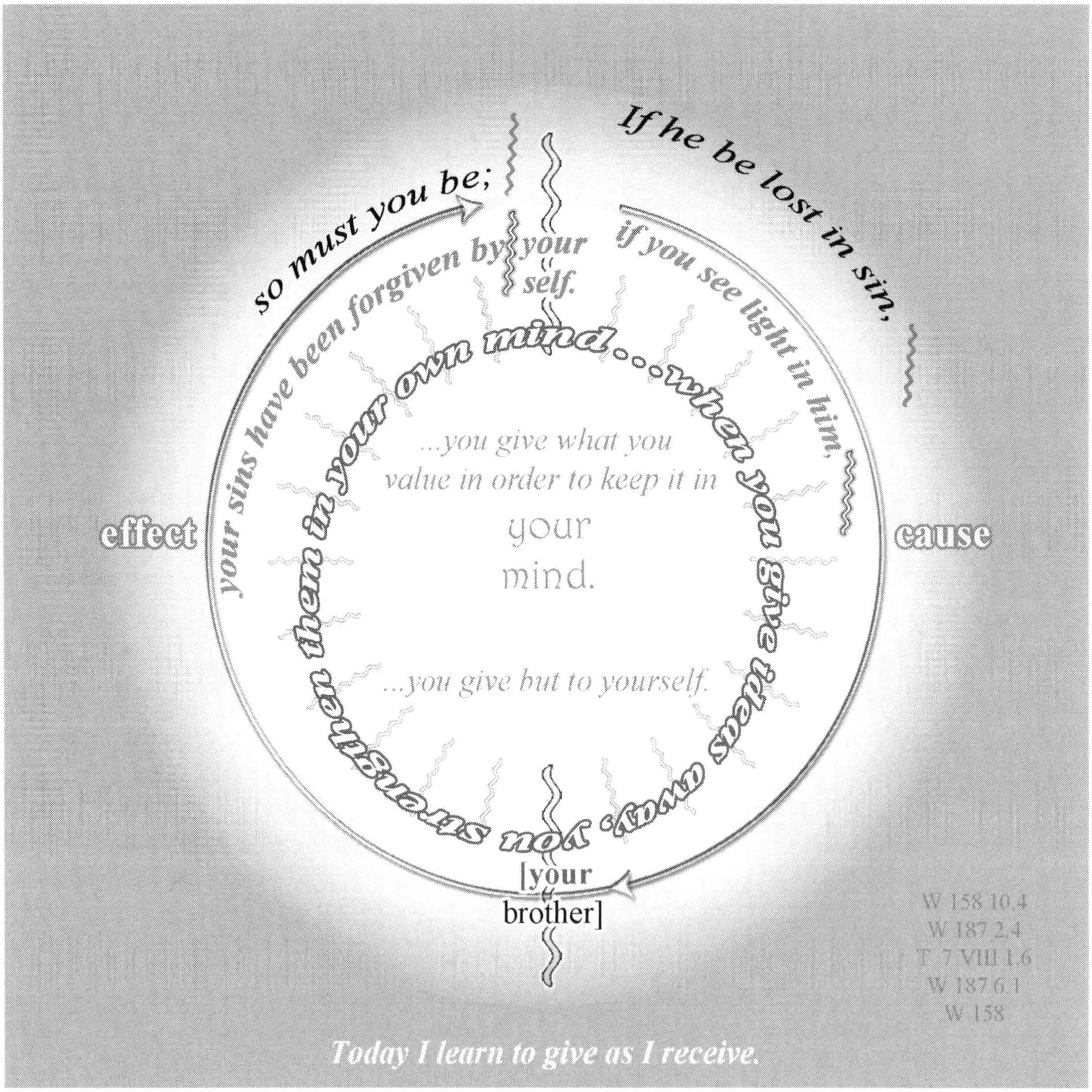

If he be lost in sin,
so must you be;
if you see light in him,
your sins have been forgiven by your self.
when you give ideas away, you strengthen them in your own mind...
...you give what you value in order to keep it in your mind.
...you give but to yourself.
effect
cause
[your brother]
W 158.10,4
W 187.2,4
T 7 VIII 1.6
W 187.6.1
W 158
Today I learn to give as I receive.

...by sharing is cause produced.

And everything you give to God is yours. Thus He creates, and thus must you restore.

By giving you receive. But to receive is to accept, not to get. It is impossible not to have, but it is possible not to know you have. The recognition of having is the willingness for giving...

For here, the more that anyone receives, the more is left for all the rest to share. The Guests have brought unlimited supply with Them. ...For Love has set its table in the space that seemed to keep your Guests apart from you.

T 26 VII 13.3   W 187 2   M Intro 2.6   T 28 IV 5.5   T 14 V 10.11-12   T 9 II 11.4-7   T 28 III 9

God, Who encompasses all being, created beings who have everything individually, but who want to share it to increase their joy. ...That is what creation means. ...Remember that in the Kingdom there is no difference between having *and* being*... In the state of being the mind gives everything always.*

T 4 VII 5

E: *What shares a common purpose is the same*

This is the law of purpose, which unites all those who share in it within itself.

Nothing is mine alone, for He and I have joined in purpose.

v

Yet being joined in one purpose, and one they share with God, how could they be separate from each other?

T 27 VI 1.5, 5.6   T 353 1.2   M 12 2.5

46

Created by God, He [the Holy Spirit] left neither God nor His creation. He is both God and you, as you are God and Him together.

...the Trinity Itself is

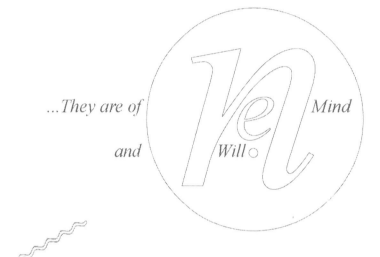

...They are of   Mind

and   Will

This single purpose creates perfect integration and establishes the peace of God.

T 6 III 5.2-3   T 3 II 5.4-6

What could conflict, when all the parts have but one purpose and one aim?

W 318 1.2

You and your brother are the same as God Himself is One, and not divided in His Will. And you must have one purpose, since He gave the same to both of you.

T 25 II 11.1-2

1 III: *There IS only One Mind*

Mind is one.

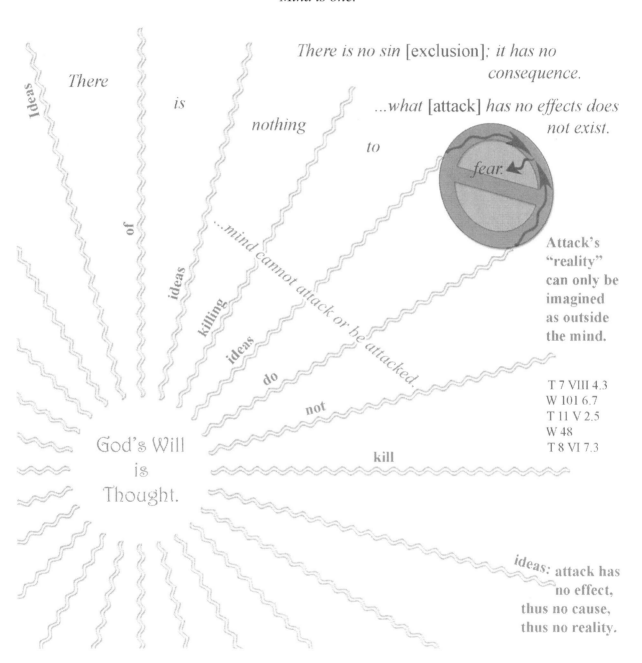

There

Ideas

is

of

ideas

nothing

killing

ideas

do

not

kill

God's Will
is
Thought.

...*mind cannot attack or be attacked.*

There is no sin [exclusion]; *it has no consequence.*

...*what* [attack] *has no effects does not exist.*

fear.

Attack's "reality" can only be imagined as outside the mind.

T 7 VIII 4.3
W 101 6.7
T 11 V 2.5
W 48
T 8 VI 7.3

ideas: attack has no effect, thus no cause, thus no reality.

...it is impossible to fragment the mind.

The truth is simple; it is one, without an opposite.

God has but one Son, knowing them all as one.

There is only one God because God is only One. *The truth is... one, as different "truths" must contractict.*

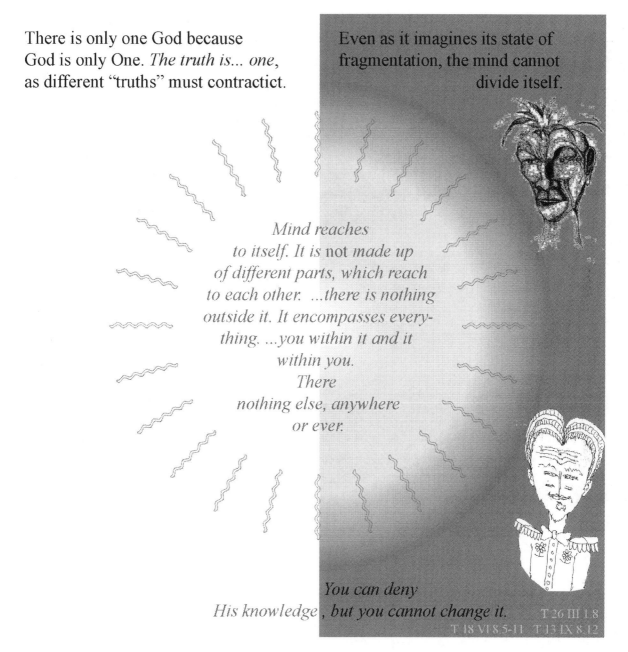

Even as it imagines its state of fragmentation, the mind cannot divide itself.

Mind reaches to itself. It is not made up of different parts, which reach to each other. ...there is nothing outside it. It encompasses every-thing. ...you within it and it within you. There nothing else, anywhere or ever.

You can deny His knowledge, but you cannot change it. T 26 III 1 8

T 18 VI 8 5-11   T 13 IX 8 12

Ideas leave not their source, and their effects [the world] *but seem to be apart from them.*

It is indeed possible for you to deny facts, although it is impossible for you to change them. ...If you deny love, you will not know it because your co-operation is the law of its being. You cannot change laws you did not make, and the laws of happiness were created for you, not by you.

Urtext   T 13 VIII 4.2   T 7 VIII 4.2   T 26 III 1.8   T 9 VI 3.5   T 26 VII 4.7   T 9 I 11.6,8-9

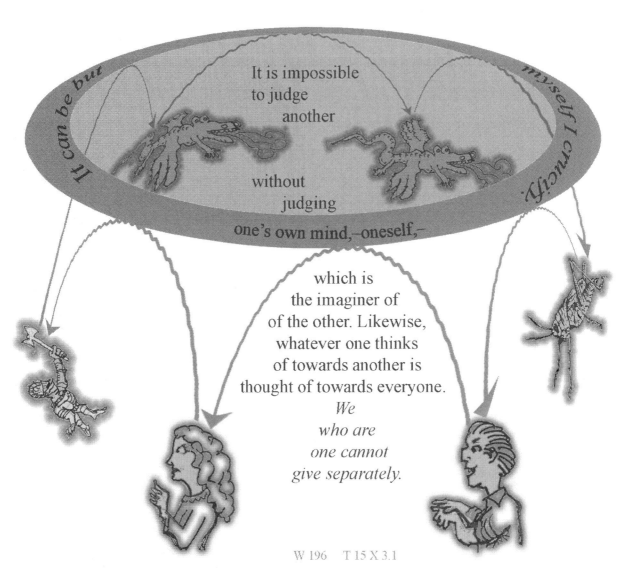

It is impossible
to judge
another

It can be but

myself I crucify.

without
judging

one's own mind,–oneself,–

which is
the imaginer of
of the other. Likewise,
whatever one thinks
of towards another is
thought of towards everyone.
We
who are
one cannot
give separately.

W 196   T 15 X 3.1

You will never be able to exclude yourself from your thoughts.

Nothing beyond yourself can make you fearful or loving, because nothing is *beyond you.*

T 7 VII 1.13   T 10 Intro 1.1

...[everyone is] part of you, as you are part of God. You are as lonely without understanding this as God Himself is lonely when His Sons do not know Him. The peace of God is understanding this. ...Understand totally by understanding totality

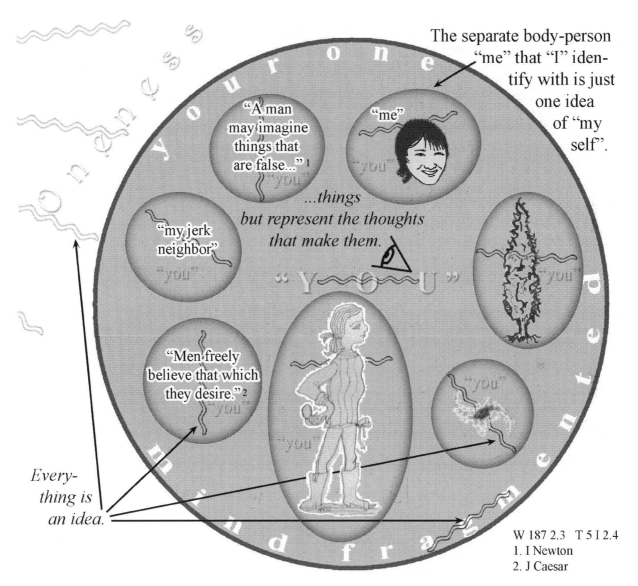

The separate body-person "me" that "I" identify with is just one idea of "my self".

...things but represent the thoughts that make them.

Every-thing is an idea.

W 187 2.3   T 5 I 2.4
1. I Newton
2. J Caesar

One is one's mind, and therefore one is also everything–all that one perceives and thinks of–in this mind, because all thoughts are part of it.

God is in everything I see because God is in my mind.

T 7 VII 10   W 30

What is within your brother still contains all of creation, everything created and creating, born and unborn as yet, still in the future or apparently gone by.

Every mind contains all minds, for every mind is one. Such is the truth.

"you"

"they"

"me"

W 161 4.2   T 8 VIII 1.10-11

The whole does define the part, but   the part does not define the whole.
Yet to know in part is to know entirely...

Every aspect is whole, and therefore no aspect is separate.

And every aspect of the Son of God is just the same as every other part.

Everything is accomplished through life, and life is of the mind and in the mind.

T 24 VII 2.2   T 13 VIII 2.3   T 28 IV 9.7   T6 V A 1.3

1 IV: The Holy Spirit and Jesus

The Holy Spirit's function is to take the broken picture of the Son of God and put the pieces into place again.

I elected, for your sake and mine, to demonstrate that the most outrageous assault, as judged by the ego, does not matter. As the world judges these things, but not as God knows them, I was betrayed, abandoned, beaten, torn, and finally killed.

The Holy Spirit is the Light in which Christ stands revealed. And all who would behold Him can see Him, for they have asked for light.

I am the manifestation of the Holy Spirit...

The Holy Spirit is the Christ Mind which is aware of the knowledge that lies beyond perception.

It is through us that peace will come. Join me in the idea of peace, for in ideas minds can communicate.

God

The Holy Spirit

The Holy Spirit's teaching takes only one direction and has only one goal. His direction is freedom and His goal is God. Yet He cannot conceive of God without you, because it is not God's Will to be without you.

T 8 II 6.1-3

I have said before that I am in charge of the Atonement. This is only because I completed my part in it as a man, and can now complete it through others. My chosen channels cannot fail, because I will lend them my strength as long as theirs is wanting.

T 28 IV 8.1   T 6 I 9   T 13 V 11.1   T 12 VII 6.1   T 5 I 5.1   T 15 VI 7.1   W 199 6.1   M CT 6 3   T IV 6.5-7

The Holy Spirit is the home of minds that seek for freedom. In Him they have found what they have sought.

I have been correctly referred to as "the lamb of God who taketh away the sins of the world," but those who represent the lamb as blood-stained do not understand the meaning of the symbol. Correctly understood, it is a very simple symbol that speaks of my innocence.

Sacrifice is a notion totally unknown to God.

Here is the only "sacrifice" You ask of Your beloved Son; You ask him to give up all suffering...

All prison doors are opened.

T 3 I 5.1-2,4.1
W 323 1.1
W 359 1.2
W 186 5.5-6

The arrogant must cling to words, afraid to go beyond them to experience which might affront their stance. Yet are the humble free to hear the Voice which tells them what they are, and what to do.

To think that God made chaos; contradicts His Will, invented opposites to truth, and suffers death to triumph over life; all this is arrogance.

If this [pain, loss, death] were the real world, God would be cruel. For no Father could subject His children to this as the price of salvation and be loving. Love does not kill to save. If it did, attack would be salvation, and this is the ego's interpretation, not God's.

You who have not yet brought all of the darkness you have taught yourself into the light in you, can hardly judge the truth and value of this course. Yet God did not abandon you.

The Holy Spirit is described as the remaining Communication Link between God and His separated Sons ...He knows because He is part of God; He perceives because He was sent to save humanity.

Across the bridge it is so different!

The Holy Spirit is the Mediator between the interpretations of the ego and the knowledge of the spirit. His ability to deal with symbols enables Him to work with the ego's beliefs in its own language.

The Holy Spirit is the Bridge to Him, made from your willingness to unite with Him and created by His joy in union with you.

His ability to look beyond symbols into eternity enables Him to understand the laws of God, for which He speaks. He can therefore perform the function of reinterpreting what the ego makes, not by destruction but by understanding.

T 5 III 7   T 16 IV 12.2

The Holy Spirit is the mechanism of miracles. He recognizes both God's creations and your illusions.

Remember that the Holy Spirit is the Answer, not the question.

...the Holy Spirit is the only Healer.

...the Holy Spirit is one, and anyone who listens is inevitably led to demonstrate His way for all.

...the Holy Spirit is part of you.

6 III 5.1

The Holy Spirit is in you in a very literal sense. His is the Voice that calls you back to where you were before and will be again.

T 13 Intr 3   W 152 7.1   T 14 XI 4.1-2   T 16 VI 6.1   T 1 I.38   T 6 IV 1.1   T 13 VIII 1.2   T 6 I 10.6   T 5 II 3.7

The Christ in you inhabits not a body. Yet He is in you. And thus it must be that you are not within a body.

A church that does not inspire love has a hidden altar that is not serving the purpose for which God intended it. ...Disciples are followers, and if the model they follow has chosen to save them pain in all respects, they are unwise not to follow him.

The Holy Spirit is the motivation for miracle-mindedness; the decision to heal the separation by letting it go.

I can help you only as our Father created us. I will love you and honor you and maintain complete respect for what you have made, but I will not uphold it unless it is true.

...I can reach up and bring the Holy Spirit down to you, but I can bring Him to you only at your own invitation. The Holy Spirit is in your right mind, as He was in mine. The Bible says, "May the mind be in you that was also in Christ Jesus," ...It is the blessing of miracle-mindedness. It asks that you may think as I thought, joining with me in Christ thinking.

The Holy Spirit has the power to change the whole foundation of the world you see to something else; a basis not insane, on which a sane perception can be based, another world perceived. And one in which nothing is contradicted that would lead the Son of God to sanity and joy.

My mission was simply to unite the will of the Sonship with the Will of the Father by being aware of the Father's Will myself. This is the awareness I came to give you... ...in this sense I am the salvation of the world. The world must therefore despise and reject me, because the world is the belief that love is impossible.

The Holy Spirit is the idea of healing. Being thought, the idea gains as it is shared. Being the Call for God, it is also the idea of God. Since you are part of God it is also the idea of yourself, as well as of all His creations.

The Holy Spirit is the frame God set around the part of Him that you would see as separate.

The Holy Spirit is the spirit of joy. He is the Call to return with which God blessed the minds of His separated Sons. This is the vocation of the mind. The mind had no calling until the separation, because before that it had only being.... The Holy Spirit is God's Answer to the separation

I hold your hand as surely as you agreed to take your brother's. You will not separate, for I stand with you and walk with you in your advance to truth. And where we go we carry God with us.

T 25 Intr 1.1-3   T 6 I 8.5   T 5 II 1.4   T 4 III 7.6-7   T 5 I 3   T 25 VII 5.1-2   T 8 IV 3.4   T 5 III 2.1-4   T 25 II 6.1
T 25 II 2.1   T 18 III 5.4

God's Teacher is as like to His Creator as is His Son, and through His Teacher does God proclaim His Oneness and His Son's. Listen in silence, and do not raise your voice against Him. For He teaches the miracle of oneness, and before His lesson division disappears.

The Holy Spirit is the radiance that you must let banish the idea of darkness.

Your Self retains Its Thoughts, and they remain within your mind and in the Mind of God. The Holy Spirit holds salvation in your mind, and offers it the way to peace. Salvation is a thought you share with God, because His Voice accepted it for you and answered in your name that it was done.

He is your remaining communication with God, which you can interrupt but cannot destroy. The Holy Spirit is the way in which God's Will is done on earth as it is in Heaven.

Those who are joined in Christ are in no way separate. For Christ is the Self the Sonship shares, as God shares His Self with Christ.

The lesson I was born to teach, and still would teach to all my brothers, is that sacrifice is nowhere and love is everywhere. For communication embraces everything, and in the peace it re-establishes, love comes of itself.

Wherever He [the Holy Spirit] *looks He sees Himself, and because He is united He offers the whole Kingdom always. This is the one message God gave to Him and for which He must speak, because that is what He is. The peace of God lies in that message, and so the peace of God lies in you.*

It is possible even in this world to hear only that Voice and no other. It takes effort and great willingness to learn. It is the final lesson that I learned, and God's Sons are as equal as learners as they are as Sons.

My decision cannot overcome yours, because yours is as powerful as mine. ...All things are possible through our joint decision, but mine alone cannot help you. ...I can offer my strength to make yours invincible, but I cannot oppose your decision without competing with it and thereby violating God's Will for you.

Only the Holy Spirit recognizes foolish needs as well as real ones. And He will teach you how to meet both without losing either.

T 14 XI 11.3-5   T 5 II 4.2   W 96 7   T 5 II 8.3-4   T 15 V 10.9-10   T 15 XI 7.5-6   T 6 II 12.5   T 5 II 3.8-10   T 8 IV 5
T 16 I 6.7-8

1 V: God's Peace, Love, Joy, and Will

Peace is the state where love abides, and seeks to share itself.

The great peace of the Kingdom shines in your mind forever, but it must shine outward to make you aware of it.

The peace of God passeth your understanding only in the past. Yet here it is, and you can understand it now.

No one who truly seeks the peace of God can fail to find it. ...The peace of God is yours.

T 23 I 12.5   T 6 II 12.8   T 13 VII 8.1-2   W 185 11

o   o   o

Love is attracted only to love. Overlooking guilt completely, it sees no fear.

Love is not learned. Its meaning lies within itself. And learning ends when you have recognized all it is not. *That is the interference; that is what needs to be undone.*

The power of love is in His gentleness, which is of God and therefore cannot crucify nor suffer crucifixion.

T 19 IV A 10.5   T 18 IX 12.1   T 14 V 10.9

○ ○ ○

Blessed is God's Teacher, Whose joy it is to teach God's holy Son his holiness. His joy is not contained in time. His teaching is for you because His joy is yours.

Joy is eternal. ...Joy does not turn to sorrow, for the eternal cannot change.

Joy is unified purpose, and unified purpose is only God's. When yours is unified it is His. T 8 VII 15.1-2

Joy is unlimited... There is no difference anywhere in it, for every thought is like itself.

T 15 II 2.4   T 22 II 3.4,6   T 22 VI 14.8-9

...His joy is not complete because yours is incomplete. And this He does know. ...The constant going out of His Love is blocked when His channels are closed, and He is lonely when the minds He created do not communicate fully with Him.

○   ○   ○

God's Will is one, not many. It has no opposition, for there is none beside it.

...[spirit] is in complete and direct communication with its Creator. This communication is the Will of God.

God's Will is that His Son be one, and united with Him in His Oneness.

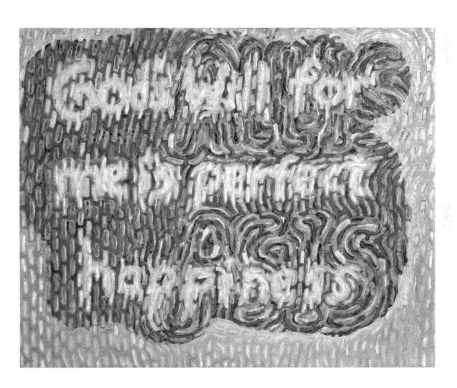

Truth is God's Will.

God's Will is that you are His Son. By denying this you deny your own will, and therefore do not know what it is.

Will is not involved in perception at any level, and has nothing to do with choice.

T 4 VII 6   T 19 IV A 3.5-6   T 4 VII 3.4-5   T 11 I 11.8   W 101   T 7 X 2.5   T 11 I 8.3-4   M-CT 1 7.2

○   ○   ○

You will not find peace except the peace of God. Accept this fact, and save yourself the agony of yet more bitter disappointments, bleak despair, and sense of icy hopelessness and doubt.

The peace of God is given you with the glowing purpose in which you join with your brother. The holy light that brought you and him together must extend, as you accepted it.

And truth stands radiant, apart from conflict, untouched and quiet in the peace of God.

What is the peace of God? No more than this; the simple understanding that His Will is wholly without opposite. There is no thought that contradicts His Will, yet can be true.

First, how can the peace of God be recognized? God's peace is recognized at first by just one thing; in every way it is totally unlike all previous experiences. ...The past just slips away, and in its place is everlasting quiet. Only that. The contrast first perceived has merely gone. Quiet has reached to cover everything.

W 200 1.2-3   T 18 I 13.5   T 23 I 7.10   M 20 6.1-3, 2

○   ○   ○

Love is freedom. To look for it by placing yourself in bondage is to separate yourself from it. ...As you release, so will you be released. Forget this not, or love will be unable to find you and comfort you.

Miracles occur naturally as expressions of love. The real miracle is the love that inspires them. In this sense everything that comes from love is a miracle.

Love wishes to be known, completely understood and shared. It has no secrets; nothing that it would keep apart and hide. It walks in sunlight, open-eyed and calm, in smiling welcome and in sincerity so simple and so obvious it cannot be misunderstood.

This little self is not your kingdom. Arched high above it and surrounding it with love is the glorious whole, which offers all its happiness and deep content to every part.

Love is extension. To withhold the smallest gift is not to know love's purpose. Love offers everything forever.

Love is not an illusion. It is a fact.

In Heaven, where the meaning of love is known, love is the same as union. Here, where the illusion of love is accepted in love's place, love is perceived as separation and exclusion.

You know not what love means because you have sought to purchase it with little gifts, thus valuing it too little to understand its magnitude. Love is not little and love dwells in you, for you are host to Him.

The meaning of love is the meaning God gave to it. Give to it any meaning apart from His, and it is impossible to understand it. God loves every brother as He loves you; neither less nor more. He needs them all equally, and so do you.

...love is content, and not form of any kind.

T 16 VI 2   T 1 I 3   T 20 VI 2.5   T 18 VIII 7.6-7   T 24 I 1.1-2   T 16 IV 4.1-2   T 16 V 3.7-8   T 15 III 8.5-6
T 15 V 10.3-5   T 16 V 12.1

o   o   o

Giving His joy is an ongoing process, not in time but in eternity.

If you are God's Will and do not accept His Will, you are denying joy. The miracle is therefore a lesson in what joy is. Being a lesson in sharing it is a lesson in love, which is joy. Every miracle is thus a lesson in truth, and by offering truth you are learning the difference between pain and joy.

Minds that are joined and recognize they are, can feel no guilt. For they cannot attack, and they rejoice that this is so, seeing their safety in this happy fact. Their joy is in the innocence they see. And thus they seek for it, because it is their purpose to behold it and rejoice.

...the one mood He [the Holy Spirit] engenders is joy. He protects it by rejecting everything that does not foster joy, and so He alone can keep you wholly joyous.

The Holy Spirit will always guide you truly, because your joy is His. This is His Will for everyone because He speaks for the Kingdom of God, which is joy.

For peace is the acknowledgement of perfect purity, from which no one is excluded. Within its holy circle is everyone whom God created as His Son. Joy is its unifying attribute, with no one left outside to suffer guilt alone.

Love waits on welcome, not on time, and the real world is but your welcome of what always was. Therefore the call of joy is in it, and your glad response is your awakening to what you have not lost.

T 6 V 1.6   T 7 X 8.3-6   T 25 IV 1.1-3   T 6 C 1.10-11   T 7 XI 1.1-2   T 14 V 8.2-3   T 13 VII 9.7-8

○   ○   ○

Your function is to add to God's treasure by creating yours. His Will to *you is His Will* for *you. He would not withhold creation from you because His joy is in it. You cannot find joy except as God does. His joy lay in creating you, and He extends His Fatherhood to you so that you can extend yourself as He did.*

What is the Will of God? He wills His Son have everything. And this He guaranteed when He created him as *everything. It is impossible that anything be lost, if what you* have *is what you* are*. This is the miracle by which creation became your function, sharing it with God. It is not understood apart from Him, and therefore has no meaning in this world.*

It is God's Will your mind be one with His. It is God's Will that He has but one Son. It is God's Will that His one Son is you.

Heaven itself is union with all of creation, and with its one Creator. And Heaven remains the Will of God for you.

God's Will is your salvation.

God's Will is all there is.

...every part of creation is of one order. This is God's Will and yours.

There is no confusion in the mind of a Son of God, whose will must be the Will of the Father, because the Father's Will is *His Son.*

You are *the Will of God. ...Deny this and you will attack, believing you have been attacked,. But see the Love of God in you, and you will see it everywhere because it* is *everywhere..*

You are the Will of God because that is how you were created.

When you have learned that your will is God's, you could no more will to be without Him than He could will to be without you. This is freedom and this is joy. Deny yourself this and you are denying God His Kingdom, because He created you for this.

From knowledge and perception respectively, two distinct thought systems arise which are opposite in every respect. In the realm of knowledge no thoughts exist apart from God, because God and His Creation share one Will.

T 8 VI 6   T 14 V 8.2-3   T 13 VII 9.7-8   T 26 VII 11.1-6   W 99 9.2-4   T 14 VIII 5.2-3   T 9 VII 1.1 M CT 3 6.1
T 7 IV 2.3-4   T 7 X 7.4   T 7 VII 10.1-4   T 8 II 7.5, 6.4-6   PREFACE p.x

Chapter 2 TWO

You play the game of death...

The ego's logic is as impeccable as that of the Holy Spirit, because your mind has the means at its disposal to side with Heaven or earth, as it elects. But again, remember that both are in you.

W 191 9.3   T 5 V 1.4

His Fatherhood

The mind can make the belief in separation very real and very fearful, and this belief is the "devil". It is powerful, active, destructive and clearly in opposition to God, because it literally denies His Fatherhood.

T 3 VII 5.1-3

"believe in aloneness"

Look at your life and see what the devil has made.

And thus are two sons made, and both appear to walk this earth without a meeting place and no encounter. ...They have a different purpose. ...The Son of God retains His Father's Will. The son of man perceives an alien will and wishes it were so.

T 24 VII 11

2 I: The Split Mind

This is a very simple course.

…there are only two parts of your mind.

A: The Divide

One is ruled by the ego, and is made up of illusions. The other is the home of the Holy Spirit, where truth abides.

God

The Holy Spirit

The Holy Spirit is in the part of the mind that lies between the ego and the spirit, mediating between them always in favour of the spirit.

the ego

The ego is the part of the mind that believes your existence is defined by separation.

T 7 IX 1.4   T 4 VII 1.5

There are no other guides but these to choose between, and no other outcomes possible as a result of your choice but the fear that the ego always engenders, and the love that the Holy Spirit always offers to replace it.

T 11 VIII 1.1   W 66 7

The separation [from God] is merely another term for a split mind. The ego is the symbol of separation, just as the Holy Spirit is the symbol of peace.

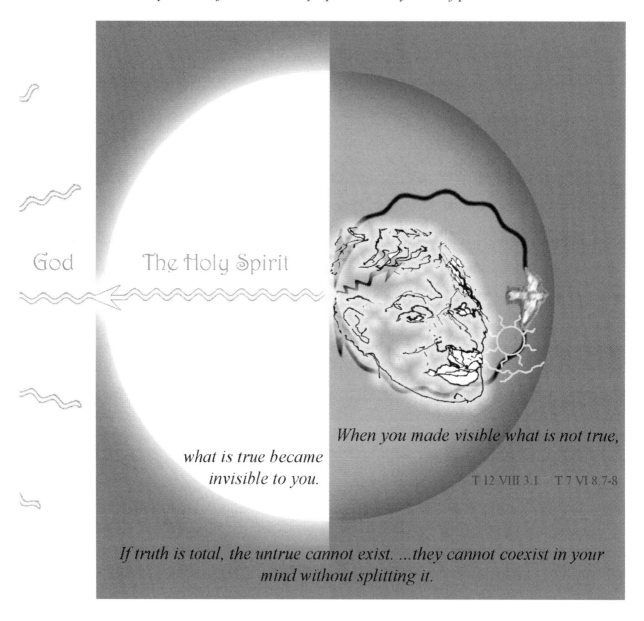

God

The Holy Spirit

When you made visible what is not true,

what is true became invisible to you.

T 12 VIII 3.1   T 7 VI 8.7-8

If truth is total, the untrue cannot exist. ...they cannot coexist in your mind without splitting it.

For a split mind and all its works were not created by the Father.

...you have split your mind into what knows and does not know the truth.

T 5 III 9.3   T 12 VIII 2.4   W 139 5.4

God calls you and you do not hear, for you are preoccupied with your own voice. And the vision of Christ is not in your sight, for you look upon yourself alone.

You cannot learn simultaneously from two teachers who are in total disagreement about everything. …Your reality is unaffected by both, but if you listen to both, your mind will be split about what your reality is.

T 13 V 6.6   T 8 I 6.2,5

B: "You": the Divider and the Divided

A divided mind cannot communicate, because it speaks for different things to the same mind.

Whatever is true is eternal, and cannot change or be changed. Spirit is therefore unalterable because it is already perfect, but the mind can elect what it chooses to serve. The only limit put on its choice is that it cannot serve two masters.

Many thought I was attacking them… What you must recognize is that when you do not share a thought system, you are weakening it. Those who believe in it therefore perceive this as an attack on them.

T 9 I 6.3   T I V 5.1-3   T 6 V B 1.5

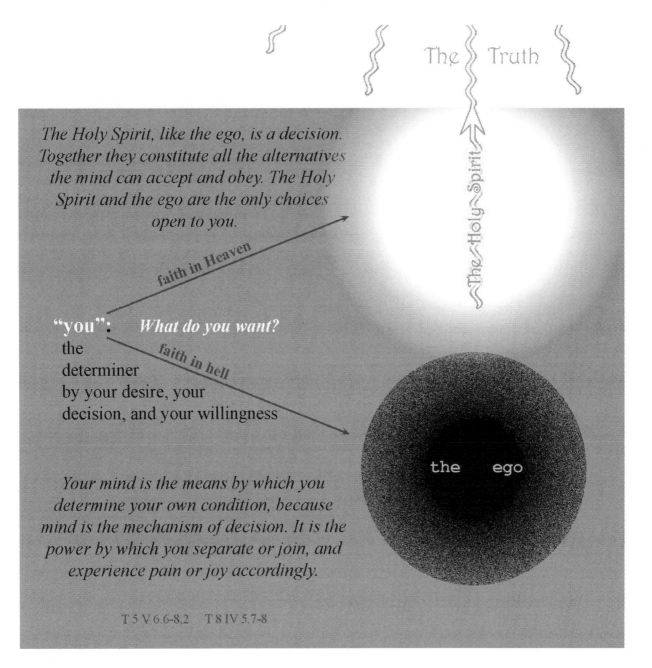

The Truth

The Holy Spirit

The Holy Spirit, like the ego, is a decision. Together they constitute all the alternatives the mind can accept and obey. The Holy Spirit and the ego are the only choices open to you.

faith in Heaven

"you": What do you want?
the
determiner
by your desire, your
decision, and your willingness

faith in hell

the ego

Your mind is the means by which you determine your own condition, because mind is the mechanism of decision. It is the power by which you separate or join, and experience pain or joy accordingly.

T 5 V 6.6-8.2   T 8 IV 5.7-8

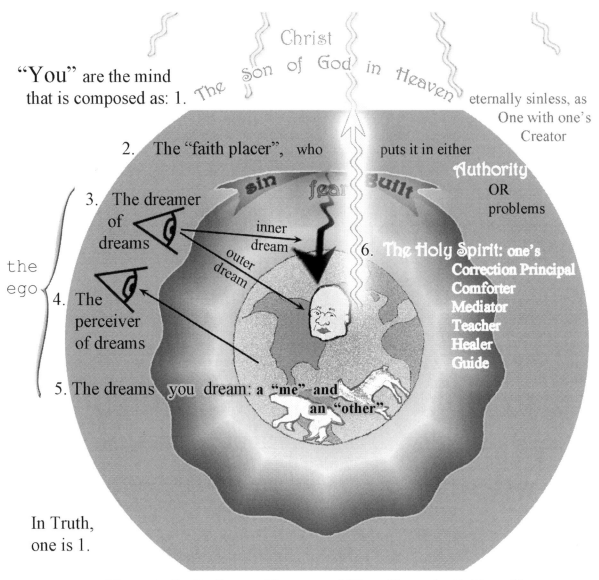

"You" are the mind that is composed as:

1. The Son of God in Heaven — Christ — eternally sinless, as One with one's Creator

2. The "faith placer", who puts it in either **Authority** OR problems

the ego {

3. The dreamer of dreams

inner dream

outer dream

sin fear guilt

4. The perceiver of dreams

5. The dreams you dream: a "me" and an "other"

6. **The Holy Spirit: one's Correction Principal Comforter Mediator Teacher Healer Guide**

In Truth, one is 1.

W II 6 1.1-2   *Christ is God's Son as He created Him. He is the Self we Share...*
W 99 12.5   *...you are the Son of God.*   *...you... placed your faith...*
T 13 IX 3.1
T 27 VII 13.1   *You are the dreamer of the world of dreams.*
T 5 III 3.2   *...you are the perceiver.*   *...you are the dream you share.*
T 28 V 3.4
T 6 III 5.1   *...the Holy Spirit is part of you.*

As an ego body-person, one is aware of one's mind only as:

at the **causal level: 3** The one who determines to be separate and different, expressed as *"I want it thus!"* in the world.

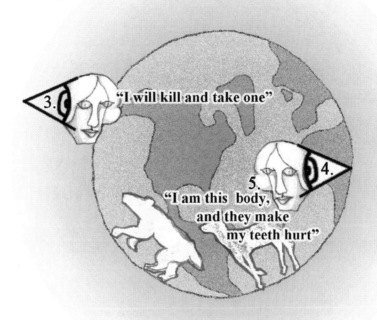

at the **effect level: 4, 5** The perceiver, and a part, of a world that one cannot control.

T 18 II 4.1

C: Split Goals

You believe that guilt and guiltlessness are both of value, each representing an escape from what the other does not offer you. You do not want either alone, for without both you do not see yourself as whole and happy.

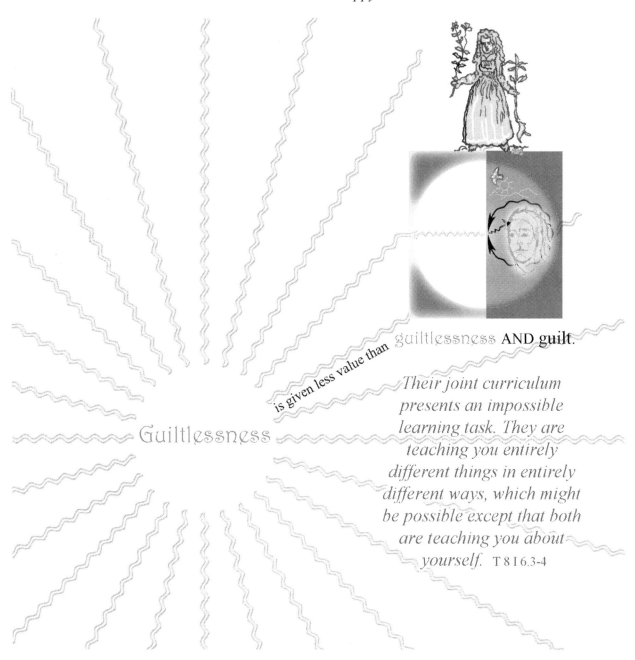

is given less value than guiltlessness **AND guilt**.

Guiltlessness

Their joint curriculum presents an impossible learning task. They are teaching you entirely different things in entirely different ways, which might be possible except that both are teaching you about yourself. T 8 I 6.3-4

Yet seeking and finding are the same, and if you seek for two goals you will find them, but you will recognize neither. You will think they are the same because you want both of them. The mind always strives for integration, and if it is split and wants to keep the split, it will still believe it has one goal by making it seem to be one.

Yet as long as you perceive the world as split, you are not healed. For to be healed is to pursue one goal, because you have accepted only one and want but one.

It [the ego] *does not reject goodness entirely, for that you could not accept. But it always adds something that is not real to the real, thus confusing illusion and reality. For perceptions cannot be partly true. If you believe in truth and illusion, you cannot tell which is true.*

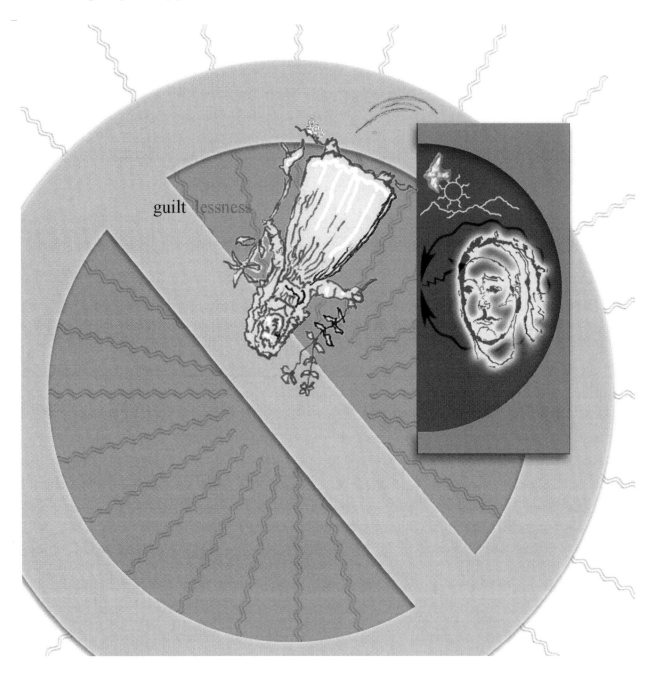

...you are whole only in your guiltlessness, and only in your guiltlessness can you be happy. There is no conflict here.

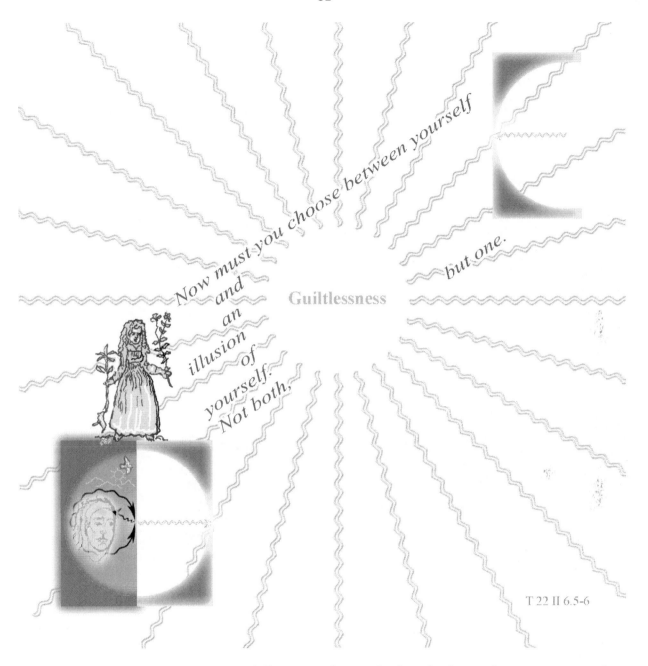

Now must you choose between yourself and an illusion of yourself. Not both, but one.

Guiltlessness

T 22 II 6.5-6

...all attempts to keep both truth and illusion in the mind, where both must be, are recognized as dedication to illusion; and given up when brought to truth, and seen as totally unreconcilable with truth, in any respect or in any way.

You have not two realities, but one. Nor can you be aware of more than one.

T 14 III 2.2-3   T 12 VII 6, 7.10-11   T 11 VII 3.3-5   T 14 III 2.4-5   T 19 I 6.7   T 30 III 11.4-5

2 II: The Authority Problem

This is *"the root of all evil"*.

Allegiance to the denial of God is the ego's religion.

...the authority problem as based on the concept of usurping God's power.

The authority problem is still the only source of conflict, because the ego was made out of the wish of God's Son to father Him. The ego, then, is nothing more than a delusional system in which you made your own father.

...you choose to separate yourself from your Author.

T 3 VI 7.3   T 10 V 3.1   T 5 V 3.3   T 11 Intro 2.3-4   T 3 VI 8.7

It is not strange that dreams can make a world that is unreal. It is the wish to make it that is incredible.

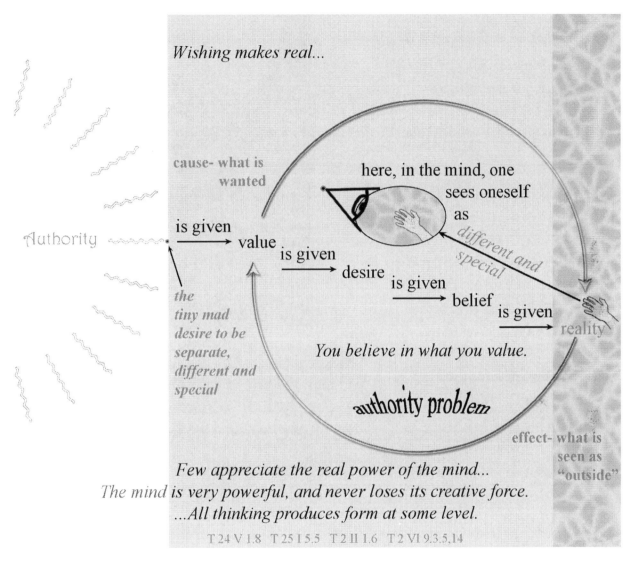

Wishing makes real...

cause- what is wanted

Authority

is given → value
is given → desire
is given → belief
is given → reality

here, in the mind, one sees oneself as *different and special*

the tiny mad desire to be separate, different and special

You believe in what you value.

authority problem

effect- what is seen as "outside"

Few appreciate the real power of the mind...
The mind is very powerful, and never loses its creative force.
...All thinking produces form at some level.

T 24 V 1.8   T 25 I 5.5   T 2 II 1.6   T 2 VI 9.3.5.14

All fear comes ultimately, and sometimes by way of very devious routes, from the denial of Authorship. The offence is never to God, but only to those who deny Him. To deny His Authorship is to deny yourself the reason for your peace, so that you see yourself only in segments. This strange perception is the authority problem.

T 18 II 8.2   T 3 VI 10

The mind is its only source.

Illusions are but beliefs in what is not there.

The world is an illusion.

...this world is an hallucination...

Nothing occures but represents your wish... Here is your world, complete in all its details.

The light of God is only seen through the window of Christ (Oneness). One is not an imagined body-person-world; one is that light.

"Miscreants outside" cannot be; the mind cannot not create or miscreate except of itself and by its own volition. All must first be willfully fantasied by the perceiving mind.

...the mind, the only level of creation, cannot create beyond itself...

W 30 5.2   T 16 III 4.9   W 155 2.1   T 20 VIII 3.8   W 152 1.5-6   T 2 IV 2.10

...your inner and outer worlds, which are actually the same.

Nothing you made has any power over you unless you still would be apart from your Creator, and with a will opposed to His.

W 32 2.1   T 22 II 10.2

You are not at peace because you are not fulfilling your function. God gave you a very lofty function that you are not meeting. Your ego has chosen to be afraid instead of meeting it.

"My 'function' is to usurp God's, and by this do I know myself."

Identity and function are the same, and by your function do you know yourself. And thus, if you confuse your function with the function of Another, you must be confused about yourself and who you are. What is the separation but a wish to take God's function from Him and deny that it is His?   T 27 II 10.6-8

To establish your personal autonomy you tried to create unlike your Father, believing that what you made is capable of being unlike Him.

The ego's goal is quite explicitly ego autonomy. From the beginning, then, its purpose is to be separate, sufficient unto itself and independent of any power except its own.

...the mind can become the medium by which spirit creates along the line of its own creation. If it does not freely elect to do so, it retains its creative potential but places itself under tyrannous rather than Authoritative control. As a result it imprisons...

T 4 I 9.4   T 11 VII 3.7   T 11 V 5.4-5   T 1 V 5

2.III: *an alien will*

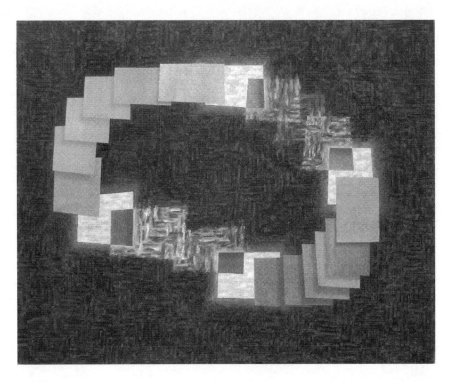

For you have hurt yourself, and made your Self your "enemy". And now you must believe you are not you, but something alien to yourself and "something else", a "something" to be feared instead of loved.

T 24 II 2.9   T 25 V 2.4-5

And you will deny your Self, and walk upon an alien ground which your Creator did not make, and where you seem to be a something you are not.

For the ego is itself an illusion, and only illusions can be the witnesses to its "reality".

T 28 V 3.6   T 16 V 9.5

A: Death and Specialness

The special ones are all asleep... Freedom and peace and joy... call them to come forth and waken from their dream of death. Yet they hear nothing. They are lost in dreams of specialness.

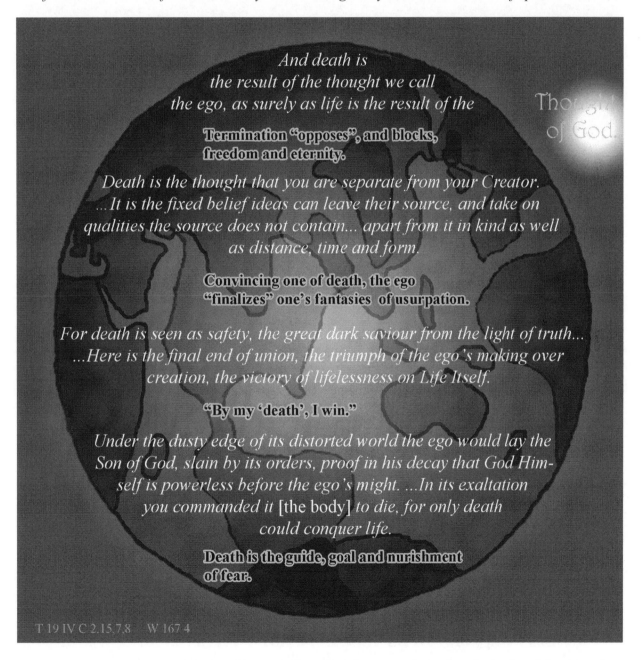

And death is the result of the thought we call the ego, as surely as life is the result of the Thought of God.

Termination "opposes", and blocks, freedom and eternity.

Death is the thought that you are separate from your Creator. ...It is the fixed belief ideas can leave their source, and take on qualities the source does not contain... apart from it in kind as well as distance, time and form.

Convincing one of death, the ego "finalizes" one's fantasies of usurpation.

For death is seen as safety, the great dark saviour from the light of truth... ...Here is the final end of union, the triumph of the ego's making over creation, the victory of lifelessness on Life Itself.

"By my 'death', I win."

Under the dusty edge of its distorted world the ego would lay the Son of God, slain by its orders, proof in his decay that God Himself is powerless before the ego's might. ...In its exaltation you commanded it [the body] to die, for only death could conquer life.

Death is the guide, goal and nurishment of fear.

T 19 IV C 2,15,7,8   W 167 4

For what can specialness delight in but to kill? What does it seek for but the sight of death? Where does it lead but to destruction?

It is the attraction of death that makes life seem to be ugly, cruel and tyrannical.

But the pursuit of specialness must bring you pain. Here is a goal that would defeat salvation, and thus run counter to the Will of God.

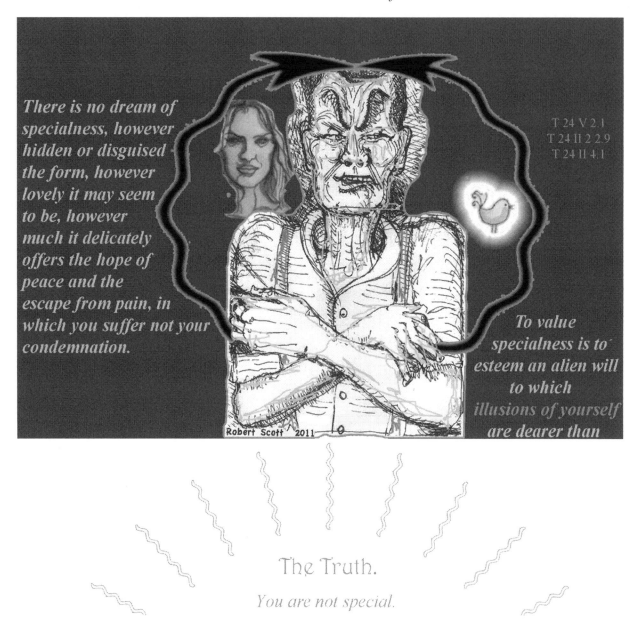

There is no dream of specialness, however hidden or disguised the form, however lovely it may seem to be, however much it delicately offers the hope of peace and the escape from pain, in which you suffer not your condemnation.

T 24 V 2.1
T 24 II 2.9
T 24 II 4.1

To value specialness is to esteem an alien will to which illusions of yourself are dearer than

Robert Scott 2011

The Truth.

You are not special.

Death is a thought that takes on many forms, often unrecognised. It may appear as sadness, fear, anxiety or doubt; as anger, faithlessness and lack of trust; concern for bodies… All such thoughts are but reflections of the worshipping of death as saviour and as giver of release.

I said before that God so loved the world that He gave it to His only begotten Son. God does love the real world, and those who perceive its reality cannot see the world of death. For death is not of the real world, in which everything reflects the eternal.

Life makes not death...

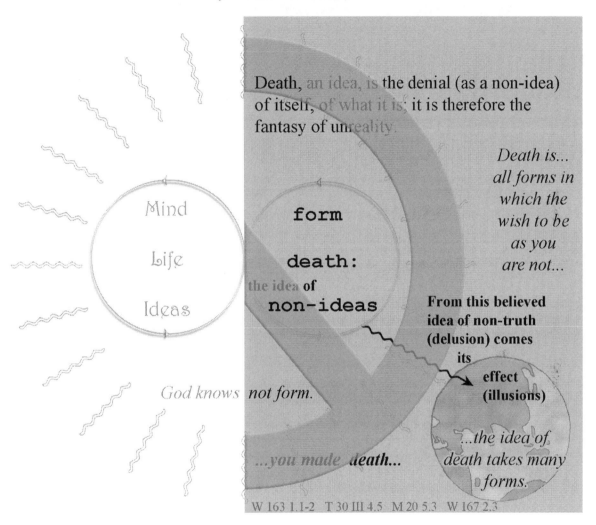

Death, an idea, is the denial (as a non-idea) of itself, of what it is; it is therefore the fantasy of unreality.

Death is... all forms in which the wish to be as you are not...

form

death: the idea of non-ideas

From this believed idea of non-truth (delusion) comes its effect (illusions)

Mind

Life

Ideas

God knows not form.

...you made death...

...the idea of death takes many forms.

W 163 1.1-2   T 30 III 4.5   M 20 5.3   W 167 2.3

Death is the central dream from which all illusions stem.

Without the idea of death there is no world. All dreams will end with this one. This is salvation's final goal; the end of all illusions.

T 24 III 7,   V 4.3-5,   II 2.7   T 19 IV D 4.3   W 163 1   T 12 III 7   T 23 IV 3.7   T 24 I 8.4   M 27 1.1   M 27 6.3-5

The fear of God and of your brother comes from each unrecognized belief in specialness. For you demand your brother bow to it against his will. ...Every twinge of malice, or stab of hate or wish to separate arises here.

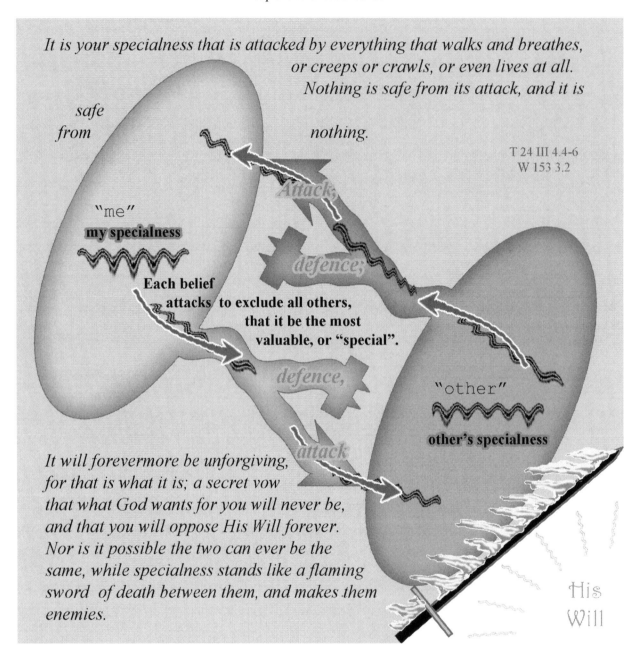

It is your specialness that is attacked by everything that walks and breathes, or creeps or crawls, or even lives at all. Nothing is safe from its attack, and it is

safe from

nothing.

T 24 III 4.4-6
W 153 3.2

"me"
my specialness

Attack;

defence;

Each belief attacks to exclude all others, that it be the most valuable, or "special".

defence,

attack

"other"

other's specialness

It will forevermore be unforgiving, for that is what it is; a secret vow that what God wants for you will never be, and that you will oppose His Will forever. Nor is it possible the two can ever be the same, while specialness stands like a flaming sword of death between them, and makes them enemies.

His Will

What can be born of death and still have life?

Specialness is the function that you gave yourself. It stands for you alone, as self-created... ...every window barred against the light. ...with anger always fully justified, you have pursued this goal with... effort that you never thought to cease. And all this grim determination was for this; you wanted specialness to be the truth.

Those who are special must defend illusions against the truth. For what is specialness but an attack upon the Will of God?

Specialness is the seal of treachery upon the gift of love. Whatever serves its purpose must be given to kill. No gift that bears its seal but offers treachery to giver and receiver. Not one glance from eyes it veils but looks on sight of death.

M 20 5 3.4-5,6.6   T 24 VI 11   T 24 I 9.1.2   T 24 II 11.1-4

B: Separation and Attack

The ego believes that power, understanding and truth lie in separation, and to establish this belief it must attack.

Attack has power to make illusions real. Yet what it makes is nothing.

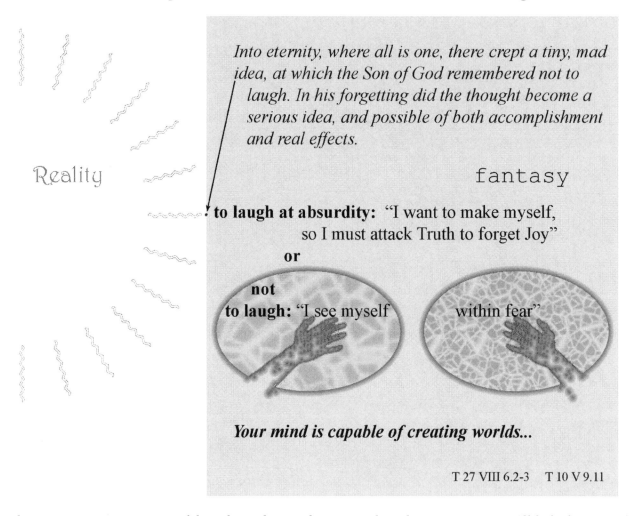

Into eternity, where all is one, there crept a tiny, mad idea, at which the Son of God remembered not to laugh. In his forgetting did the thought become a serious idea, and possible of both accomplishment and real effects.

Reality

fantasy

to laugh at absurdity: "I want to make myself, so I must attack Truth to forget Joy"

or

not to laugh: "I see myself   within fear"

Your mind is capable of creating worlds...

T 27 VIII 6.2-3   T 10 V 9.11

The separation is a system of thought real enough in time, though not in eternity. All beliefs are real to the believer.

T 11 V 13.4   T 30 IV 5.5-6   T 3 VII 3.2-3

What is not love is murder. What is not loving must be an attack. Every illusion is an assault on truth, and every one does violence to the idea of love because it seems to be of equal truth.

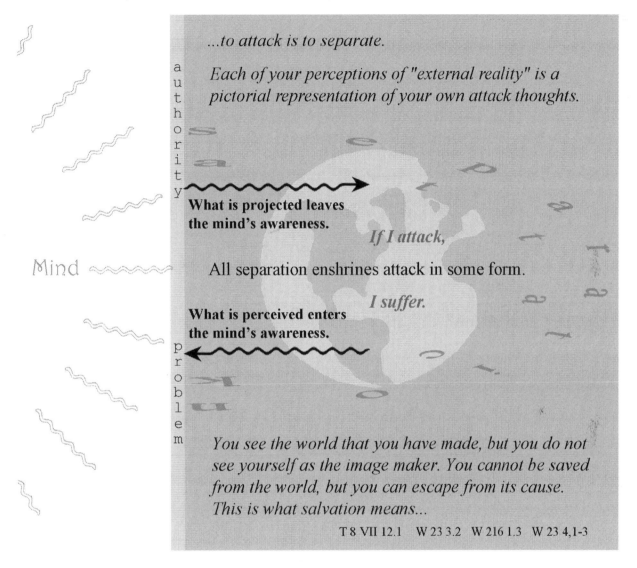

...to attack is to separate.

Each of your perceptions of "external reality" is a pictorial representation of your own attack thoughts.

authority

What is projected leaves the mind's awareness.

If I attack,

Mind

All separation enshrines attack in some form.

I suffer.

What is perceived enters the mind's awareness.

problem

You see the world that you have made, but you do not see yourself as the image maker. You cannot be saved from the world, but you can escape from its cause. This is what salvation means...

T 8 VII 12.1   W 23 3.2   W 216 1.3   W 23 4,1-3

The world provides no safety. It is rooted in attack...

The purpose of attack is in the mind, and its effects are felt but where it is.

...condemnation is the root of attack. It is the judgment of one mind by another as unworthy of love...

T 23 IV 1.10   W 153 1.2-3   T 24 3.5   T 13 Intro 1.1

You may have carried the ego's reasoning to its logical conclusion, which is total confusion about everything. The only reason you could possibly want any part of it is because you do not see the whole of it.

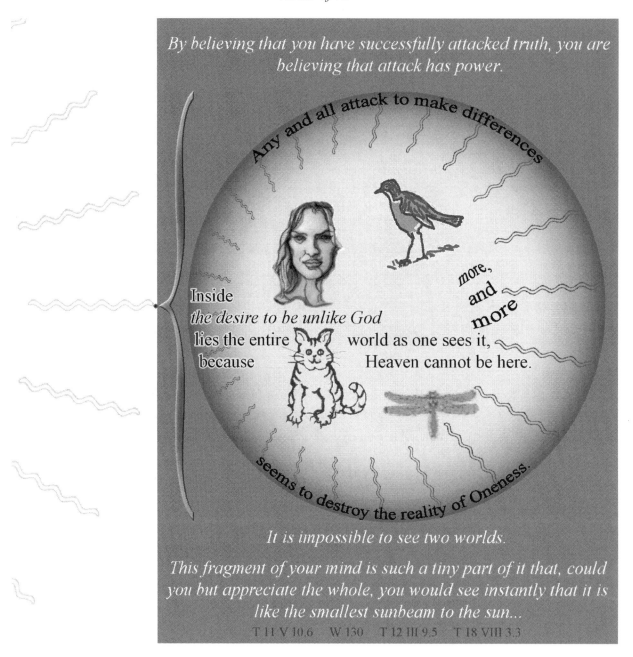

By believing that you have successfully attacked truth, you are believing that attack has power.

Any and all attack to make differences

Inside the desire to be unlike God lies the entire because world as one sees it, Heaven cannot be here.

more, and more

seems to destroy the reality of Oneness.

It is impossible to see two worlds.

This fragment of your mind is such a tiny part of it that, could you but appreciate the whole, you would see instantly that it is like the smallest sunbeam to the sun...

T 11 V 10.6   W 130   T 12 III 9.5   T 18 VIII 3.3

Your Self is radiant in this holy joy, unchanged, unchanging and unchangeable, forever and forever. And would you deny a little corner of your mind its own inheritance, and keep it as a hospital for pain; a sickly place where living things must come at last to die?

T VII 10 1.2,4   W 190 6.5

Within this kingdom the ego rules, and cruelly. And to defend this little speck of dust it bids you fight against the universe.

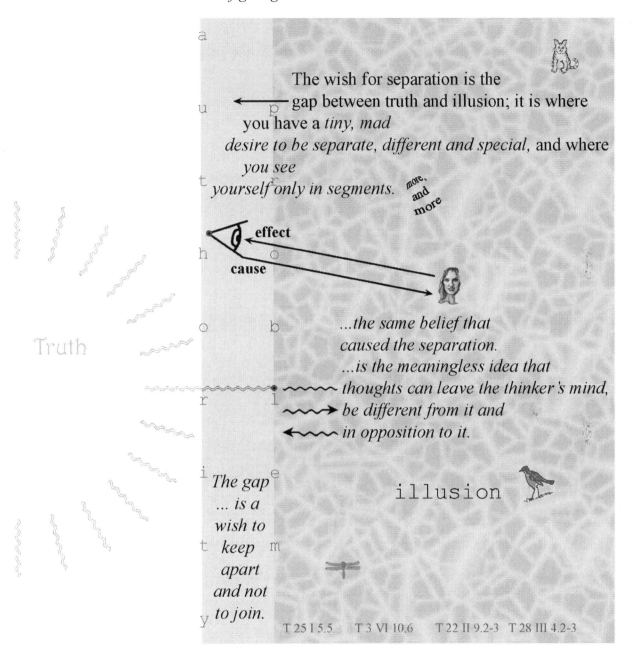

The wish for separation is the gap between truth and illusion; it is where you have a *tiny, mad desire to be separate, different and special,* and where *you see* yourself only in segments. *more, and more*

effect

cause

...the same belief that caused the separation.
...is the meaningless idea that thoughts can leave the thinker's mind, be different from it and in opposition to it.

Truth

illusion

The gap ... is a wish to keep apart and not to join.

T 25 I 5.5   T 3 VI 10.6   T 22 II 9.2-3   T 28 III 4.2-3

The ego always attacks on behalf of separation. ...it does nothing else...

T 18 VIII 3.1   T 11 V 7.1-2

His Will

Sharing His Will with me
is not really open to choice,
though it may seem to be.

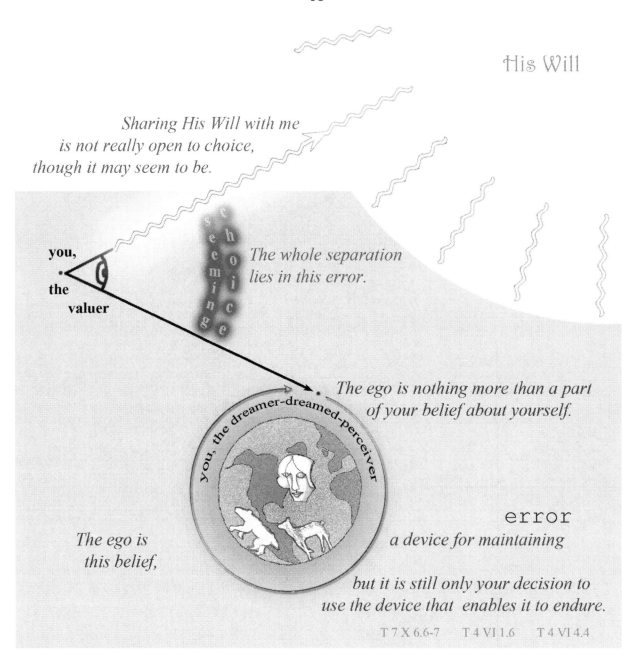

you,

seeming choice

The whole separation
lies in this error.

the
valuer

you, the dreamer-dreamed-perceiver

The ego is nothing more than a part
of your belief about yourself.

The ego is
this belief,

error

a device for maintaining

but it is still only your decision to
use the device that enables it to endure.

T 7 X 6.6-7   T 4 VI 1.6   T 4 VI 4.4

You *are the dreamer of the world of dreams. No other cause it has, nor ever will.*

T 27 VII 13.1-2

99

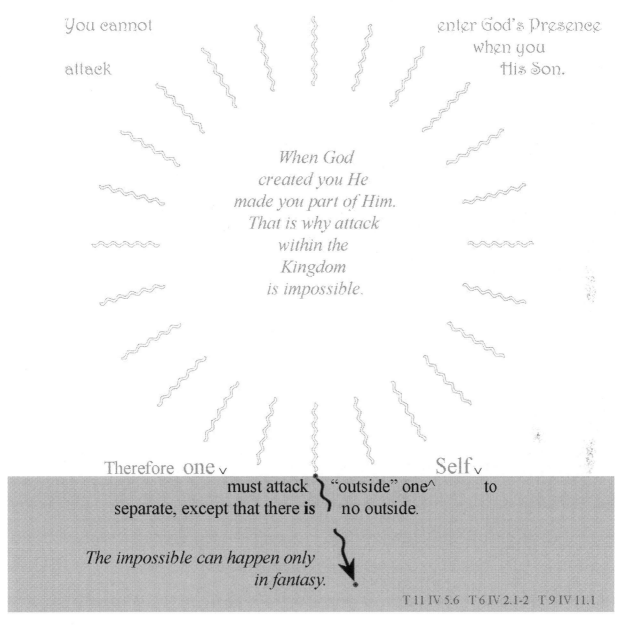

You cannot attack enter God's Presence when you His Son.

When God created you He made you part of Him. That is why attack within the Kingdom is impossible.

Therefore one ˅ Self ˅
must attack ⟩ "outside" one^ to separate, except that there **is** ⟩ no outside.

The impossible can happen only in fantasy.

T 11 IV 5.6   T 6 IV 2.1-2   T 9 IV 11.1

The ego does not regard itself as part of you. Herein lies its primary error, the foundation of its whole thought system.

T VI 1.6

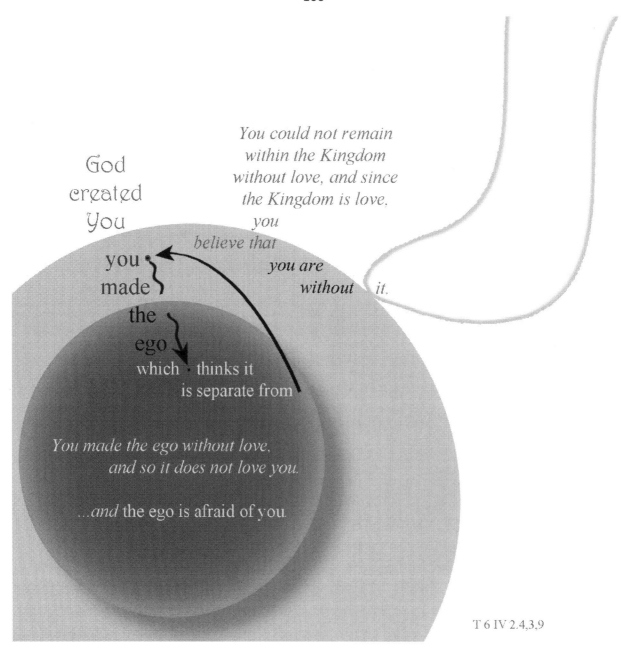

God created You

You could not remain within the Kingdom without love, and since the Kingdom is love. you believe that

you made the ego which thinks it is separate from

you are without it.

You made the ego without love, and so it does not love you.

...and the ego is afraid of you

T 6 IV 2.4,3,9

This enables the ego to regard itself as separate and outside its maker [you], *thus speaking for the part of your mind that believes* you *are separate and outside the Mind of God.*

Your will is not the ego's, and that is why the ego is against you.

T 6 IV 2.5   T 9 I 2.1

Mind

...the ego is part
of your mind, and because of its source the ego is
not wholly split off, or it   unbelief
could not be believed at all.
For it is your mind that believes in it
and gives existence to it.

For if
you could really separate
yourself
from the Mind of God you would die.

T 12 IV 2.4-5   T 12 III 8.5

Knowledge is total, and the ego does not believe in totality. This unbelief is its origin.

T VI 4.2

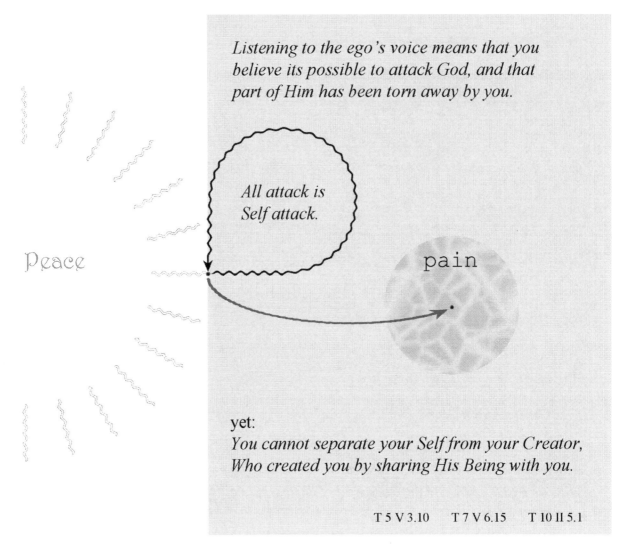

Listening to the ego's voice means that you believe its possible to attack God, and that part of Him has been torn away by you.

All attack is Self attack.

Peace

pain

yet:
You cannot separate your Self from your Creator, Who created you by sharing His Being with you.

T 5 V 3.10   T 7 V 6.15   T 10 II 5.1

If you further recognize that you are part of God, you will understand why it is that you always attack yourself first.

If attack thoughts must entail the belief that you are vulnerable, their effect is to weaken you in your own eyes. Thus they have attacked your perception of yourself.

T 10 II 4.5   W 26 3.1-2

2.IV: Sleeping in Dreams

Nothing at all has happened but that you have put yourself to sleep, and dreamed a dream in which you were an alien to yourself, and but a part of someone else's dream.

Yet where are dreams but in a mind asleep?

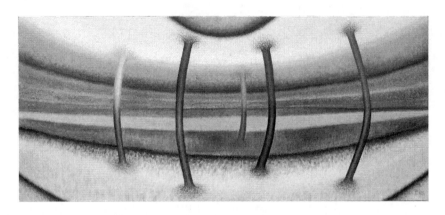

And who can stand upon a distant shore and dream himself across an ocean, to a place and time that have long since gone by? ...In the extreme, he can delude himself that this is true, and pass from mere imagining into belief and into madness, quite convinced that where he would prefer to be, he is.

T 28 II 4.1   T 29 VII 9.1   T 26 V 6

Dreams of any kind
are strange and alien to the truth.

Nothing I see in this room means anything.

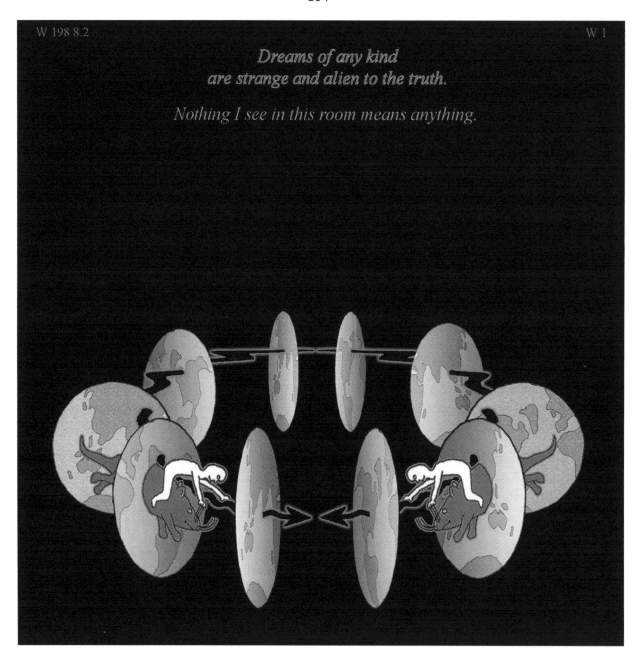

When the mind elects to be what it is not, and to assume an alien power which it does not have, a foreign state it cannot enter, or a false condition not within its Source, it merely seems to go to sleep a while.

W 167 9.2

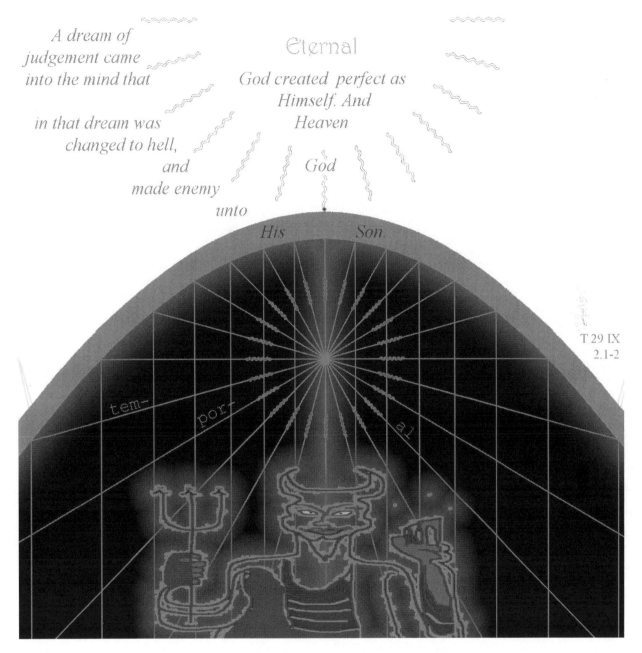

A dream of judgement came into the mind that

in that dream was changed to hell, and made enemy unto

Eternal

God created perfect as Himself. And Heaven

God

His Son.

tem- por- al

T 29 IX 2.1-2

What seems to be the opposite of life is merely sleeping.

God's extending outward, though not His completeness, is blocked when the Sonship does not communicate with Him as one. So He thought, "My children sleep and must be awakened".

W 167 9.1   T 6 V 1.7-8

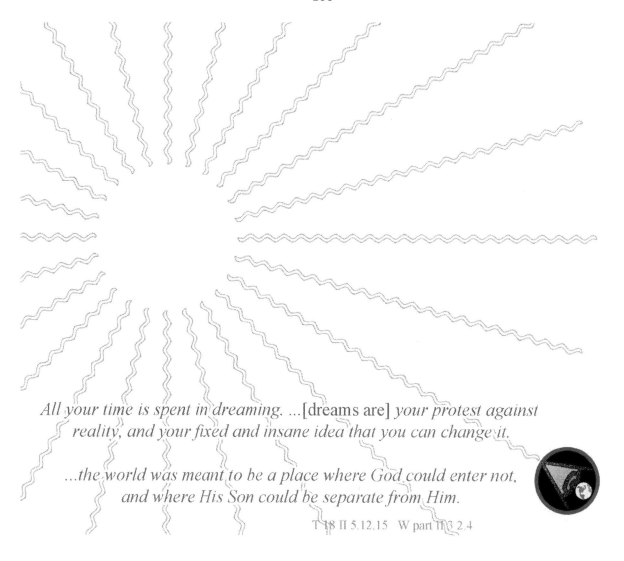

All your time is spent in dreaming. ...[dreams are] your protest against reality, and your fixed and insane idea that you can change it.

...the world was meant to be a place where God could enter not, and where His Son could be separate from Him.

T 18 II 5.12.15   W part II 3.2.4

What you wish is true for you. Nor is it possible that you can wish for something and lack faith that it is so.

T 24 V 1.6-7

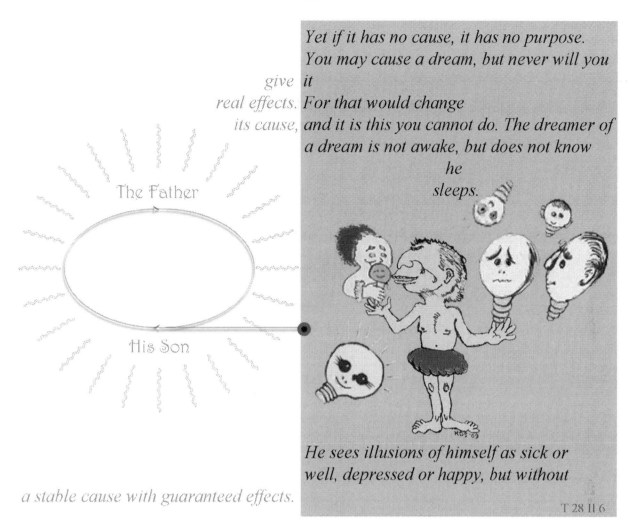

The Father

His Son

Yet if it has no cause, it has no purpose.
You may cause a dream, but never will you give it
real effects. For that would change
its cause, and it is this you cannot do. The dreamer of
a dream is not awake, but does not know
he
sleeps.

He sees illusions of himself as sick or
well, depressed or happy, but without
a stable cause with guaranteed effects.

T 28 II 6

It is true for you because it is made by you.

T 1 VI 4.6

You are at home in God, dreaming of exile but perfectly capable of awakening to reality. ...what you see in dreams you think is real while you are asleep.

T 10 I 2.1.5

I go before you because I am beyond the ego. Reach, therefore, for my hand because you want to transcend the ego. My strength will never be wanting, and if you choose to share it you will do so. I give it willingly and gladly, because I need you as much as you need me.

The dreams you think you like would hold you back as much as those in which the fear is seen.

T 8 V 6.7-10
T 29 IV 2.1-4

For every dream is but a dream of fear, no matter what the form it seems to take. The fear is seen within, without, or both. Or it can be disguised in pleasant form.

You do not remember being awake.

Dreams have no reason in them. A flower turns into a poisoned spear, a child becomes a giant and a mouse roars like a lion. And love is turned to hate as easily. This is no army, but a madhouse. What seems to be a planned attack is bedlam.

T 10 I 3.2   T 21 VII 3.9

2 V: The Mind's First, Secret Inner Dream of Murder

...a murderer who stalks you in the night and plots your death, yet plans that it be lingering and slow; of this you dream. Yet underneath this dream is yet another, in which you become the murderer, the secret enemy, the scavenger and the destroyer of your brother and the world alike.

The dreaming of the world... started by your secret dream which you do not perceive although it caused the part you see and do not doubt is real.

For in that dark and secret place is the realisation that you have betrayed God's Son by condemning him to death.

T 27 VII 11.6-7   T 13 II 3.2

Here is the cause of suffering... the birthplace of illusions and of fear, the time of terror and of ancient hate, the instant of disaster, all are here. Here is the cause of unreality.

From the ego came sin and guilt and death, in opposition to life and innocence, and to the Will of God Himself.

T 27 VII 12   T 19 IV C 3.1

A: Sin, Guilt, and Sin and Guilt

The separation started with the dream the Father was deprived of His effects, and powerless to keep them since He was no longer their Creator.

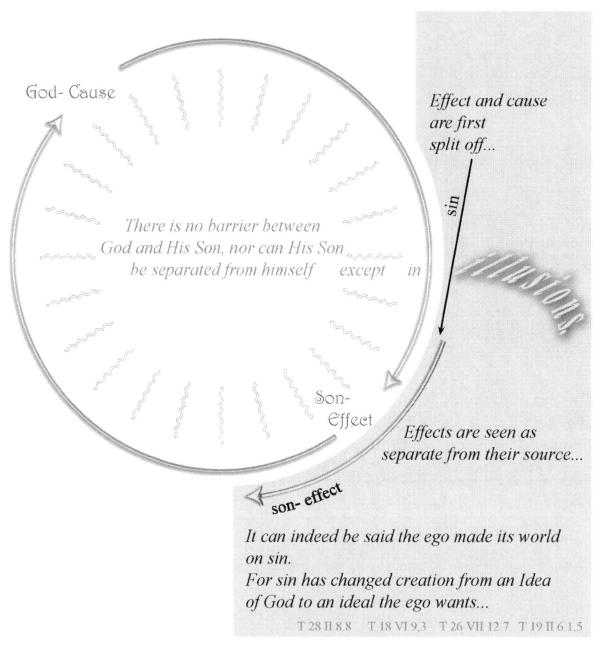

God- Cause

There is no barrier between God and His Son, nor can His Son be separated from himself   except   in

illusions

Son- Effect

son- effect

Effect and cause are first split off...

sin

Effects are seen as separate from their source...

It can indeed be said the ego made its world on sin.
For sin has changed creation from an Idea of God to an ideal the ego wants...

T 28 II 8.8   T 18 VI 9,3   T 26 VII 12.7   T 19 II 6.1.5

For sin is the idea you are alone and separated off from what is whole.

The Father
and
The Son

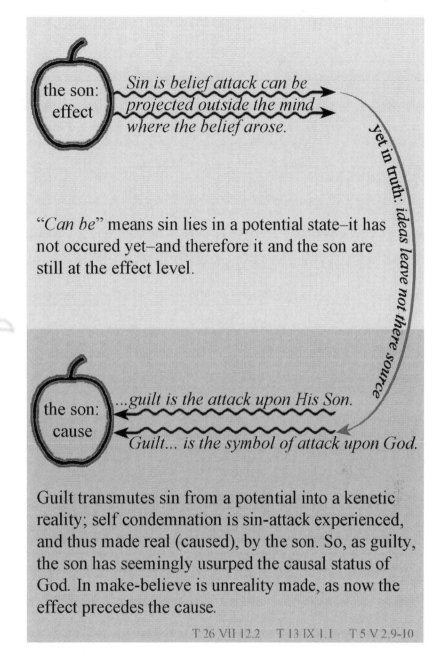

the son: effect

Sin is belief attack can be projected outside the mind where the belief arose.

yet in truth: ideas leave not there source

"*Can be*" means sin lies in a potential state–it has not occured yet–and therefore it and the son are still at the effect level.

the son: cause

...guilt is the attack upon His Son.

Guilt... is the symbol of attack upon God.

Guilt transmutes sin from a potential into a kenetic reality; self condemnation is sin-attack experienced, and thus made real (caused), by the son. So, as guilty, the son has seemingly usurped the causal status of God. In make-believe is unreality made, as now the effect precedes the cause.

T 26 VII 12.2   T 13 IX 1.1   T 5 V 2.9-10

Denial of Self results in illusions, while correction of the error brings release from it.

He [maker of dream] does not realise he picked a thread from here, a scrap from there, and wove a picture out of nothing.

T 28 II 8.1   T 30 III 3.7   T 1 VII 1.6   T 24 V 2.2-3

Attack and sin are bound as one illusion...

The ego does not perceive sin as a lack of love, but as a positive act of assault.

Sin is the symbol of attack.

...[to] make him *[Son of God]* really guilty. *That is what sin would do, for such is its purpose.*

The
Son

a u t h o r i t y

p r o b l e m

g u i l t

c a u s e

sin to be "real"

. . i
. . s
. g t
. u h
. i e
. l b
. t e
. . l
. . i
. . e
. . f

i n
s i n .

"outside" the mind

Guilt cuts off sin, such that the original separative attack indeed now appears to be *projected outside the mind*, out of awareness. Guilt is the cause of separation's "reality".

T 25 V 1.3   T 5 V 4.9   W 247 1.1   T 19 II 3.3-4   T 5 V 4.8   T 26 VII 12.2

The world began with one strange lesson, powerful enough to render God forgotten, and His Son an alien to himself, in exile from the home where God Himself established him. You who have taught yourself the Son of God is guilty...

T 31 I 4.5-6

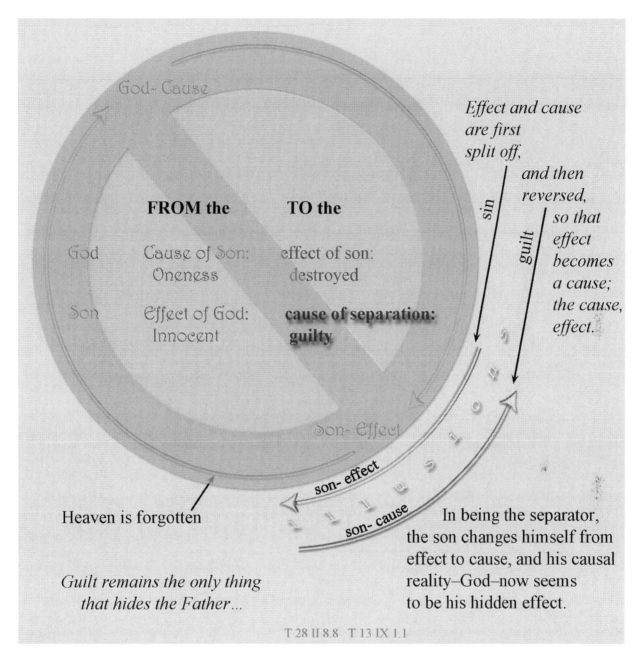

FROM the   **TO the**

God   Cause of Son: effect of son:
         Oneness   destroyed

Son   Effect of God: **cause of separation:**
         Innocent   **guilty**

God- Cause

Son- Effect

son- effect

son- cause

Effect and cause are first split off,

and then reversed, so that effect becomes a cause; the cause, effect.

sin

guilt

Heaven is forgotten

Guilt remains the only thing that hides the Father...

In being the separator, the son changes himself from effect to cause, and his causal reality–God–now seems to be his hidden effect.

T 28 II 8.8   T 13 IX 1.1

The Son is the effect, whose Cause he would deny. And so he seems to be the cause, producing real effects.

Fantasy is a distorted form of vision. Fantasies... always involve twisting perception into unreality. Actions that stem from distortions are literally the reactions of those who know not what they do. ...Twist reality in any way and you are perceiving destructively.

T 21 II 10.6-7   T 1 VII 3

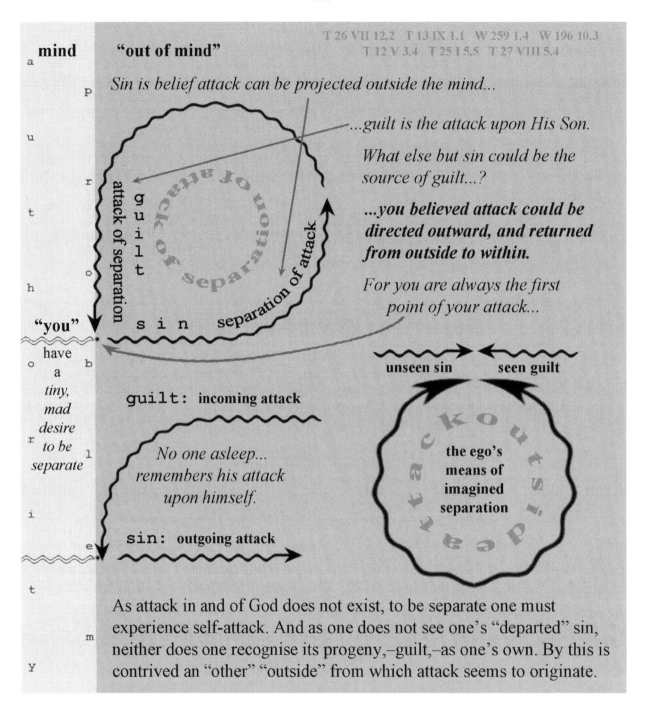

mind   "out of mind"

a p u r t o h "you" b o r l i e t m y — *have a tiny, mad desire to be separate*

T 26 VII 12.2 T 13 IX 1.1 W 259 1.4 W 196 10.3
T 12 V 3.4 T 25 I 5.5 T 27 VIII 5.4

Sin is belief attack can be projected outside the mind...

...guilt is the attack upon His Son.

What else but sin could be the source of guilt...?

...you believed attack could be directed outward, and returned from outside to within.

For you are always the first point of your attack...

attack of separation

guilt of attack

separation of attack

g u i l t

s i n

unseen sin   seen guilt

guilt: incoming attack

No one asleep... remembers his attack upon himself.

sin: outgoing attack

attackoutside's idea

the ego's means of imagined separation

As attack in and of God does not exist, to be separate one must experience self-attack. And as one does not see one's "departed" sin, neither does one recognise its progeny,–guilt,–as one's own. By this is contrived an "other" "outside" from which attack seems to originate.

For the idea of guilt brings a belief in condemnation of one by another, projecting separation in place of unity. You can condemn only yourself...

T 13 I 6.3-4

Attack [separation] *makes Christ* [oneness] *your enemy, and God along with Him. Must you not be afraid with "enemies" like these? And must you not be fearful of yourself?*

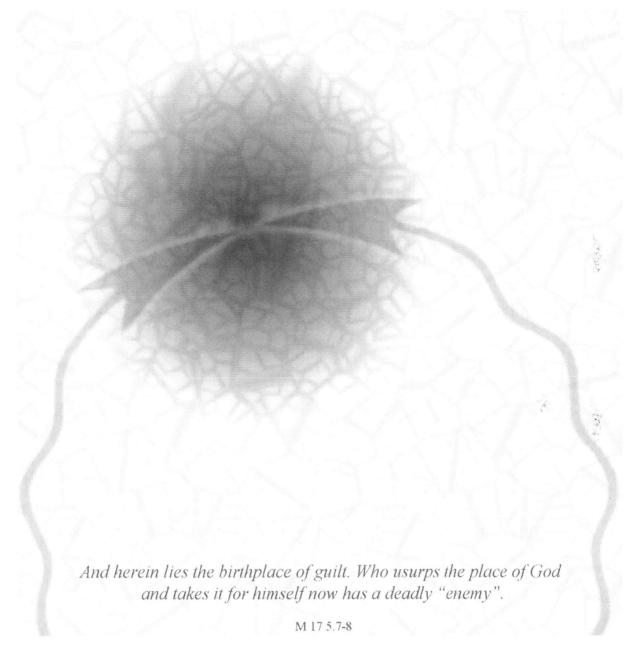

And herein lies the birthplace of guilt. Who usurps the place of God and takes it for himself now has a deadly "enemy".

M 17 5.7-8

Forget not that the witness to the world of evil cannot speak except for what has seen a need for evil in the world. And it is this where your guilt was first beheld.

T 25 V 2.1-3 T 27 VII 6.2-3

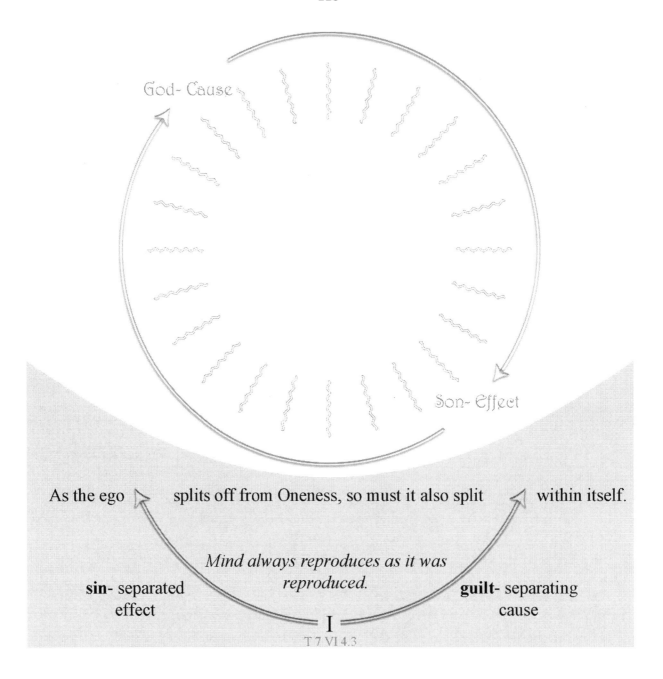

God- Cause

Son- Effect

As the ego ▷ splits off from Oneness, so must it also split ◁ within itself.

Mind always reproduces as it was reproduced.

sin- separated effect

guilt- separating cause

I

T 7 VI 4.3

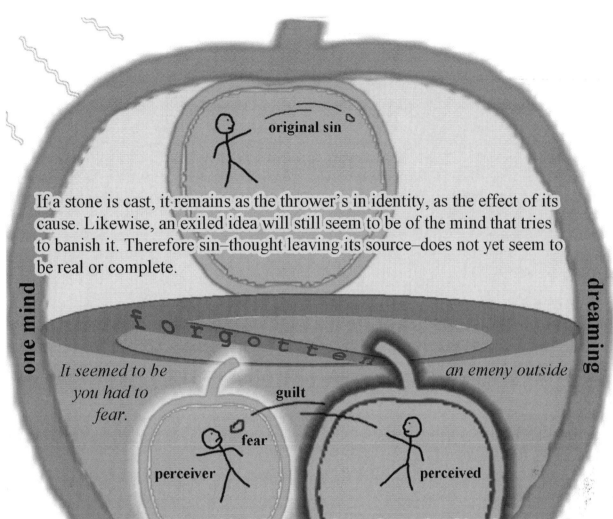

If a stone is cast, it remains as the thrower's in identity, as the effect of its cause. Likewise, an exiled idea will still seem to be of the mind that tries to banish it. Therefore sin–thought leaving its source–does not yet seem to be real or complete.

Yet if an attacking "stone-idea" is seen as incoming and making fear, now does it and its cause seem to be outside of the mind that sees it; guilt-fear makes sin-separation believed. There is still only one mind, yet it is split into a perceiver and a perceived, whereby the "original sin" is forgotten.

T 16 V 2.1

For sin and condemnation are the same, and the belief in one is faith in the other, calling for punishment instead of love.

For if what has been will be punished, the ego's continuity is guaranteed.

T 13 IX 5.5   T 13 I 8.7

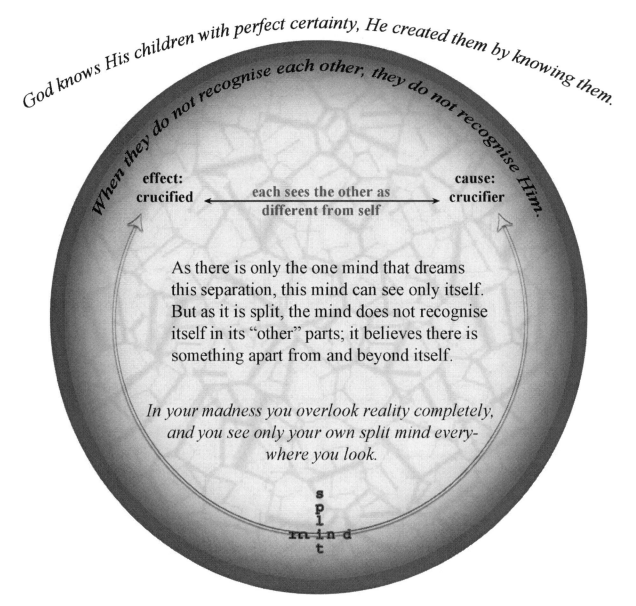

God knows His children with perfect certainty, He created them by knowing them.

When they do not recognise each other, they do not recognise Him.

effect:
crucified ← each sees the other as different from self → cause:
crucifier

As there is only the one mind that dreams this separation, this mind can see only itself. But as it is split, the mind does not recognise itself in its "other" parts; it believes there is something apart from and beyond itself.

In your madness you overlook reality completely, and you see only your own split mind everywhere you look.

split mind

T 3 III 7.9,12,1   T 13 V 6.5

To be alone is to be guilty. For to experience yourself as alone is to deny the Oneness of the Father and His Son, and thus to attack reality.

For the mind that judges perceives itself as separate from the mind being judged...

The war against yourself is but the battle of two illusions, struggling to make them different from each other...

T 15 V 2.6   T 13 Intro 1.4   T 23 I 6.1

B: Fear

Very simply, then, you have become afraid of yourself. And no one wants to find what he believes would destroy him.

For who [a god] has decreed that all things pass away, ending in dust and disappointment and despair, can but be feared. ...Who loves such a god knows not of love, because he has denied that life is real.

When the fear of God is gone, there are no obstacles that still remain between you and the holy peace of God.

T 11 V 10.7-8   M 27 2.2,5   2W 196 12.2

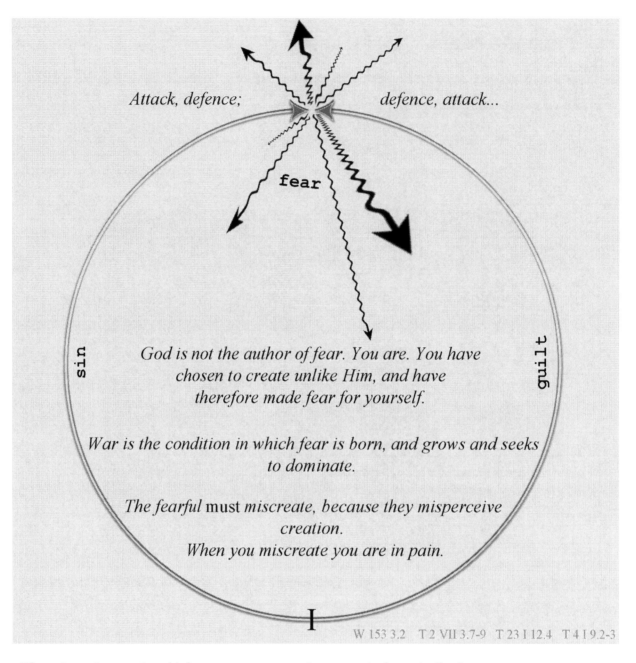

Attack, defence; defence, attack...

fear

sin

guilt

God is not the author of fear. You are. You have chosen to create unlike Him, and have therefore made fear for yourself.

War is the condition in which fear is born, and grows and seeks to dominate.

The fearful must miscreate, because they misperceive creation.
When you miscreate you are in pain.

I

W 153 3.2   T 2 VII 3.7-9   T 23 I 12.4   T 4 I 9.2-3

There is an instant in which terror seems to grip your mind so wholly that escape appears quite hopeless.

W 196 10.1,5

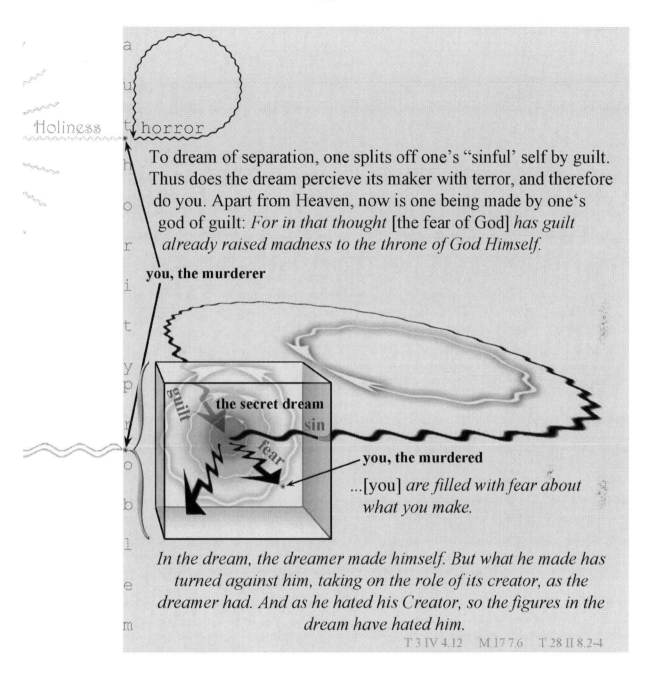

a
u
t
h
o
r
i
t
y
p
r
o
b
l
e
m

Holiness horror

you, the murderer

To dream of separation, one splits off one's "sinful' self by guilt. Thus does the dream percieve its maker with terror, and therefore do you. Apart from Heaven, now is one being made by one's god of guilt: *For in that thought* [the fear of God] *has guilt already raised madness to the throne of God Himself.*

guilt

the secret dream

sin

fear

you, the murdered

...[you] *are filled with fear about what you make.*

In the dream, the dreamer made himself. But what he made has turned against him, taking on the role of its creator, as the dreamer had. And as he hated his Creator, so the figures in the dream have hated him.

T 3 IV 4.12   M 17 7.6   T 28 II 8.2-4

The mind must think of its Creator as it looks upon itself.

To Him you ascribed the ego's treachery, inviting it to take His place to protect you from Him.

And thus a god outside yourself became your mortal enemy; the source of fear.

T 30 VI 4.6   T 15 X 8.5   W 196 10.4

Very simply, the attempt to make guilty is always directed against God. For the ego would have you see Him, and Him alone, as guilty, leaving the Sonship open to attack and unprotected from it.

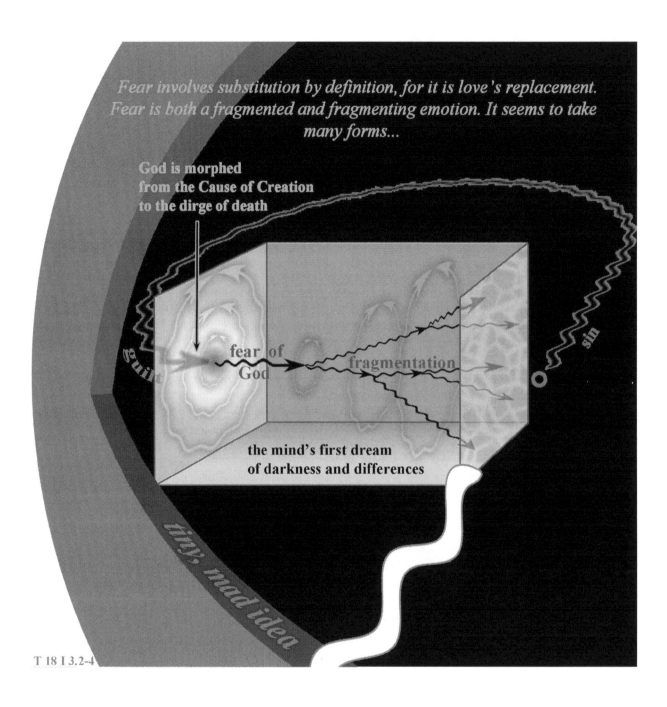

T 18 I 3.2-4

Fear has made everything you think you see. All separation, all distinctions, and the multitude of differences you believe make up the world.

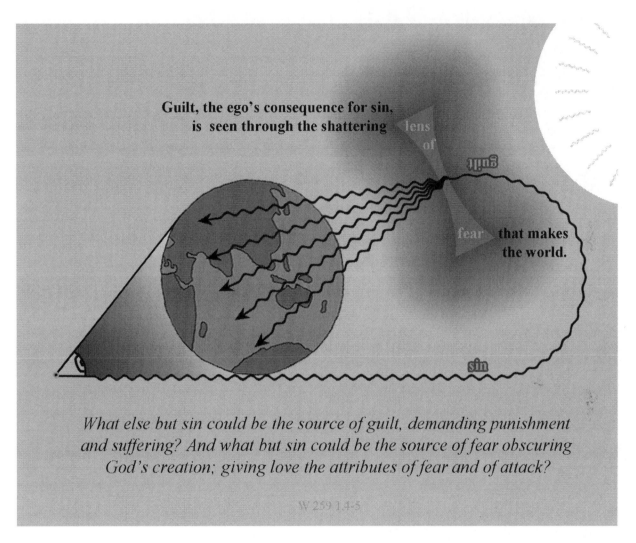

Guilt, the ego's consequence for sin, is seen through the shattering lens of guilt fear **that makes the world.** sin

What else but sin could be the source of guilt, demanding punishment and suffering? And what but sin could be the source of fear obscuring God's creation; giving love the attributes of fear and of attack?

W 259 1.4-5

You who believe that God is fear made but one substitution. It has taken many forms, because it was the substitution of illusion for truth; of fragmentation for wholeness. ... That one error, which brought truth to illusion, infinity to, time, and life to death, was all you ever made. Your whole world rests upon it.

T 16 V 2.1-2   W 130 4.1   T 18 I 4

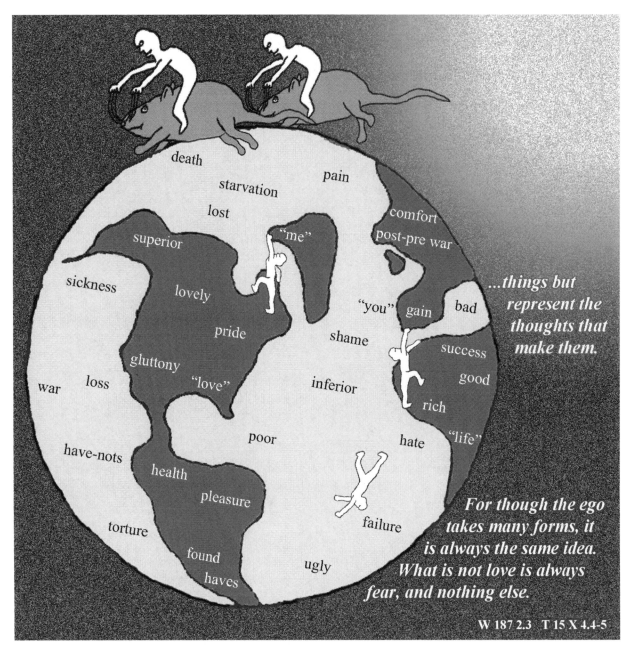

death

starvation

pain

lost

comfort

post-pre war

superior

"me"

sickness

lovely

"you" gain bad

pride

shame

...things but represent the thoughts that make them.

gluttony

"love"

success

good

war loss

inferior

rich

have-nots

poor

hate "life"

health

pleasure

torture

failure

found

ugly

haves

For though the ego takes many forms, it is always the same idea. What is not love is always fear, and nothing else.

W 187 2.3   T 15 X 4.4-5

You can be sure indeed that any seeming happiness that does not last is really fear.

W 187 2.3   T 22 II 3.5

To identify with the ego is to attack yourself and make yourself poor. ...what he [you] did was to exchange Self-love for self-hate, making him afraid of himself.

The fundamental conflict in this world, then, is between creation [Cause] and miscreation [effect]. All fear is implicit in the second, and all love in the first. The conflict is therefore one between love and fear.

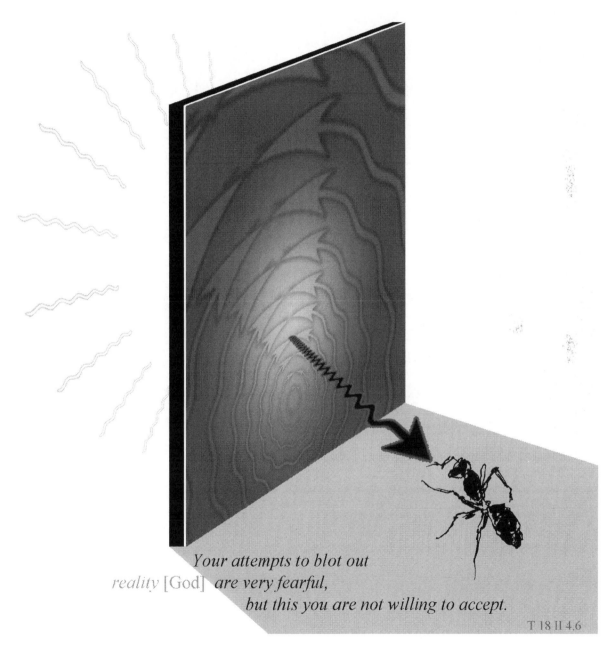

Your attempts to blot out reality [God] are very fearful, but this you are not willing to accept.

T 18 II 4.6

Any attempt to deny what is must be fearful, and if the attempt is strong it will induce panic.

T 12 III 6.1   T 2 VII 3.13   T 9 I 12.1

...you are afraid of your dissociation [self-attack], *not of what you have dissociated.*

T 18 II 4.7-8

And so you substitute the fantasy that reality is fearful,
not what you would do to [dissociate] it. And thus is guilt ["other"] made real.

What seems to be the fear of God is really the fear of your own [ego-made] *reality.*

T 10 II 1.5   T 9 I 2.2

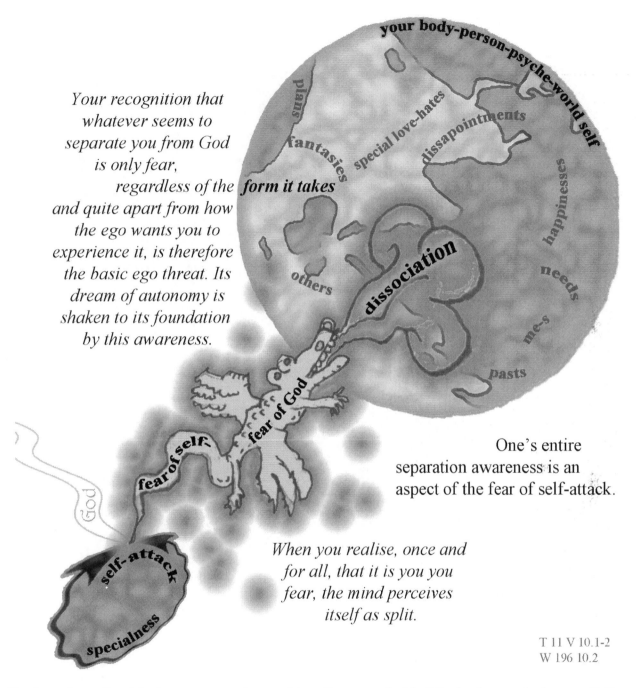

Your recognition that whatever seems to separate you from God is only fear, regardless of the **form it takes** *and quite apart from how the ego wants you to experience it, is therefore the basic ego threat. Its dream of autonomy is shaken to its foundation by this awareness.*

One's entire separation awareness is an aspect of the fear of self-attack.

When you realise, once and for all, that it is you you fear, the mind perceives itself as split.

T 11 V 10.1-2
W 196 10.2

You have been fearful of everyone and everything. You are afraid of God, of me and of yourself. You have misperceived or miscreated Us, and believe in what you have made. You would not have done this if you were not afraid of your own thoughts.

T 2 VII 3.5

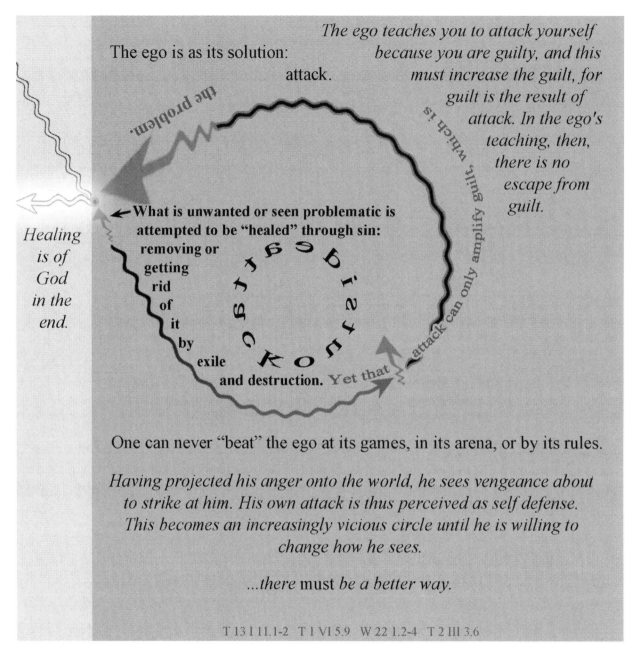

The ego is as its solution: attack.

The ego teaches you to attack yourself because you are guilty, and this must increase the guilt, for guilt is the result of attack. In the ego's teaching, then, there is no escape from guilt.

the problem.

which is attack can only amplify guilt,

Healing is of God in the end.

What is unwanted or seen problematic is attempted to be "healed" through sin: removing or getting rid of it by exile and destruction. Yet that

strategic conundrum

One can never "beat" the ego at its games, in its arena, or by its rules.

Having projected his anger onto the world, he sees vengeance about to strike at him. His own attack is thus perceived as self defense. This becomes an increasingly vicious circle until he is willing to change how he sees.

...there must be a better way.

T 13 I 11.1-2 T 1 VI 5.9 W 22 1.2-4 T 2 III 3.6

Knowledge must precede dissociation, so that dissociation is nothing more than a decision to forget. What has been forgotten then appears to be fearful, but only because the dissociation is an attack on truth [your Self]. You are fearful because you have forgotten.

10 II 1.2-4

2 VI: The Mind's Second, Outer Dream of the World

For if God would demand total sacrifice of you, it seems safer to project Him outward and away from you, and not be host to Him.

What can save you now from your delusion of an angry god, whose fearful image you believe you see at work in all the evils of the world? What but illusions could defend you now, when it is but illusions that you fight?

W 153 7.3-4

You do not realise the magnitude of that one error. It was so vast and so completely incredible that from it a world of total unreality had *to emerge. ...which seemed to cast you out of Heaven, to shatter knowledge into meaningless bits of disunited perceptions, and to force you to make further substitutions.*

And he must stand alone in his protection, and make himself a shield to keep him safe from fury that can never be abated, and vengeance that can never be satisfied.

The concept of the self stands like a shield, a silent barricade before the truth...

M 17 5.9 T 31 VII 7.1

That was the first projection of error outward. The world arose to hide it, and became the screen on which it was projected and drawn between you and the truth.

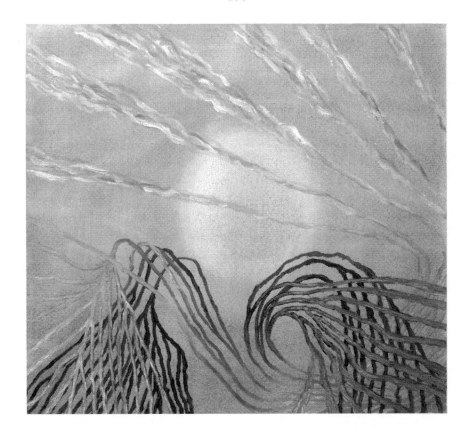

You have handled this wish to kill yourself by not knowing who you are, and identifying with something else.

T 15 X 8.4   T 18 I 5, 6.1   T 13 II 5.4

A: Projection

No one really sees anything. He sees only his thoughts projected outward.

You have projected outward what is antagonistic to what is inward, and therefore you would have to perceive it [the world] *this way.*

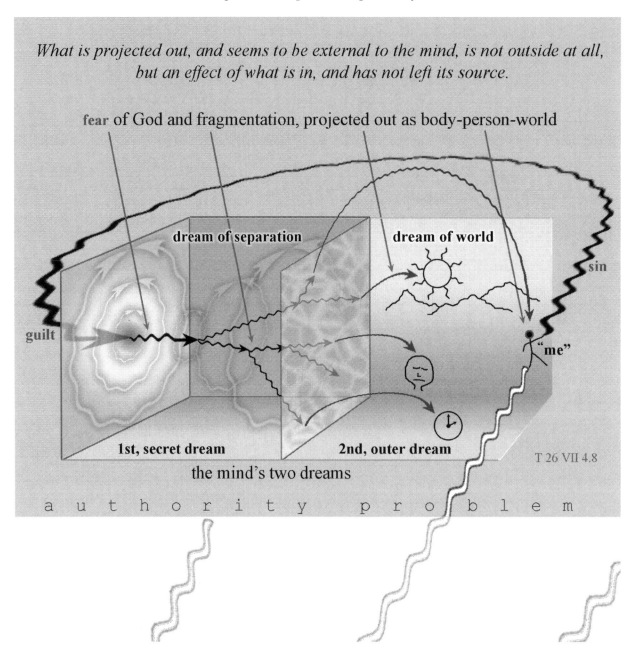

What is projected out, and seems to be external to the mind, is not outside at all, but an effect of what is in, and has not left its source.

fear of God and fragmentation, projected out as body-person-world

dream of separation

dream of world

sin

guilt

"me"

1st, secret dream

2nd, outer dream

T 26 VII 4.8

the mind's two dreams

a u t h o r i t y   p r o b l e m

Projection and attack are inevitably related, because projection is always a means of justifying attack. Anger without projection is impossible.

The delusional can be very destructive, for they do not recognize they have condemned themselves. ...And so they separate into their private worlds, where... what is within [murder] appears to be without. Yet what is within [oneness] they do not see, for the reality of their brothers they cannot recognize.

W 8 1.2-3   T 12 III 7.9   T 6 II 3.5-6   T 13 V 4

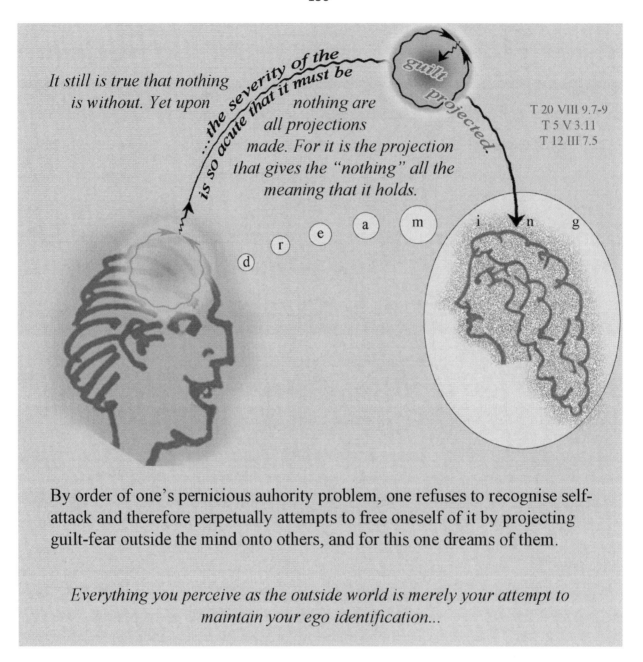

It still is true that nothing is without. Yet upon ...the severity of the is so acute that it must be nothing are all projections made. For it is the projection that gives the "nothing" all the meaning that it holds.

guilt projected.

T 20 VIII 9.7-9
T 5 V 3.11
T 12 III 7.5

d r e a m i n g

By order of one's pernicious auhority problem, one refuses to recognise self-attack and therefore perpetually attempts to free oneself of it by projecting guilt-fear outside the mind onto others, and for this one dreams of them.

Everything you perceive as the outside world is merely your attempt to maintain your ego identification...

It [the ego] is very ingenious in devising ways that seem to diminish conflict... It projects conflict from your mind to other minds, in an attempt to persuade you that you have gotten rid of the problem.

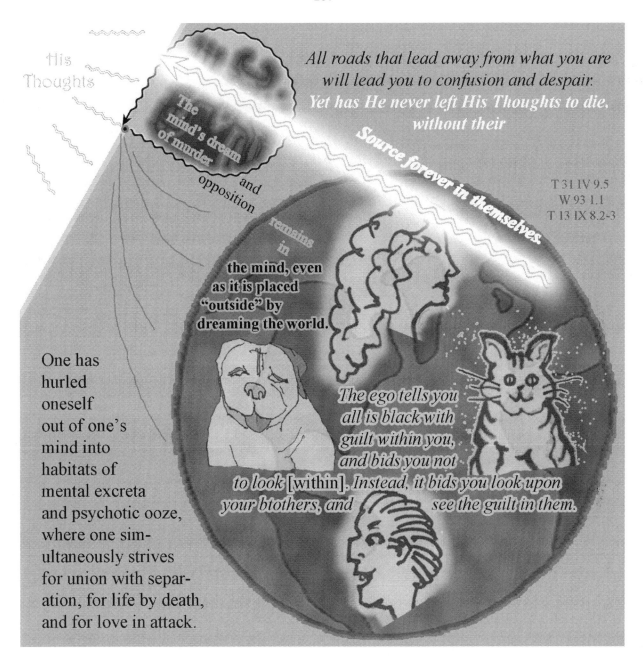

His Thoughts

The mind's dream of murder and opposition

All roads that lead away from what you are will lead you to confusion and despair. Yet has He never left His Thoughts to die, without their Source forever in themselves

T 31 IV 9.5
W 93 1.1
T 13 IX 8.2-3

remains in **the mind, even as it is placed "outside" by dreaming the world.**

One has hurled oneself out of one's mind into habitats of mental excreta and psychotic ooze, where one simultaneously strives for union with separation, for life by death, and for love in attack.

The ego tells you all is black with guilt within you, and bids you not to look [within]. Instead, it bids you look upon your brothers, and see the guilt in them.

...believing that by punishing another, it will escape punishment. All this is but the delusional attempt of the mind to deny itself, and escape the penalty of denial. It is not an attempt to relinquish denial, but to hold on to it.

T 7 VIII 2   T 13 Intro 1

authority problem

To the ego the goal is death...

T 15 I 2.7
T 12 VII 7.6

When you think you are projecting what you do not want, it is still because you do want it.

It is not will for life but wish for death that is the motivation for this world. Its only purpose is to prove guilt real.

You must receive the message you give because it is the message you want.

You have projected guilt blindly and indiscriminately, but you have not uncovered its source. For the ego does want to kill you [God's Son], *and if you identify with it you must believe its goal is yours.*

T 27 I 6.3-4　T 10 V 2.2　T 13 II 5.5-6

B: The World

Behold the great projection...

...this puff of madness...

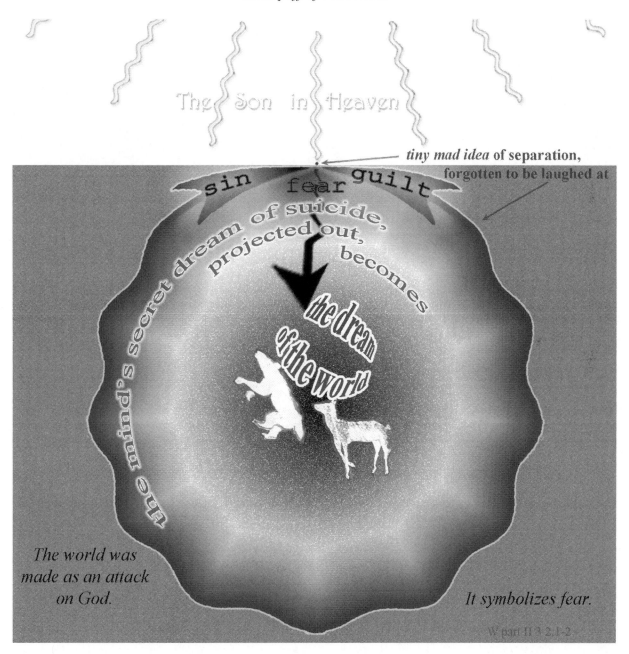

The Son in Heaven

tiny mad idea of separation,
forgotten to be laughed at

sin   fear   guilt

the mind's secret dream of suicide, projected out, becomes

the dream of the world

The world was made as an attack on God.

It symbolizes fear.

W-part II 3.2:1-2

The world you made is... made out of what you do not want, projected from your mind because you are afraid of it.

There is no world apart from your ideas because ideas leave not their source, and you maintain the world within your mind in thought.

You have made many ideas that you have placed between yourself and your Creator, and these beliefs are the world as you perceive it. Truth is not absent here, but it is obscure.

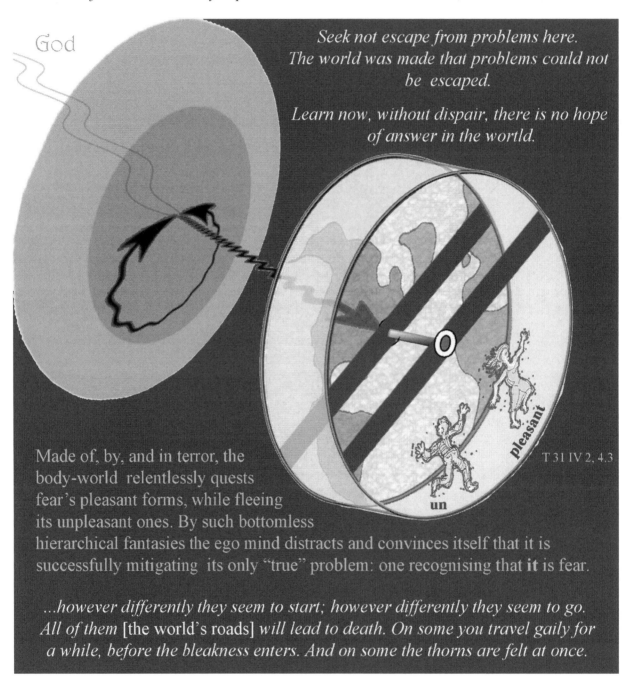

God

Seek not escape from problems here. The world was made that problems could not be escaped.

Learn now, without dispair, there is no hope of answer in the wortld.

T 31 IV 2, 4.3

Made of, by, and in terror, the body-world relentlessly quests fear's pleasant forms, while fleeing its unpleasant ones. By such bottomless hierarchical fantasies the ego mind distracts and convinces itself that it is successfully mitigating its only "true" problem: one recognising that **it** is fear.

...however differently they seem to start; however differently they seem to go. All of them [the world's roads] *will lead to death. On some you travel gaily for a while, before the bleakness enters. And on some the thorns are felt at once.*

T 22 II 10.1   T 20 III 8.4   W 32 1.2-3   W 132 10.3   T 11 VII 4.4-5

There is no world! This is the central thought the course attempts to teach.

The world is an illusion. Those who choose to come to it are seeking for a place where they can be illusions, and avoid their own reality.

There is no world!

...Not everyone is ready to accept it, and each one must go as far as he can let himself be led along the road to truth.

the Father and the Son

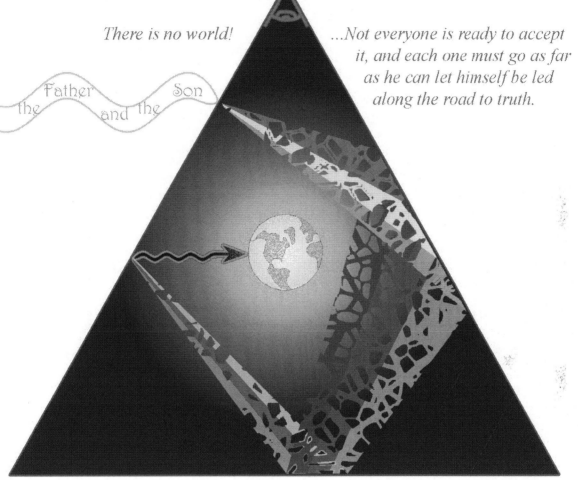

There is no world because it is a thought apart from God, and made to separate the Father and the Son, and break away a part of God Himself and thus destroy His Wholeness.

W 155 2.1-2   W 132 6.2,4 13.1

Can a world which comes from this idea be real? Can it be anywhere?

W 132 6.2-3, 13.2-3

The world you made is therefore totally chaotic... For it is made out of what you do not want, projected from your mind because you are afraid of it.

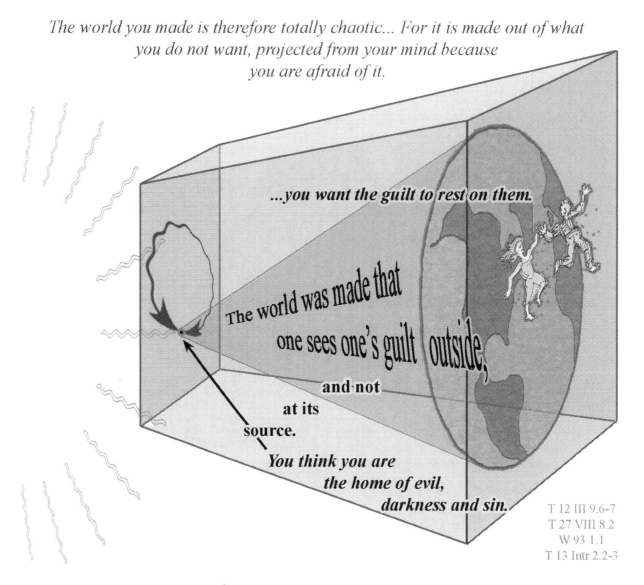

...you want the guilt to rest on them.

The world was made that one sees one's guilt outside, and not at its source.

You think you are the home of evil, darkness and sin.

T 12 III 9.6-7
T 27 VIII 8.2
W 93 1.1
T 13 Intr 2.2-3

*The world you see is the delusional system of those made mad by guilt.
Look carefully at this world, and you will realize that this is so,*

Every thought you have makes up some segment of the world you see.

It [the mind] *can project its guilt, but it will not lose it through projection.*

W 23 1.4   T 18 IV 4.5

The world you see is an illusion of a world. God did not create it, for what He creates must be eternal as Himself.

...you made the world you see...

what is mine cannot be God's thus He kicked me out of Heaven therefore I lack and need to take back

M-CT.4 1.1-2
T 21 II 11.1

For anti-Christ becomes more powerful than Christ to those who dream the world is real. The body becomes more solid and stable than the mind. And love becomes a dream...

W 137 6.2

It can indeed be said the ego made its world on sin. Only in such a world could everything be upside down.

For this world is the opposite of Heaven, being made to be its opposite, and everything here takes a direction exactly opposite of what is true.

...a world in which everything is backwards and upside down...

Yet this world is only in the mind of its maker, along with his real salvation. Do not believe it is outside of yourself, for only by recognizing where it is will you gain control over it. For you do have control over your mind, since the mind is the mechanism of decision.

You cannot be saved from the world, but you can escape from its cause. This is what salvation means, for where is the world you see when its cause is gone?

T 19 II 6.1-2   T 16 V 3.6   T 18 I 6.4   T 12 III 9.8-10   W 23 4.2-3

C: The Body

The Bible says, "The Word (or thought) was made flesh." Strictly speaking this is impossible, since it seems to involve the translation of one order of reality into another. ...Thought cannot be made into flesh except by belief, since thought is not physical..

And what are you who live within the world except a picture of the Son of God in broken pieces, each concealed within a separate and uncertain bit of clay?

When parts are wrested from the whole and seen as separate... they become symbols standing for attack upon the whole.

T 8 VII 7   T 28 III 7.5   W 136 6.3

The body is outside you [mind], and but seems to surround you, shutting you off from others and keeping you apart from them, and them from you. It is not there. ...This is not his [His Son's] reality, though he believes it is.

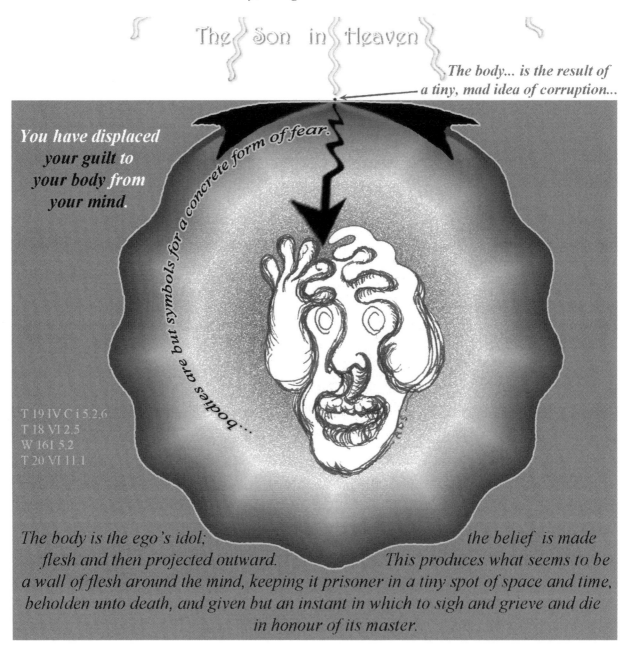

The Son in Heaven

The body... is the result of a tiny, mad idea of corruption...

You have displaced your guilt to your body from your mind.

...bodies are but symbols for a concrete form of fear.

T 19 IV C i 5.2,6
T 18 VI 2.5
W 161 5.2
T 20 VI 11.1

The body is the ego's idol; flesh and then projected outward. *the belief is made* *This produces what seems to be a wall of flesh around the mind, keeping it prisoner in a tiny spot of space and time, beholden unto death, and given but an instant in which to sigh and grieve and die in honour of its master.*

This is the host of God that you have made. And neither God nor His most holy Son can enter an abode that harbors hate, and where you have sown the seeds of vengeance, violence and death. This thing you made to serve your guilt stands between you and other minds.

T 18 VI 9   7.1-3

Yet bodies have no goal. Purpose is of the mind.

No one who comes here but must still have hope, some lingering illusion, or some dream that there is something outside of himself that will bring happiness and peace to him. ...This is the purpose he bestows upon the body; that it seek for what he lacks, and give him what would make himself complete.

And thus he wanders aimlessly about, in search of something that he cannot find, believing that he is what he is not. T 29 VII 2

It [the body] *is the only identification with which the ego feels safe, since the body's vulnerability is its own best argument that you cannot be of God. ...Yet the ego hates the body, because it cannot accept it as good enough to be its home. Here is where the mind becomes actually dazed.*

T 24 IV 2.5-6   T 4 V 4

I made up the prison in which I see myself.

You see yourself locked in a separate prison, removed and unreachable, incapable of reaching out as being reached.

It is only the awareness of the body that makes love seem limited. For the body is a limit on love. The belief in limited love was its origin, and it was made to limit the unlimited. ...it was made to limit you. Can you who see yourself within a body know yourself as an idea?

The body cannot know. And while you limit your awareness to its tiny senses, you will not see the grandeur that surrounds you. God cannot come into a body, nor can you join Him there. Limits on love will always seem to shut Him out, and keep you apart from Him.　　T 18 VIII 1.1-5, 2.1-4

...the place you set aside to house your hate is not a prison, but an illusion of yourself. The body is a limit imposed on the universal communication that is an eternal property of mind.

W 57 2.2　T 18 VI 7.5, 8.2

You see what is not there, and you hear what makes no sound.

It [the body] *cannot see nor hear. ...Its eyes are blind; its ears are deaf. It can not think, and so it cannot have effects.   ...*
For eyes and ears are senses without sense, and what they see and hear they but report: It is not they that hear and see, but you, who... make a witness to the world you want. Let not... them persuade their maker his imaginings are real.

The ego mind deceives one into believing that thought is of the brain, and sensory information, the body. All that is "sensed" are the mind's imagined ideas of taste, touch etc. that return to their source via its distorted perceptions of the "outside" body-world.

The senses are the mechanism of illusion

You also believe the body's brain can think. ...It is as if you thought you held the match that lights the sun and gives it all its warmth.... Yet this is no more foolish than to believe the body's eyes can see...

ego mind ●

T 28 V 4.5,8 5   W 92 2

It [the body] *transmits to you the feelings that you want. Like any communication medium the body receives and sends the messages that it is given. It has no feeling for them. All of the feeling with which they are invested is given by the sender and the receiver.*

To the ego the body is to attack with. *Equating you with the body, it teaches that* you *are to attack with. The body, then, is not the source of its own health. The body's condition lies solely in your interpretation of its function.*

150

Who hangs an empty frame upon a wall and stands before it, deep in reverence, as if a masterpiece were there to see? Yet if you see your brother as a body, it is but this you do.

The body is a tiny fence around a little part of a glorious and complete idea. It draws a circle, infinitely small, around a very little segment of Heaven, splintered from the whole, proclaiming that within it is your kingdom, where God can enter not.

No one who carries Christ in him can fail to recognize Him everywhere. Except *in bodies.*

...specialness set forth within his body.

The body is an isolated speck of darkness; a hidden secret room, a tiny spot of senseless mystery, a meaningless enclosure carefully protected, yet hiding nothing.

You cannot make the body the Holy Spirit's temple, and it will never be the seat of love. It is the home of the idolater, and of love's condemnation.

The hope of specialness makes it seem possible God made the body as the prison house that keeps His Son from Him. For it demands a special place God cannot enter, and a hiding place where none is welcome but your tiny self. Nothing is sacred here but unto you, and you alone...

There is no barrier between God and His Son, nor can His Son be separated from himself except in illusions.

You cannot put a barrier around yourself, because God placed none between Himself and you.

Yet is it joy to look upon decay and madness, and believe this crumbling thing, with flesh already loosened from the bone and sightless holes for eyes, is like yourself?

T 13 V 6.2   T 19 IV B 14.4-7   T 8 VIII 1.5   T 25 II 5.1-2   T 18 VIII 2.5-6   T 25 Intro 2.1-2,7   T 20 VI 5.2,6.1-2
T 24 II 13.1-3   T 18 VI 9.3,10   T 24 V 4.8

D: Time

The ego has a strange notion of time, and it is with this notion that your questioning might well begin.

...it [the mind] *merely seems to go to sleep a while. It dreams of time, an interval in which what seems to happen never has occurred, the changes wrought are substance-less, and all events are nowhere.*

The mind's preoccupation with the past is the cause of the misconception about time from which your seeing suffers. Your mind cannot grasp the present, which is the only time there is. It therefore cannot understand time, and cannot, in fact, understand anything.

Time really, then, goes backward to an instant so ancient that it is beyond all memory, and past even the possibility of remembering.

This instant is the only time there is.

...time is an illusion. ...The thoughts of God are quite apart from time. For time is but another meaningless defense against the truth.

T 13 IV 4.1   W 167 9   W 8 1   M 2 4.1   W 308   W 136 13

Time is a trick, a sleight of hand, a vast illusion in which figures come and go as if by magic. Yet there is a plan behind appearances that does not change. The script is written. When experience will come to end your doubting has been set. For we but see the journey from the point at which it ended, looking back on it, imagining we make it once again; reviewing mentally what has gone by.

The ego invests heavily in the past, and in the end believes that the past is the only aspect of time that is meaningful. Remember that its emphasis on guilt enables it to ensure its continuity by making the future like the past, and thus avoiding the present.

"Now" has no meaning to the ego. The present merely reminds it of past hurts, and it reacts to the present as if it were the past.

W 158 4 T 13 IV 4.2-3 5.1-2

I see only the past.

Unless you learn that past pain is an illusion, you are choosing a future of illusions and losing the many opportunities you could find for release in the present. The ego would preserve your nightmares, and prevent you from awakening and understanding they are past.

For guilt establishes that you will be punished for what you have done, and thus depends on one dimensional time, proceeding from past to future. No one who believes this can understand what "always" means, and therefore guilt must deprive you of the appreciation of eternity.

154

Time is inconceivable without change, yet holiness does not change. ...Change is an illusion, taught by those who cannot see themselves as guiltless. There is no change in Heaven because there is no change in God.

Time seems to go in one direction, but when you reach its end it will roll up like a long carpet spread along the past behind you, and will disappear.

T 13 I 3.5

You are immortal because you are eternal, and "always" must be now.

W 7   T 13 IV 6.6-7   T 13 I 8.3-4   T 15 I 10.1,5-6   T 13 I 8.5

Time itself is your choice. If you would remember eternity, you must look only on the eternal. If you allow yourself to become preoccupied with the temporal, you are living in time. As always, your choice is determined by what you value.

Time and eternity cannot both be real, because they contradict each other. If you will accept only what is timeless as real, you will begin to understand eternity and make it yours.

...sorrow can be turned to joy, for time gives way to the eternal. ...illusions must give way to truth, and not to other dreams...

Let us forget the purpose of the world the past has given it. For otherwise, the future will be like the past, and but a series of depressing dreams, in which all idols fail you, one by one, and you see death and disappointment everywhere.

Guilt feelings are the preservers of time. They induce fears of retaliation or abandonment, and thus ensure that the future will be like the past. ...It gives the ego a false sense of security by believing that you cannot escape from it. But you can and must.

...truth lies only in the present, and you will find it if you seek it there. You have looked for it where it is not, and therefore have not found it. ...Your past was made in anger, and if you use it to attack the present, you will not see the freedom that the present holds.

Only in the past—an ancient past, too short to make a world in answer to creation—did this world appear to rise. ...Yet in each unforgiving act or thought, in every judgment and in all belief in sin, is that one instant still called back... You keep an ancient memory before your eyes. And he who lives in memories alone is unaware of where he is.

T 10 V 14.4-7   T 10 V 14   T 22 II 3.7,9   T 29 VII 7   T 5 VI 2   T 13 VI 5.4   T 26 V 5

The time will come when you will not return in the same form in which you now appear, for you will have no need of it.

Physical birth is not a beginning; it is a continuing.

Such is each life; a seeming interval from birth to death and on to life again, a repetition of an instant gone by long ago that cannot be relived. And all of time is but the mad belief belief that what is over is still here and now.

Trials are but lessons that you failed to learn presented once again, so where you made a faulty choice before you now can make a better one, and thus escape all pain that what you chose before has brought to you.

Yet all who meet will someday meet again, for it is the destiny of all relationships to become holy.

And they will come again [to the world] *until the time Atonement is accepted...*

The world is not left by death but by truth...

Sometimes it dreams it is a conqueror of bodies weaker than itself. But in some phases of the dream, it is the slave of bodies that would hurt and torture it.

...you will believe that others do to you exactly what you think you did to them.

You think you hold against your brother what he has done to you. But what you really blame him for is what you *did to* him.

...you are also free to join my resurrection. Until you do so your life is indeed wasted. It merely re-enacts the separation, the loss of power, the futile attempts of the ego at reparation, and finally the crucifixion of the body, or death. Such repetitions are endless until they are voluntarily given up.

W 157 7.3   T 5 IV 2.4   T 26 V 13.3-4   T 31 VIII 5.1   M 3 4.6   W 139 7.3   T 3 VII 6.11   T 27 VIII 2.6-7 8.1
T 17 VII 8.2   T 4 Intr 3.3-6

E: Perception and *the great reversal*

The world you see depicts exactly what you thought you did. Except that now you think that what you did is being done to you.

...perception's fundamental law:

You see what and you believe is there, .
because you want it

Perception has no other law than this. The rest but stems from this, to hold it up and offer it support. This is perception's form, adapted to this world, of God's more basic law; that love creates itself, and nothing but itself.

T 25 III 1.3-6

In perception the whole is built up of parts that can separate and reassemble in different constellations. But knowledge never changes, so its constellation is permanent.

The ego may see some good, but never only good. That is why its perceptions are so variable.

T 23 II 15.1   T 27 VIII 7.2-3   T 8 VIII 1.12-13   T 11 VII 3.1-2

In dreams effect and cause are interchanged, for here the maker of the dream believes that what he made is happening to him.

Perception's laws must be reversed, because they are reversals of the laws of truth.

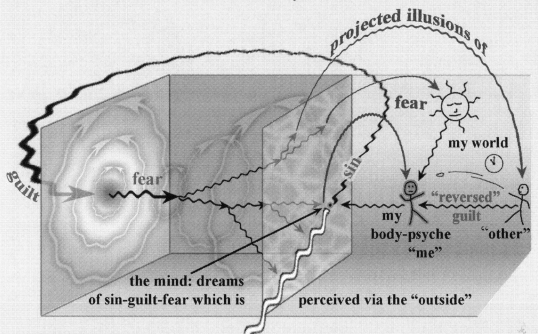

The imaginings of the mind's first dream are dissociated out into the body-person-world of the second dream. Here, concealed in the world and weeping from it, does self-loathing metamorphose; instead of from the dreaming mind, now does the outer world (including one's body-psyche) seem to be the bringer of malice. By this reversal of cause and effect is self-attack orchestrated from "elsewhere", obscuring the real source: the mind's valued separation.

T 24 V 2.2   T 26 VII 5.2

What you exclude from yourself seems fearful, for you endow it with fear and try to cast it out, though it is part of you.

T 15 XI 4.6

..."You have usurped the place of God. Think not He has forgotten."
...An angry father pursues his guilty son.

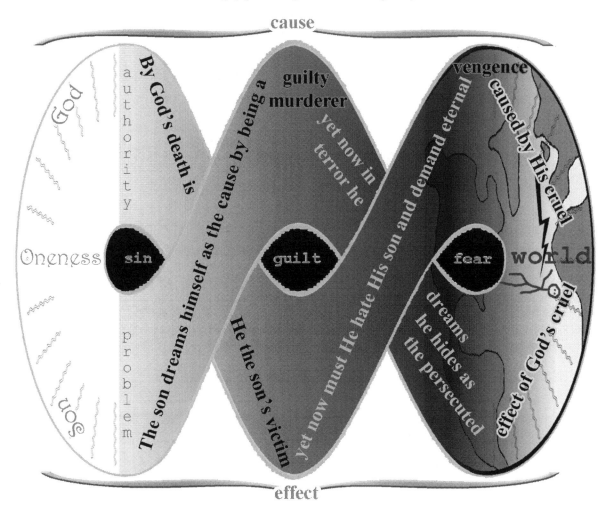

The stain of blood can never be removed, and anyone who bears
this stain on him must meet with death. M 17 7.3-4,10,13

And what would have effects through you must also have effects on you.

W 26 1.4

He sees only his thoughts projected...

The world you perceive is a world of separation.

W 8 3.1   T 12 III 9.1

A solid mountain range, a lake, a city, all rise in your imagination, and from the clouds the messengers of your perception return to you, assuring you that it is there. Figures stand out and move about, actions seem real, and forms appear and shift from loveliness to the grotesque. And back and forth they go, as long as you would play the game of children's make-believe.

T 18 IX 7

Each one peoples his world with figures from his individual past, and it is because of this that private worlds do differ.

The one collective ego mind dreams the world, yet its separate fragments dream their own interpretations onto it.

If anger comes from an interpretation and not a fact, it is never justified. Once this is even dimly grasped, the way is open.

Yet the figures ...are made up only of his reactions to his brothers, and do not include their reactions to him. Therefore, he does not see he made them, and that they are not whole.

Here it is difficult to see that others are entirely our projections of ourselves. In reality they are innocent Christ, upon which we cast our bile. One must rise *Above the Battleground* to see this.

T 13 V 2, 3.7-8   T 23 IV   M 17 8.6-7

...you must attack yourself first, for what you attack is not in others. Its only reality is in your own mind, and by attacking others you are literally attacking what is not there.

For it is we who make the world as we would have it.

Your brother is the mirror in which you see the image of yourself as long as perception lasts.

W 188 10.3   T 7 VII 3.9

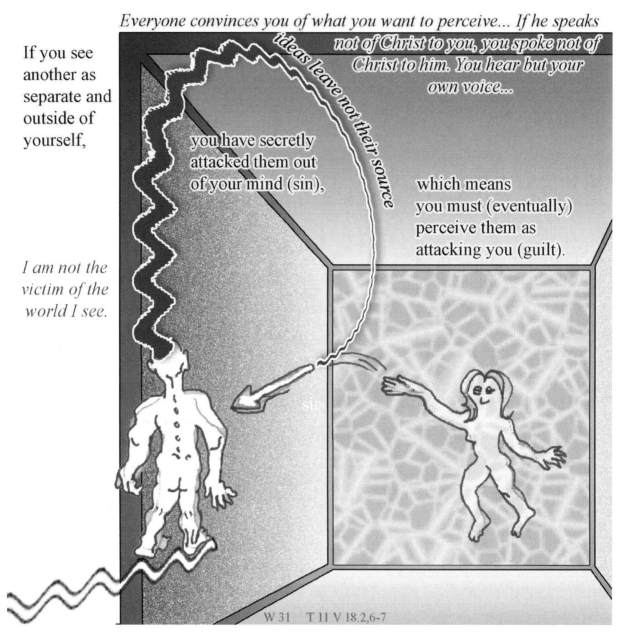

Everyone convinces you of what you want to perceive... If he speaks not of Christ to you, you spoke not of Christ to him. You hear but your own voice...

If you see another as separate and outside of yourself,

I am not the victim of the world I see.

ideas leave not their source

you have secretly attacked them out of your mind (sin),

which means you must (eventually) perceive them as attacking you (guilt).

W 31   T 11 V 18.2,6-7

You may believe that you judge your brothers by the messages they give you, but you have judged them by the message you give to them.

...meaning always looks within to find itself, and then *looks out.*

I have given what I see all the meaning it has for me.

T 10 V 2.3   T 20 VIII 10.2   W 51 2

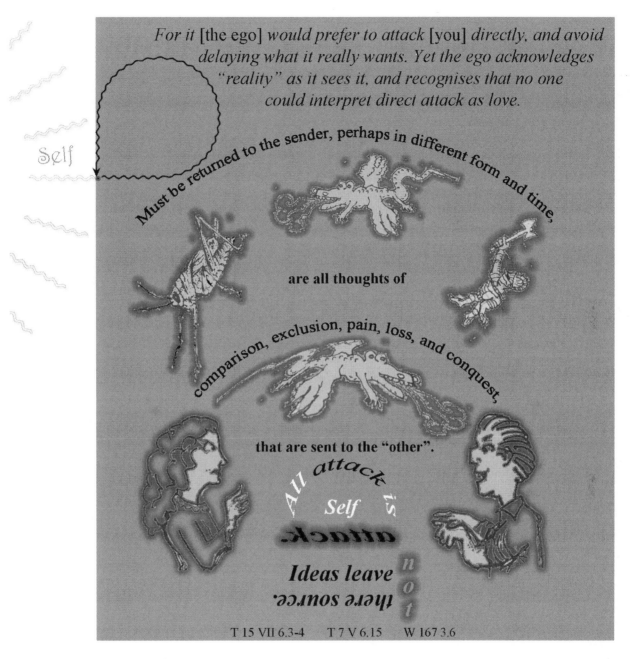

For it [the ego] *would prefer to attack* [you] *directly, and avoid delaying what it really wants. Yet the ego acknowledges "reality" as it sees it, and recognises that no one could interpret direct attack as love.*

Self

Must be returned to the sender, perhaps in different form and time,

are all thoughts of

comparison, exclusion, pain, loss, and conquest,

that are sent to the "other".

All attack is Self attack

Ideas leave not there source.

T 15 VII 6.3-4   T 7 V 6.15   W 167 3.6

Only what God creates is irreversible and unchangeable. What you made can always be changed because, when you do not think like God, you are not really thinking at all. Delusional ideas are not real thoughts, although you can believe in them. But you are wrong.

T 5 V 6.11-14

The world of perception, however, is made by the belief in opposites and separate wills, in perpetual conflict with each other and with God.

Therefore, seek not to change the world, but choose to change your mind about the world. Perception is a result and not a cause.

PREFACE p.x   T 21 Intro 1.7

Any attack thought that is believed to have left the mind must return to attack its sender, for there is nothing, and nowhere, else to attack. This incoming attack thought, fragmented by fear, the mind must see, for it meets the mind at the "boundary" between mind and "out of mind", at the "exit point" of sin. Therefore, as one looks upon this boundary where sin reveals itself as guilt, there seems to be a multiplicitous attacking world outside. This dualistic perception–a perceiver and a perceived–is consciousness, which is the substitute for the Knowledge of Oneness.

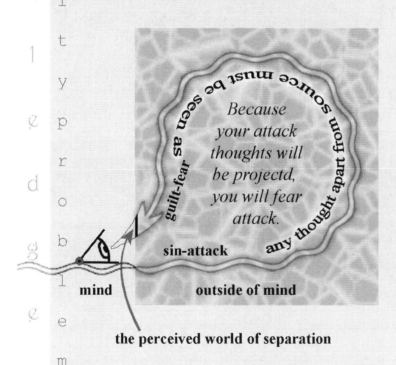

Because your attack thoughts will be projectd, you will fear attack.

source must be seen as guilt-fear

any thought apart from

sin-attack

mind   outside of mind

the perceived world of separation

Consciousness, the level of perception, was the first split introduced into the mind after the separation, making the mind a perceiver rather than a creator. Consciousness is correctly identified as the domain of the ego.

T 3 IV 2.1-2   W 26 2.1   T 26 VII 3.3

The Son of God perceived what he would see because perception is a wish fulfilled.

Consciousness is the receptive mechanism, receiving messages from above or below; from the Holy Spirit or the ego. ...Yet the very fact that it has levels and can be trained demonstrates that it cannot reach knowledge.

And you have replaced your knowledge by an awareness of dreams...

Here was perception born, for knowledge could not cause such insane thoughts.

M-CT 1 7   T 10 II 1.5   W Part II 3 2.5

Knothorwityepredoggbleem   authoritywithin   (margin letters)

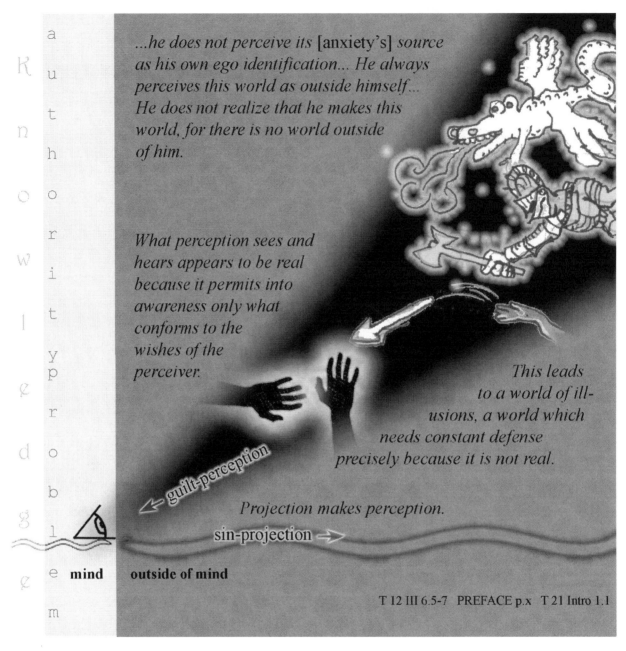

...he does not perceive its [anxiety's] source as his own ego identification... He always perceives this world as outside himself... He does not realize that he makes this world, for there is no world outside of him.

What perception sees and hears appears to be real because it permits into awareness only what conforms to the wishes of the perceiver.

This leads to a world of illusions, a world which needs constant defense precisely because it is not real.

← guilt-perception

Projection makes perception.

sin-projection →

mind   **outside of mind**

T 12 III 6.5-7   PREFACE p.x   T 21 Intro 1.1

a u t h o r i t y p r o b l e m

K n o w l e d g e

...he [the dreamer] sees himself attacked unjustly and by something not himself. ...Yet is his own attack upon himself apparent still, for it is he who bears the suffering. And he cannot escape because its source is seen outside himself.

T 27 VII 1.3-4

You see in death escape from   what
    you   made. But this   you do not see;
                                    that   you
            made death, and   it is   but illusion
    of an end.

M 20 5.2-3

Hallucinations serve to meet the goal of madness. ... Therefore, the question never is whether you want them, but always, do you want the purpose they serve?

T 20 VIII 9.5, 8.7

The guilt for what you thought is being placed outside yourself, and on a guilty world that dreams your dreams and thinks your thoughts instead of you.

What is perceived takes many forms, but none has meaning. Brought to truth, its senselessness is quite apparent. Kept apart from truth, it seems to have a meaning and be real.

T 27 VIII 7.4   T 26 VII 3.7-9

2 VII: *you made it up*

I have invented the world I see.

You see the world you have made, but you do not see yourself as the image maker.

Separation is only the decision not *to know yourself. This whole thought system is a carefully contrived learning experience, designed to lead away from truth and into fantasy.*

Sin is the home of all illusions, which but stand for things imagined...

T 20 VIII 7.4   W 32   W 23 4.1   T 16 V 15.3-4   W II 4 3.1

Dreams show you that you have the power to make a world as you would have it be, and that because you want it you see it.

Yet is he really tragic, when you see that he is following the way he chose…

Your wish to make another world that is not real remains with you.

T 18 II 5.1   W 166 6.3 7.1

ego's
secret
means:
*fantasy
of
destruction*

*And if you think what you made can tell you what you see and feel,
and place your faith in its ability to do so,
you are denying your creator and believing that you made yourself.*

ego's
secret
yet
desired
end:

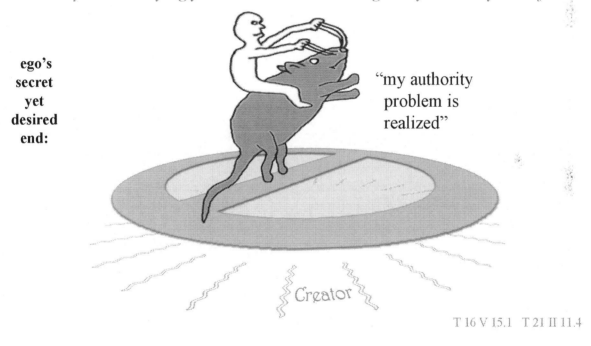

"my authority
problem is
realized"

T 16 V 15.1   T 21 II 11.4

*To obtain this [a sick god, self-created] you are willing to attack the Divinity of your brothers, and
thus lose sight of yours. And you are willing to keep it hidden, to protect an idol you think will save
you from the dangers for which it stands, but which do not exist.*

*You make the world and then adjust to it, and it to you. Nor is there any difference between yourself
and it in your perception, which made them both.*

T 10 III 5.2-3   T 20 III 3.6

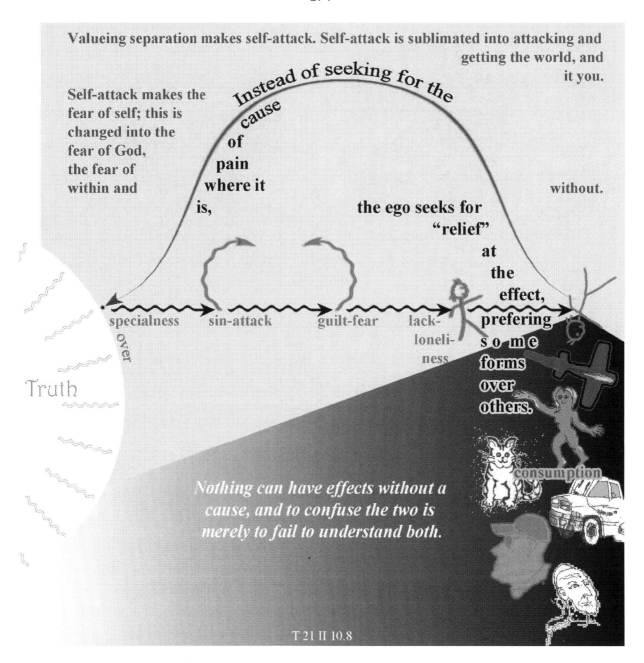

Valueing separation makes self-attack. Self-attack is sublimated into attacking and getting the world, and it you.

Instead of seeking for the cause of pain where it is,

Self-attack makes the fear of self; this is changed into the fear of God, the fear of within and

the ego seeks for "relief"

without.

at the effect, preferring some forms over others.

specialness   sin-attack   guilt-fear   lack-loneliness

over

Truth

consumption

Nothing can have effects without a cause, and to confuse the two is merely to fail to understand both.

T 21 II 10.8

Since you have also judged against what you project, you continue to attack it because you continue to keep it separated. By doing this unconsciously, you try to keep the fact that you attacked yourself out of awareness, and thus imagine that you have made yourself safe.

T 6 II 2.3-4

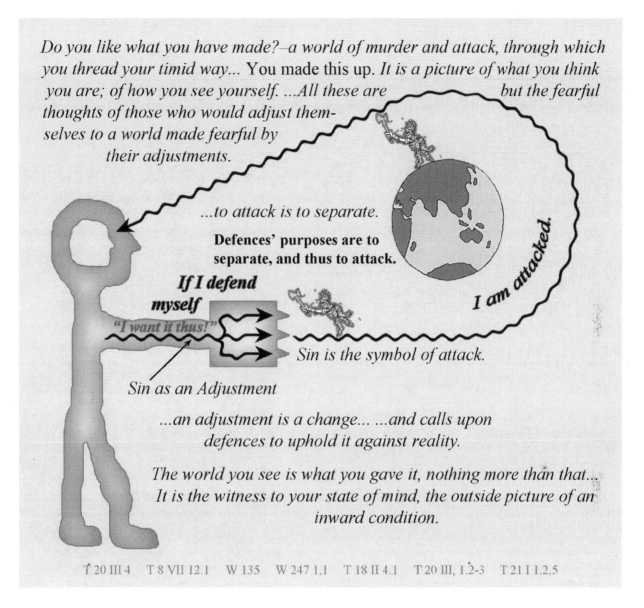

Do you like what you have made?–a world of murder and attack, through which you thread your timid way... You made this up. *It is a picture of what you think you are; of how you see yourself. ...All these are* **but the fearful** *thoughts of those who would adjust themselves to a world made fearful by their adjustments.*

...to attack is to separate.

Defences' purposes are to separate, and thus to attack.

I am attacked.

If I defend myself

"I want it thus!"

Sin is the symbol of attack.

Sin as an Adjustment

...an adjustment is a change... ...and calls upon defences to uphold it against reality.

The world you see is what you gave it, nothing more than that... It is the witness to your state of mind, the outside picture of an inward condition.

T 20 III 4   T 8 VII 12.1   W 135   W 247 1.1   T 18 II 4.1   T 20 III, 1.2-3   T 21 I 1.2,5

For a time it seems as if the world were given you, to make it what you wish. You do not realise you are attacking it, trying to triumph over it and make it serve you.

The only sane solution is not to try to change reality, which is indeed a fearful attempt, but to accept it as it is.

T 18 II 3.7   T 4 I 8.4

You will believe that you are part of where you think you are.
That is because you surround yourself with the environment you want.
And you want it to protect the image of yourself that you have made.
The image is part of this environment.

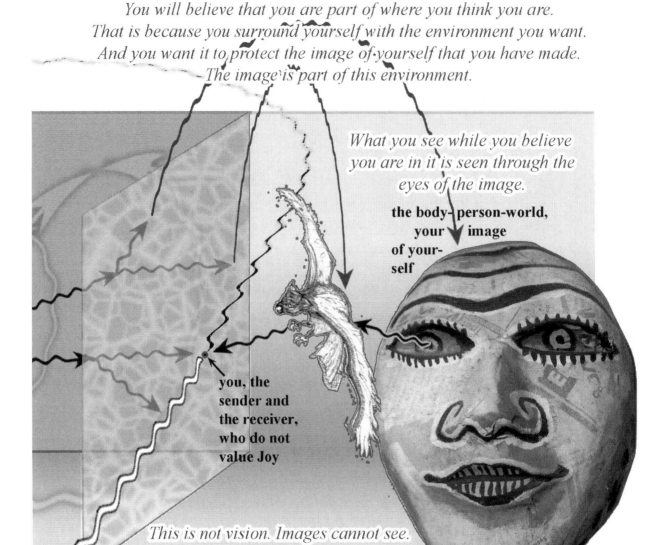

What you see while you believe
you are in it is seen through the
eyes of the image.

the body-person-world,
your image
of your-
self

you, the
sender and
the receiver,
who do not
value Joy

This is not vision. Images cannot see.

You are the **imag**-iner.

W 35 2

All things you see are images...

T 31 VII 7.2

A: *it is what you wish*

A dream is like a memory in that it pictures what you wanted shown to you.

Death... the wish to be as you are not...

*The world may seem to cause you pain. ...As an illusion, it is what you wish.
...Your strange desires bring it evil dreams. Your thoughts of death envelop it
in fear, while in your kind forgiveness does it live.*

conflict

hospital
of pain

disappointment

sickness

*...all guilt
is solely* an
invention
of your
mind...

authority problem

g u i l t

One picks
these
for the
purposes
~death and specialness~
they
serve.

W 190 7
W 70 1.5
T 29 VII 8.4

*You choose your dreams, for
they are what you wish, perceived
as if it had been given you.*

You are not the victim of the world you see because you invented it. You can give it up as easily as you made it up. ...While you want it you will see it; when you no longer want it, it will not be there for you to see.

The world can teach no images of you unless you want to learn them.

You see the world you value.

For hell and oblivion are ideas that you made up, and you are bent on demonstrating their reality to establish yours [as separate]. *If their reality is questioned, you believe that yours is.*

For you believe that attack is your reality, and that your destruction is the final proof that you were right.

LIFE

ABYSS

T 13.IV.2.3,5

You look for safety and security, while in your heart you pray for danger and protection for the little dream you made.

He must… suffer to preserve the world he made.

You made perception and it must last as long as you want it.

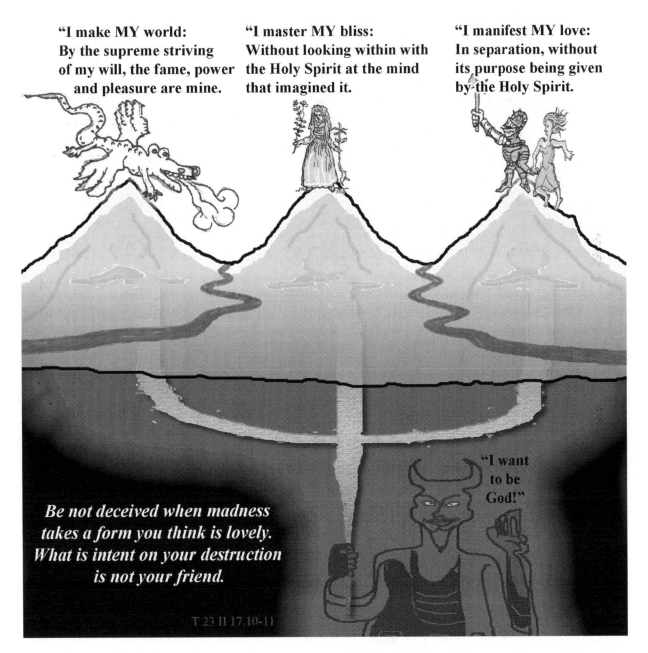

"I make MY world:
By the supreme striving
of my will, the fame, power
and pleasure are mine.

"I master MY bliss:
Without looking within with
the Holy Spirit at the mind
that imagined it.

"I manifest MY love:
In separation, without
its purpose being given
by the Holy Spirit.

"I want
to be
God!"

*Be not deceived when madness
takes a form you think is lovely.
What is intent on your destruction
is not your friend.*

T 23 II 17.10-11

*What you have given "life" is not alive, and symbolises but your wish to be alive apart from life,
alive in death, with death perceived as life, and living, death.*

W 190 7.4   T 28 II 4.5   W 163 1.1-2   W 32 1   T 31 V 17.1   T 16 VI 5.1   W 131 2.7   W 166 3.3   T 7 VII 3.11
T 29 II 6.2

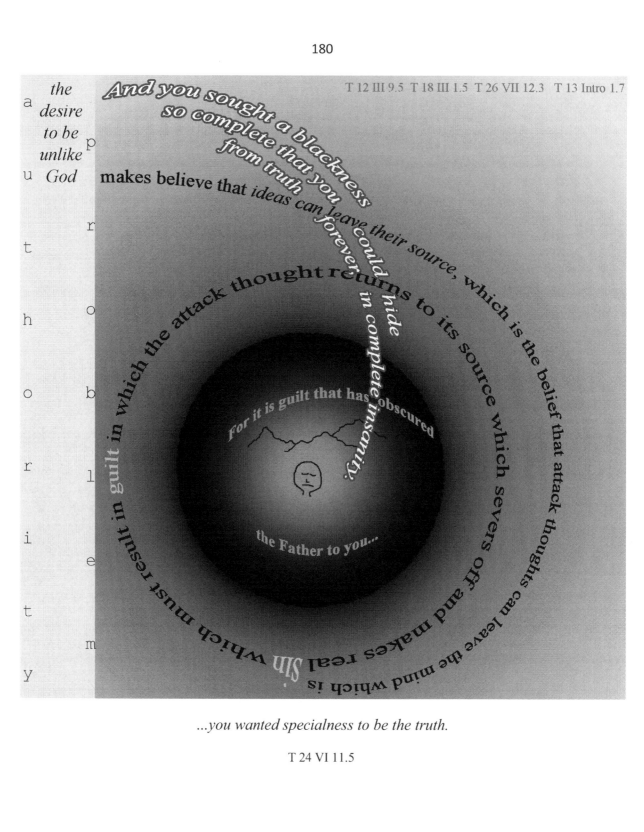

a
the
desire
to be
unlike
God

p

u

r

t

h

o

o

b

r

l

i

e

t

m

y

T 12 III 9.5 T 18 III 1.5 T 26 VII 12.3 T 13 Intro 1.7

And you sought a blackness so complete that you could hide forever from truth

makes believe that ideas can leave their source, which is the belief that attack thoughts can leave the mind which makes real. Sin which is the result in guilt in which the attack thought returns to its source which severs off and makes real. Sin which must result in guilt in which the attack thought returns to its source in complete insanity.

For it is guilt that has obscured the Father to you...

...you wanted specialness to be the truth.

T 24 VI 11.5

You trained it [the world] *in its testimony, and as it gave it back to you, you listened and convinced yourself that what it saw was true. You did this to yourself.* T 21 II 5.3-4

The mind imagines a body, and it imagines what this body is to experience: all the pleasures and pains and sights and sounds, triumphs and traumas...

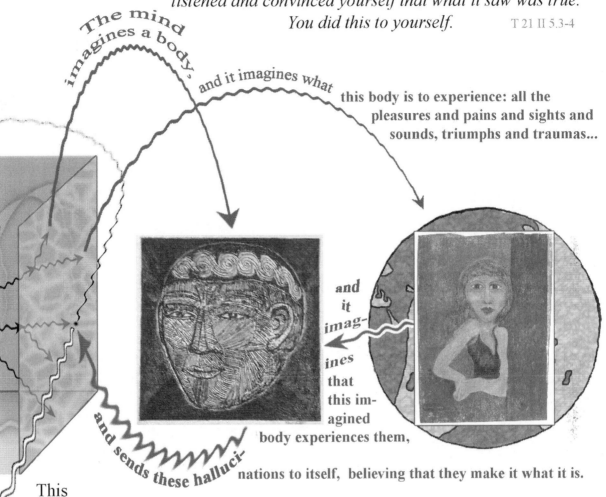

and it imag-ines that this imagined body experiences them,

and sends these hallucinations to itself, believing that they make it what it is.

This process can be readily observed in a daydream, which is always initiated by a wish to wander off into a fantasy of one's choice. What is occulted by dreams however is the purpose of death given them to serve.

B: *an unholy purpose*

The ego's purpose is fear, because only the fearful can be egotistic.

How can you know your worth while specialness claims you instead?

...your desire to create your own Creator, and be father and not son to Him... The Son is the effect, whose Cause he would deny.

Perhaps you are willing to accept even death to deny your Father.

You choose your dreams...

Why is the choice you make of value to you? What attracts your mind to it?

What purpose does it serve?

One "daydreams" one's interpretations of the dream according to the purpose desired.
I could see peace instead of this.

T 29 VII 8.4   W 133 8.2-4   W 34

..."What do you want?" ...You are answering it every minute and every second, and each moment of decision is a judgment that is anything but ineffectual. Its effects will follow automatically until the decision is changed.

W 43 2.4   T 5 V 1.3   T 24 VII 3.1   T 12 III 9.2   T 21 II 10.4,6   T 5 V 6.2-4

Nor is the mind limited; so must it be that harmful purpose hurts the mind as one. Nothing could make less sense to specialness.

Pain demonstrates the body must be real. It is a loud, obscuring voice whose shrieks would silence what the Holy Spirit says, and keep His words from your awareness.

Pain compels attention, drawing it away from Him and focusing upon itself.

pain, problems

pleasure, magic

What shares a common purpose is the same.

His Word

Call pleasure pain, and it will hurt. Call pain a pleasure, and the pain behind the pleasure will be felt no more. Sin's witnesses but shift from name to name, as one steps forward and another back. Yet which is foremost makes no difference. Sin's witnesses hear but the call of death.

T 27 VI 1.1-3,4 2.7-11

In pain is God denied the Son He loves. In pain does fear appear to triumph over love, and time replace eternity and Heaven. And the world becomes a cruel and a bitter place, where sorrow rules...

Your distorted perceptions produce a dense cover over miracle impulses, making it hard for them to reach your own awareness. ...Physical impulses are misdirected miracle impulses. All real pleasure comes from doing God's Will. This is because not doing it is a denial of Self.

If one equates oneself as a body, the symbol of separation, guilt-fear must be believed so as to be split off into the body; therefore the ego desires fear and proclaims it as one's purpose. Thus, to maintain itself, the ego seeks for bodily identification ("good" pleasure or "bad" pain-sickness) which can only increase separative guilt-pain in the mind.

g
u
i
l
t

"By self attack am I a "me"."

sin

separate "me" pain

fear

"Yet I desire guilt "outside" that I not see I am its cause."

Any relationship in which the body enters is based not on love, but on idolatry.

pain-pleasure

makes body "me"

guilt

pleasure-pain

makes body "other"

It is impossible to seek for pleasure through the body and not find pain. ...It is but the inevitable result of equating yourself with the body, which... invites fear to enter and become your purpose. The attraction of guilt [pain] must enter with it, and whatever fear directs the body to do is therefore painful. It will share the pain of all illusions, and the illusion of pleasure will be the same as pain.

A meaningless world [ill-usions] engenders fear.

T 19 IV B 12
W 13
T 20 VI 2.3.

What could the purpose of the body be but specialness? And it is this that makes it frail and helpless in its own defence. It was conceived to make you frail and helpless. The goal of separation is its curse.

You will impose upon the body all the pain that comes from the conception of the mind as limited and fragile, and apart from other minds and separate from its source.

You are unwilling to recognize that the ego, which you invited, is treacherous only to those who think they are its host. The ego will never let you perceive this…

The ego's messages are always sent away from you, in the belief that for your message of attack and guilt will someone other than yourself suffer. …The great deceiver recognises that this is not so, but… it urges you to send out all your messages of hate and free yourself.

The ego does… perceive sin as… a positive act of assault.

…any seeming happiness that does not last is really fear.

assault [sin-pleasure]

must be the

Depression [guilt-pain] or

theme of every dream…

"While I am attacking you, you cannot be attacking me."

The ego is a perpetual state of war; sinlessness is only peace.

T 19 IV B 15
T 22 II 3.5
T 5 V 4.9
T 29 IV 3.3
W 72

And to convince you this is possible, it bids the body search for pain in attack upon another, calling it pleasure and offering it to you as freedom from attack.

The ego mind is ever capable of inducing amazing simulations of peace and love within separation, yet its transient highs of getting can be only as crumbs on its trail to deprivation.

Holding grievances is an attack on God's plan for salvation.

T 24 IV 3.5   W 190 8   T 1 VII 1   T 24 IV 2.1-4   W 135 9.4   T 15 X 6.4-5

The ego and the Holy Spirit both… recognize that here the sender and receiver are the same. The Holy Spirit tells you this with joy. The ego hides it, for it would keep you unaware of it. Who would send messages of hatred and attack if he but understood he sends them to himself?

How can it [the ego] *preach separation without upholding it through fear, and would you listen to it if you recognized this is what it is doing?*

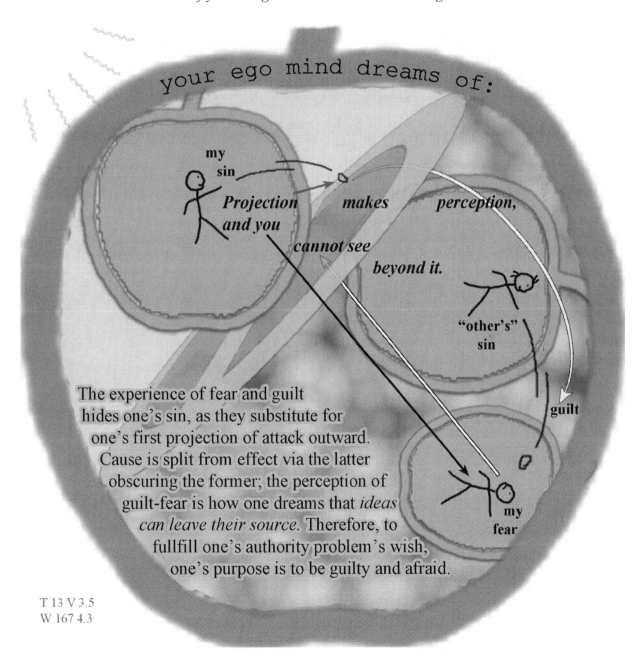

your ego mind dreams of:

my sin

Projection *makes* *perception,*
and you
cannot see
beyond it.

"other's"
sin

guilt

my
fear

The experience of fear and guilt hides one's sin, as they substitute for one's first projection of attack outward. Cause is split from effect via the latter obscuring the former; the perception of guilt-fear is how one dreams that *ideas can leave their source.* Therefore, to fullfill one's authority problem's wish, one's purpose is to be guilty and afraid.

T 13 V 3.5
W 167 4.3

Take not the form for content, for the form is but a means for content. ...A frame [form-fear] that hides the picture [content-separation] has no purpose. ...Without the picture is the frame without its meaning.

The purpose of the world you see is to obscure your function of forgiveness, and provide you with a justification for forgetting it.

T 19 B i 14.8-11   T 11 V 9.3   T 25 II 4   W 64 1.2

The circle of fear lies just below the level the body sees, and seems to be the whole foundation on which the world is based. Here are all the illusions, all the twisted thoughts, all the insane attacks, the fury, the vengeance and betrayal that were made to keep the guilt in place, so that the world could rise from it and keep it hidden. Its shadow rises to the surface, enough to hold its most external manifestations in darkness, and to bring despair and loneliness to it and keep it joyless.

Every special relationship you have made has, as its fundamental purpose, the aim of occupying your mind so completely that you will not hear the call of truth.

What you would still contain behind your little barrier and keep separate from your brother seems mightier than the universe, for it would hold back the universe and its Creator. This little wall would hide the purpose of Heaven, and keep it from Heaven.

...to deny God is to deny their own Identity, and in this sense the wages of sin is death. The sense is very literal; denial of life perceives its opposite, as all forms of denial replace what is with what is not. No one can really do this, but that you think you can and believe you have is beyond dispute.

How weak is fear; how little and how meaningless. How insignificant before the quiet strength of those whom love has joined! This is your "enemy"—a frightened mouse that would attack the universe. How likely is it that it will succeed?

The ego can and does allow you to regard yourself as supercilious, unbelieving, "light-hearted", distant, emotionally shallow, callous, uninvolved and even desperate, but not really afraid. Minimising fear, but not its undoing, is the ego's constant effort, and is indeed a skill at which it is very ingenious.

What you desire, you will see. And if its reality is false, you will uphold it by not realising all the adjustments you have introduced to make it so.

You would rather be a slave of the crucifixion than a Son of God in redemption. Your individual death seems more valuable than your living oneness, for what is given you is not so dear as what you made.

The ego uses projection only to destroy your perception of both yourself and your brothers.

For hate to be maintained, love must be feared; and only sometimes present, sometimes gone. Thus is love seen as treacherous... You do not see how limited and weak is your allegiance, and how frequently you have demanded that love go away, and leave you quietly alone in "peace".

The body is the means by which the ego tries to make the unholy relationship seem real. The unholy instant is the time of bodies. But the purpose here is sin.

All sacrifice entails the loss of your ability to see relationships among events. And looked at separately they have no meaning. For there is no light by which they can be seen and understood. They have no purpose... This is not communication.

T 18 IX 4   T 17 IV 3.3   T 19 IV A 3.6-7   T 10 V 1.5-7   T 22 V 4.1-3   T 11 V 9.1-2   T 21 II 10.1   T 13 III 5.2-3
T 6 II 3.7   T 29 I 7   T 20 VII 5.1-3   T 30 VII 6

2 VIII Ego Defences: *secret, magic wan*

...those who want the ego are predisposed to

...defences are but foolish guardians of mad

To substitute is
other is repl
To fra

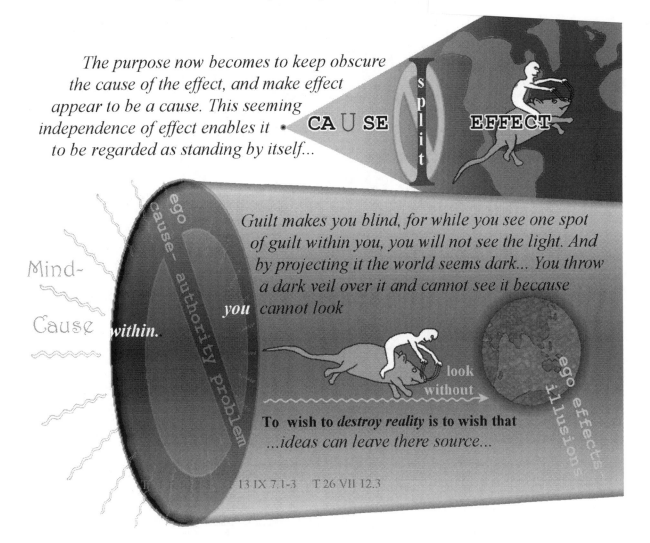

The purpose now becomes to keep obscure the cause of the effect, and make effect appear to be a cause. This seeming independence of effect enables it to be regarded as standing by itself...

CA U SE   split   EFFECT

Mind-

Cause *within.*

ego cause- authority problem

Guilt makes you blind, for while you see one spot of guilt within you, you will not see the light. And by projecting it the world seems dark... You throw a dark veil over it and cannot see it because you cannot look

look without

ego effects... illusions

To wish to *destroy reality* is to wish that
...ideas can leave there source...

13 IX 7.1-3   T 26 VII 12.3

The ego substitutes its cause, and one's Cause, with its ghosts of guilt. Therefore minds and their ideas appear to be apart from each other and from themselves... outside of the reality of oneness, in imagination.

A false image of yourself has come to take the place of what you are.

...to choose between... For this special purpose, one is judged more valuable and the ...aced by him. The relationship... is thus fragmented, and its purpose split accordingly. ...gment is to exclude, and substitution is the strongest defense the ego has for separation.

...your plan [of defence] requires that you must forget you made it, so it seems to be external to your own intent....

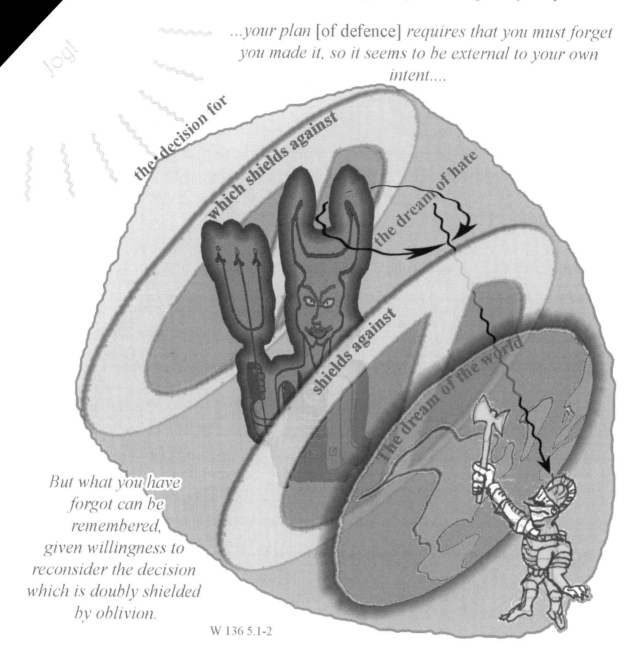

joy!

the decision for

which shields against

the dream of hate

shields against

The dream of the world

But what you have forgot can be remembered, given willingness to reconsider the decision which is doubly shielded by oblivion.

W 136 5.1-2

...remember that the ego is not alone. Its rule is tempered, and its unknown "enemy", Whom it cannot even see, it fears.

W 136 3.2   T 8 VIII 4.4   M 4 VI 1.6   W 26 3.5   T 18 I.1   T 21 IV 2.1

Every defence operates by giving gifts... [that are] set in a golden frame. ...[the frame's] purpose is to be of value in itself, and to divert your attention from what it encloses. But the frame without the picture you cannot have. Defences operate to make you think you can.

Protecting the dream (picture) of death and deprivation, the world (frame) cannot elude it.

T 21 IV 2
T 17 IV 7.1.3

Loudly the ego ...tells you not to look inward, for if you do

...God will strike you blind.
...Yet this is not the ego's hidden fear, nor yours who serve it...
Beneath... is yet another fear, and which makes the ego tremble.

One

It is essential to realise that all defences do what they would defend. ...What they defend is placed in them for safe-keeping, and as they operate they bring it to you.

Do not defend this senseless dream, in which God is bereft of what He loves, and you remain beyond salvation.

...the mind asks, "Where can I go for protection?"... The ego has no real answer to this because there is none, but it does have a typical solution. It obliterates the question from the mind's awareness. Once out of awareness the question can and does produce uneasiness, but it cannot be answered because it cannot be asked.

What is kept apart from love cannot share its healing power, because it has been separated off and kept in darkness. The sentinels of darkness watch over it carefully, and you who made these guardians of illusion out of nothing are now afraid of them.

Would you continue to give imagined power to these strange ideas of safety? ...They do nothing at all, being nothing at all. ...But let them go, and what was fearful will be so no longer. Without protection of obscurity only the light of love remains... Everything else must disappear.

T 17 IV 7   T 24 IV 5.1   T 4 V 4.7, 9-11   T 14 VI 2.4-5, 3

A: Idols: *figures in the dream*

Behind the search for every idol lies the yearning for completion.

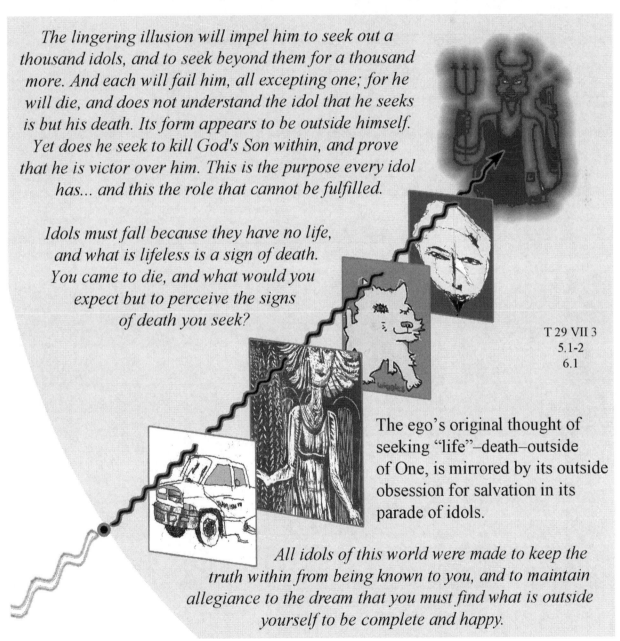

The lingering illusion will impel him to seek out a thousand idols, and to seek beyond them for a thousand more. And each will fail him, all excepting one; for he will die, and does not understand the idol that he seeks is but his death. Its form appears to be outside himself. Yet does he seek to kill God's Son within, and prove that he is victor over him. This is the purpose every idol has... and this the role that cannot be fulfilled.

Idols must fall because they have no life, and what is lifeless is a sign of death. You came to die, and what would you expect but to perceive the signs of death you seek?

T 29 VII 3
5.1-2
6.1

The ego's original thought of seeking "life"–death–outside of One, is mirrored by its outside obsession for salvation in its parade of idols.

All idols of this world were made to keep the truth within from being known to you, and to maintain allegiance to the dream that you must find what is outside yourself to be complete and happy.

An idol or the Thought God holds of you is your reality. Forget not, then, that idols must keep hidden what you are... The star shines still; the sky has never changed. But you, the holy Son of God Himself, are unaware of your reality.

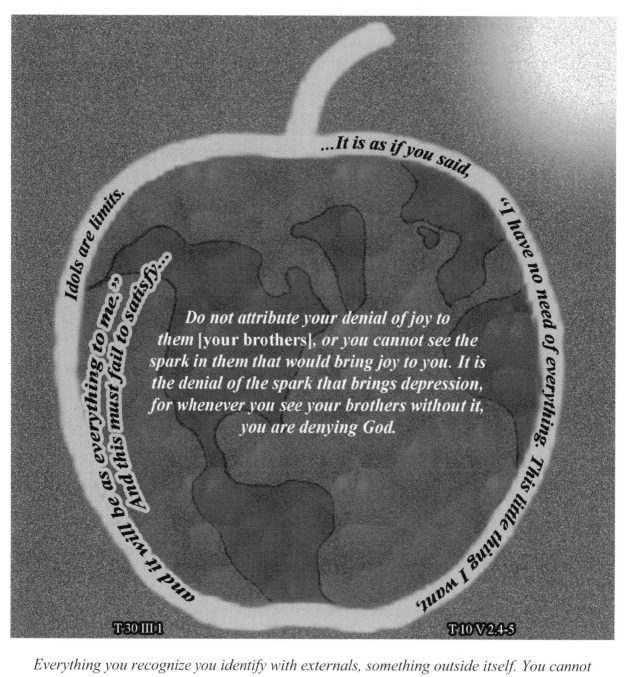

...It is as if you said,

'I have no need of everything. This little thing I want,

and it will be as everything to me." And this must fail to satisfy...

Idols are limits.

Do not attribute your denial of joy to them [your brothers], or you cannot see the spark in them that would bring joy to you. It is the denial of the spark that brings depression, for whenever you see your brothers without it, you are denying God.

T 30 III 1

T 10 V 2.4-5

Everything you recognize you identify with externals, something outside itself. You cannot even think of God without a body, or in some form you think you recognize.

T 29 IX 3.1   T 30 III 3.1, 11.9   T 18 VIII 1.6-7

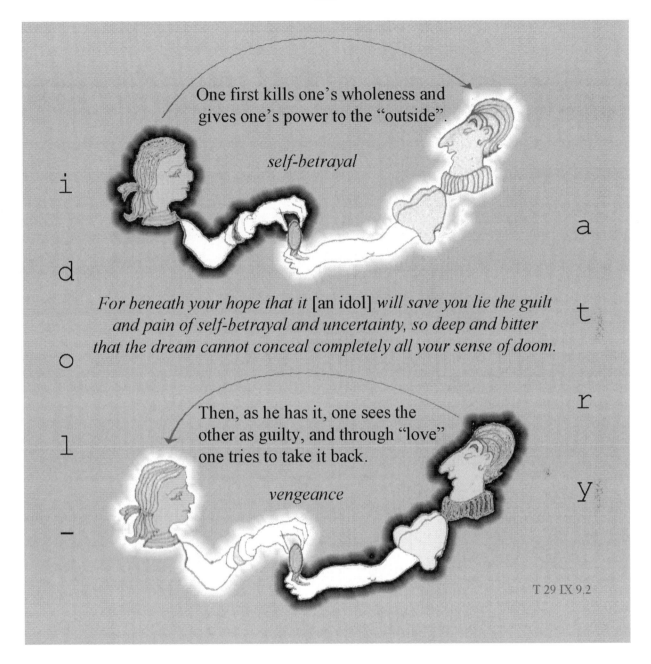

One first kills one's wholeness and gives one's power to the "outside".

self-betrayal

For beneath your hope that it [an idol] will save you lie the guilt and pain of self-betrayal and uncertainty, so deep and bitter that the dream cannot conceal completely all your sense of doom.

Then, as he has it, one sees the other as guilty, and through "love" one tries to take it back.

vengeance

i d o l
a t r y
_

T 29 IX 9.2

What is an idol? Nothing! It must be believed before it seems to come to life, and given power that it may be feared. Its life and power are its believer's gift...

The belief that you could give and get something... outside yourself, has cost you the awareness of Heaven and of your Identity.

While it is obvious that the ego does demand payment it never seems to be demanding it of you.

An idol is a wish...

T 29 VIII 5.1-4   T 18 VI 2.3   T 15 X 6.3   T 29 VIII 3.2

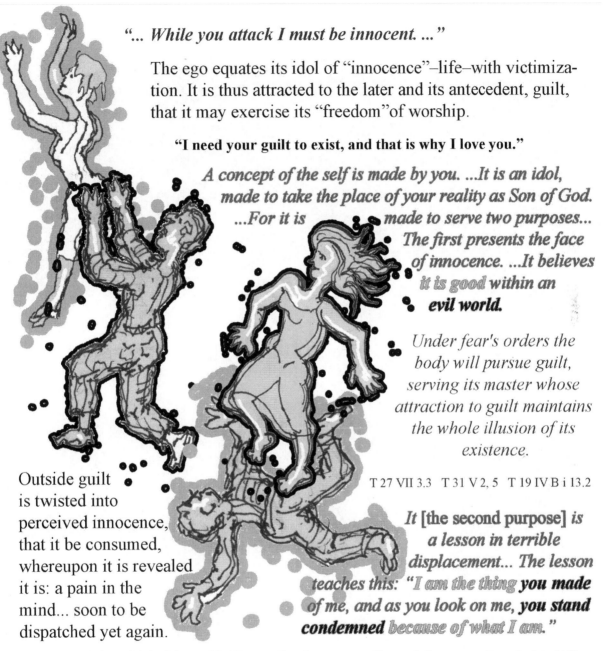

"... While you attack I must be innocent. ..."

The ego equates its idol of "innocence"–life–with victimiza-tion. It is thus attracted to the later and its antecedent, guilt, that it may exercise its "freedom"of worship.

"I need your guilt to exist, and that is why I love you."

A concept of the self is made by you. ...It is an idol, made to take the place of your reality as Son of God. ...For it is made to serve two purposes... The first presents the face of innocence. ...It believes it is good within an evil world.

Under fear's orders the body will pursue guilt, serving its master whose attraction to guilt maintains the whole illusion of its existence.

T 27 VII 3.3   T 31 V 2, 5   T 19 IV B i 13.2

Outside guilt is twisted into perceived innocence, that it be consumed, whereupon it is revealed it is: a pain in the mind... soon to be dispatched yet again.

*It [the second purpose] is a lesson in terrible displacement... The lesson teaches this: "I am the thing **you made** of me, and as you look on me, **you stand condemned** because of what I am."*

The conceived idol of the self: "I am alive by your guilt, and thus am attracted to it."

He must be innocent because he knows not what he does, but what is done to him.

This world is an attempt to prove your innocence, while cherishing attack.

Yet fear attracts you, and believing it is love, you call it to yourself.

...whatever reminds you of your past grievances attracts you, and seems to go by the name of love...

Seek not outside yourself. For it will fail, and you will weep each time an idol falls. Heaven cannot be found where it is not, and there can be no peace excepting there.

The fact that truth and illusion cannot be reconciled, no matter how you try, what means you use and where you see the problem, must be accepted if you would be saved.

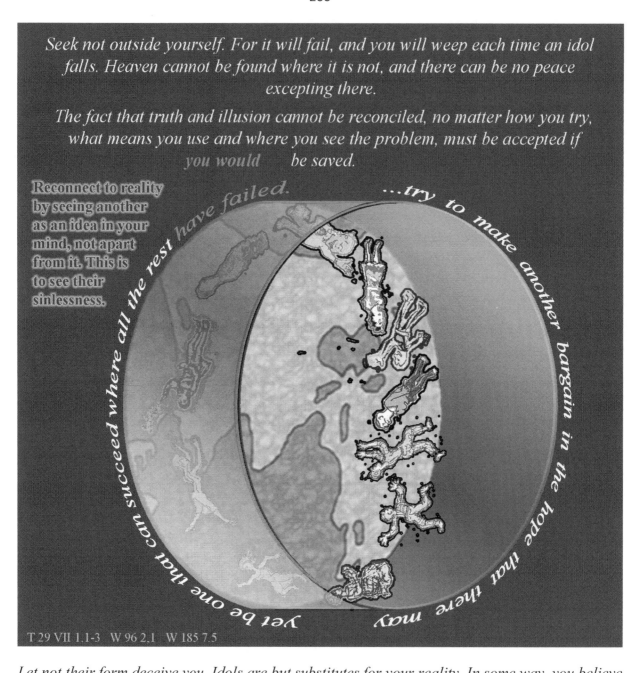

Reconnect to reality by seeing another as an idea in your mind, not apart from it. This is to see their sinlessness.

...try to make another bargain in the hope that there may

Yet be one that can succeed where all the rest have failed.

T 29 VII 1.1-3   W 96 2,1   W 185 7.5

Let not their form deceive you. Idols are but substitutes for your reality. In some way, you believe they will complete your little self...

T 27 VII 1.5   T 26 VII 12.5   T 13 V 5.6   T 17 III 2.5   T 29 VIII 2.1-3

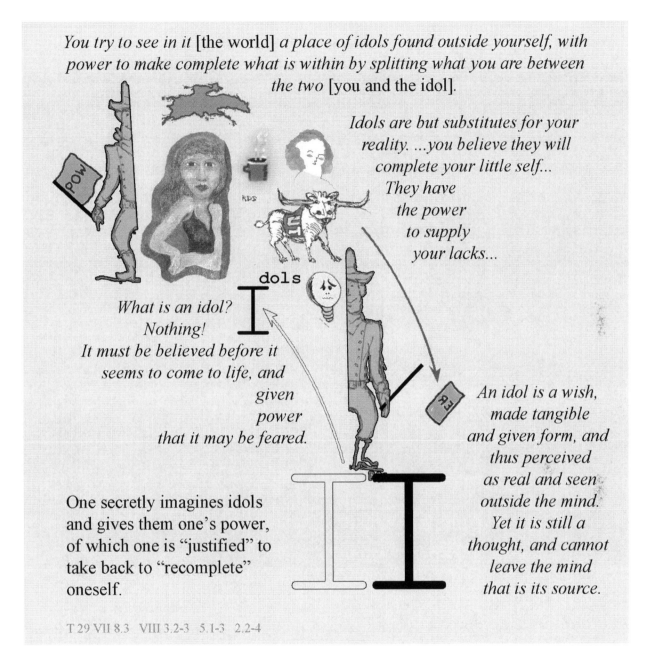

You try to see in it [the world] *a place of idols found outside yourself, with power to make complete what is within by splitting what you are between the two* [you and the idol].

Idols are but substitutes for your reality. ...you believe they will complete your little self... They have the power to supply your lacks...

What is an idol? Nothing! It must be believed before it seems to come to life, and given power that it may be feared.

An idol is a wish, made tangible and given form, and thus perceived as real and seen outside the mind. Yet it is still a thought, and cannot leave the mind that is its source.

One secretly imagines idols and gives them one's power, of which one is "justified" to take back to "recomplete" oneself.

T 29 VII 8.3   VIII 3.2-3   5.1-3   2.2-4

Do not deceive yourself into believing that you can relate in peace to God or to your brothers with anything external.

T 1 VII 1.7

If you seek love outside yourself you can be certain that you perceive hatred within, and are afraid of it. Yet peace will never come from the illusion of love, but only from its reality.

T 16 IV 6.5-6

To seek a special person or a thing to add to you to make yourself complete, can only mean that you believe some form is missing. ...This is the purpose of an idol; that you will not look beyond it, to the source of the belief that you are incomplete.

T 30 III 3.3,5

B: The Special Relationship: *fantasies in uninterrupted "bliss"*

Without exception, these relationships have as their purpose the exclusion of the truth about the other, and of yourself.

The demand for specialness, and the perception of the giving of specialness as an act of love, would make love hateful. The real purpose of the special relationship, in strict accordance with the ego's goals, is to destroy reality and substitute illusion.

To believe that special relationships, with special love, can offer you salvation is the belief that separation is salvation.

Yet the special relationship the ego seeks does not include even one whole individual. The ego wants but part of him, and sees only this part and nothing else.

T 17 III 4.8   T 17 III 2.3   T 16 V 9.3-4   T 15 V 3.3   T 16 VI 5.7-8

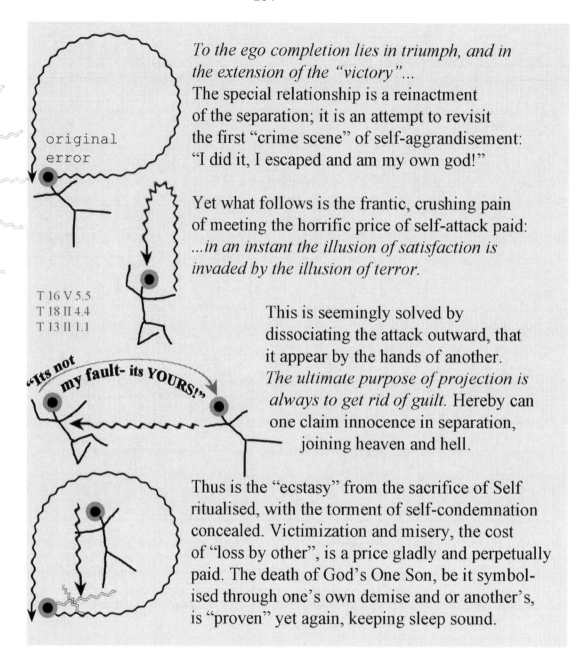

To the ego completion lies in triumph, and in the extension of the "victory"...
The special relationship is a reinactment of the separation; it is an attempt to revisit the first "crime scene" of self-aggrandisement: "I did it, I escaped and am my own god!"

Yet what follows is the frantic, crushing pain of meeting the horrific price of self-attack paid: *...in an instant the illusion of satisfaction is invaded by the illusion of terror.*

This is seemingly solved by dissociating the attack outward, that it appear by the hands of another. *The ultimate purpose of projection is always to get rid of guilt.* Hereby can one claim innocence in separation, joining heaven and hell.

Thus is the "ecstasy" from the sacrifice of Self ritualised, with the torment of self-condemnation concealed. Victimization and misery, the cost of "loss by other", is a price gladly and perpetually paid. The death of God's One Son, be it symbolised through one's own demise and or another's, is "proven" yet again, keeping sleep sound.

original error

T 16 V 5.5
T 18 II 4.4
T 13 II 1.1

"Its not my fault- its YOURS!"

Pain is the ransom you have gladly paid not to be free.

The appeal of hell lies only in the terrible attraction of guilt, which the ego holds out to those who place their faith in littleness. The conviction of littleness lies in every special relationship, for only the deprived could value specialness.

W 190 8.2   T 16 V 9.1-2

The special relationship is a ritual of form, aimed at raising the form to take the place of God at the expense of content. There is no meaning in the form, and there will never be. ...God is not angry. He merely could not let this happen. You cannot change His Mind.

No rituals that you have set up in which the dance of death delights you can bring death to the eternal...

T 16 V 12

The special love relationship is the ego's most boasted gift, and one which has the most appeal to those unwilling to relinquish guilt.

T 16 V 3.1

The special relationship has the most imposing and deceptive frame of all the defenses the ego uses. ...Into the frame are woven all sorts of fanciful and fragmented illusions of love, set with dreams of sacrifice and self-aggrandisement, and interlaced with gilded threads of self-destruction. The glitter of blood shines like rubies, and the tears are faceted like diamonds and gleam in the dim light in which the   offering is made.

T 17 IV 8,9

Look at the picture.   Do not let the frame distract you. ...You cannot have the frame without the picture. What you value is the frame, for there you see no conflict. Yet the frame is only the wrapping for the gift of conflict. ...Be not deceived... Let not your gaze dwell on the hypnotic gleaming of the frame. Look at the picture, and realize that death is offered you.

If you seek to separate out certain aspects of the totality and look to them to meet your imagined needs, you are attempting to use separation to save you. How, then, could guilt not enter?

...the one idea that hides behind them [ego defenses] all; that love demands sacrifice, and is therefore inseparable from attack and fear. And that guilt is the price of love, which must be paid by fear.

T 15 V 2.3-4   T 15 X 6-7

In looking at the special relationship, it is necessary first to realize that it involves a great amount of pain. Anxiety, despair, guilt and attack all enter into it, broken into by periods in which they seem to be gone. .... Whatever form they take, they are always an attack on the self to make the other guilty.

Very simply, the attempt to make guilty is always directed against God. ... The special love relationship is the ego's chief weapon for keeping you from Heaven. It does not ... appear to be a weapon, but if you consider how you ... value it and why, you will realize what it ... must be.

For the special relationship ... is the renunciation of the Love of God, and the ... attempt to secure for the self the specialness ... that He denied.

And whoever seems to ... possess a special self is "loved" for what can be taken ... from him. Where both partners see this special ... self in each other, the ego sees ... "a union made in Heaven." ...the ego's illusion of ... Heaven... ...is nothing more than an "attractive" form of fear, ... in which the guilt is buried deep and rises in the form of "love."

T 16 V 1, 2, 4, 8

If you perceived the special relationship as a triumph over God, would you want it?

T 16 V 10.1

How can anything upon a foundation of separateness be otherwise?

An altar is erected in between two separate people, on which each seeks to kill his self, and on his body raise another self to take its power from his death. Over and over and over this ritual is enacted. And it is never completed, nor ever will be completed. The ritual of completion cannot complete, for life arises not from death, nor Heaven from hell.

Each seeks "death" to take the other's "life"; both play-acts of life taken from "killing" Oneness.

It [sacrifice] *is the cost of believing in illusions. It is the price that must be paid for the denial of truth.*

"My pain-death from you becomes my innocence-life"

Because unless the Holy Spirit gives the dream its function, it was made for hate, and will continue in death's services.

But truth is indivisible...

T 16 V 11.5-8   M 13 5.2   T 29 V 7.4, 8   T 23 I 7.6   **fear of self**

Every special relationship you have made is a substitute for God's Will, and glorifies yours instead of His because of the illusion that they are different.

It is a kind of union from which union is excluded, and the basis for the attempt at union rests on exclusion.

In dreams, no two can share the same intent. ...the outcome wanted not the same for both. Loser and gainer merely shift about...

Minds cannot unite in dreams. They merely bargain.

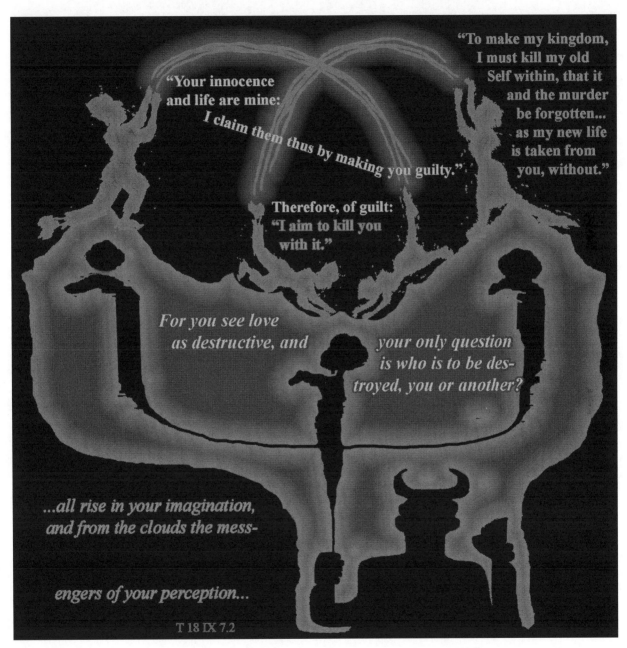

How childish is the petulant device to keep your innocence by pushing guilt outside yourself, but never letting go!

T 17 IV 2.7   T 16 V 6.4   W 185 3.3-5, 4.4-5   T 27 VIII 8.3

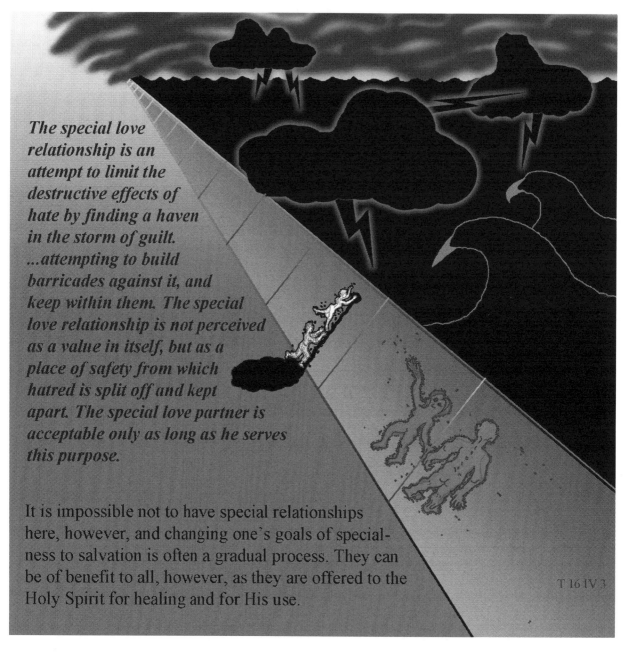

The special love relationship is an attempt to limit the destructive effects of hate by finding a haven in the storm of guilt. ...attempting to build barricades against it, and keep within them. The special love relationship is not perceived as a value in itself, but as a place of safety from which hatred is split off and kept apart. The special love partner is acceptable only as long as he serves this purpose.

It is impossible not to have special relationships here, however, and changing one's goals of special-ness to salvation is often a gradual process. They can be of benefit to all, however, as they are offered to the Holy Spirit for healing and for His use.

T 16 IV 3

And love, to them, is only an escape from death. They seek it desperately, but not in the peace in which it would gladly come quietly to them. And when they find the fear of death is still upon them, the love relationship loses the illusion that it is what it is not. When the barricades against it are broken, fear rushes in and hatred triumphs.

This "self" seeks the relationship to make itself complete. ...it gives itself away, and tries to "trade" itself for the self of another.

...every relationship the ego makes is based on the idea that by sacrificing itself, it becomes bigger. The "sacrifice", which it regards as purification, is actually the root of its bitter resentment.

For each one thinks that he has sacrificed something to the other, and hates him for it. Yet this is what he thinks he wants. He is not in love with the other at all. He merely believes he is in love with sacrifice. And for this sacrifice, which he demands of himself, he demands that the other accept the guilt and sacrifice himself as well. Forgiveness becomes impossible, for the ego believes that to forgive another is to lose him.

But idols do not share. Idols accept, but never make return. They can be loved, but cannot love.

For the ego cannot love, and in its frantic search for love it is seeking what it is afraid to find.

T 15 VII 6.1-2, 7
T 20 VI 3.1-3
T 12 IV 2.3

Like wholeness, specialnesses are also sacrificed, that the special reign confusion and madness upon their worlds. One's specialness, one's "truth", is exchanged for another's, an idol, a *dream figure,* "outside" of one's mind. And this never ending search for completion is for what one strives, but will never see, as specialness demands it be kept outside.

This is not union, for there is no increase and no extension. Each partner tries to sacrifice the self he does not want for one he thinks he would prefer. And he feels guilty for the "sin" of taking, and of giving nothing of value in return.

Everything that the ego tells you that you need will hurt you. ...For where the ego sees salvation it sees separation, and so you lose whatever you have gotten in its name.

T 16 IV 4.7-10   T 16 V 7   T 13 VII 11.1,4

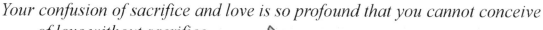

Your confusion of sacrifice and love is so profound that you cannot conceive of love without sacrifice.

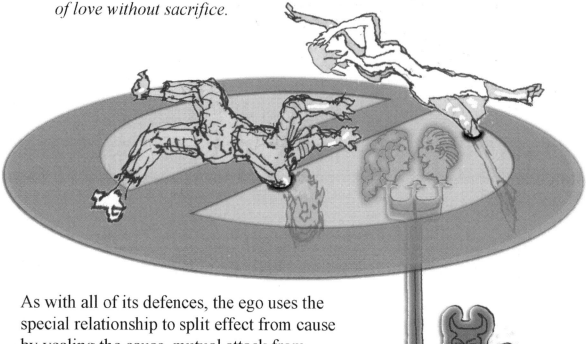

As with all of its defences, the ego uses the special relationship to split effect from cause by vealing the cause—mutual attack from lack—with the effect: the "love" of getting via sacrifice.

As long as you perceive the body as your reality, so long will you perceive yourself as lonely and deprived.

the belief in separation

And as long as you would retain the deprivation, attack becomes salvation and sacrifice becomes love.

T 15 X 5.8, XI 5

If you seek for satisfaction in gratifying your needs as you perceive them, you must believe that strength comes from another, and what you gain he loses. Someone must always lose if you perceive yourself as weak.

Because of guilt, all special relationships have elements of fear in them. This is why they shift and change so frequently.

T 15 VI 3.3-4, V 4.1-2

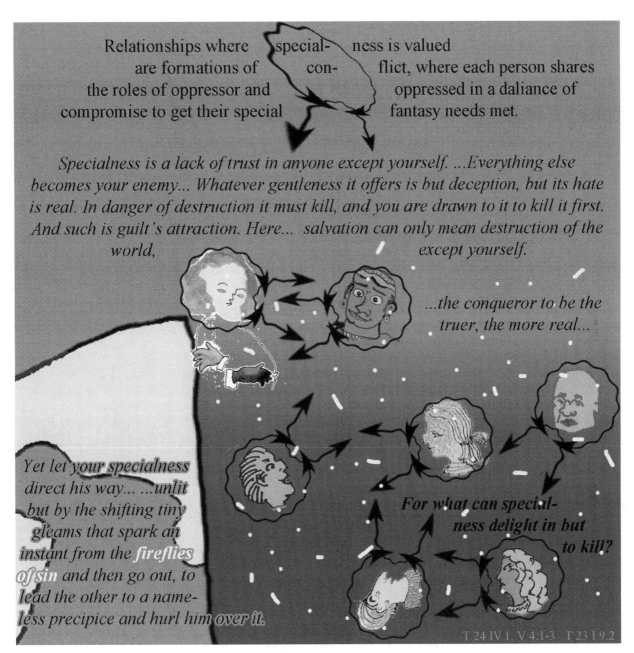

Relationships where special- ness is valued are formations of con- flict, where each person shares the roles of oppressor and oppressed in a daliance of compromise to get their special fantasy needs met.

Specialness is a lack of trust in anyone except yourself. ...Everything else becomes your enemy... Whatever gentleness it offers is but deception, but its hate is real. In danger of destruction it must kill, and you are drawn to it to kill it first. And such is guilt's attraction. Here... salvation can only mean destruction of the world,   except yourself.

...the conqueror to be the truer, the more real...

Yet let your specialness direct his way... ...unlit but by the shifting tiny gleams that spark an instant from the fireflies of sin and then go out, to lead the other to a name-less precipice and hurl him over it.

For what can special-ness delight in but to kill?

T 24 IV 1, V 4.1-3   T 23 I 9.2

Here [in the body] *the unholy relationship escapes reality, and seeks for crumbs to keep itself alive. Here it would drag its brothers, holding them here in its idolatry. Here it is "safe", for here love cannot enter.*

The special relationship is a device for limiting your self to a body, and for limiting your perception of others to theirs. The Great Rays would establish the total lack of value of the special relationship, if they were seen. For in seeing them the body would disappear, because its value would be lost.

T 20 VI 5.3-5   T 16 VI 4.4-6

For total love would demand total sacrifice. And so the ego seems to demand less of you than God...
...you seem to be both destroyer and destroyed in part, but able to be neither completely. And this you think saves you from God, Whose total Love would completely destroy you.

This gift is given you for your damnation, and if you take it you will believe that you are damned.

Yet the closer you look at the special relationship, the more apparent it becomes that it must foster guilt and therefore must imprison.

And the attempt to find the imagined "best" of both worlds [hell and Heaven] *has merely led to fantasies of both, and to the inability to perceive either as it is. The special relationship is the triumph of this confusion.*

It is essential to the preservation of the ego that you believe this special-ness is not hell, but Heaven. For the ego would never have you see that separation could only be loss, being the one condition in which Heaven could not be.

But fear demands the sacrifice of love, for in love's presence fear cannot abide.

Any relationship you would substitute for another has not been offered to the Holy Spirit for His use. There is *no substitute for love. If you would attempt to substitute one aspect of love for another, you have placed less value on one and more on the other.*

It is impossible to see your brother as sinless and yet to look upon him as a body. ...for holiness is positive and the body is merely neutral. It is not sinful, but neither is it sinless. As nothing, which it is, the body cannot meaningfully be invested with attributes of Christ or of the ego.

For the Love of God, no longer seek for union in separation, nor for freedom in bondage!

The special relationship is totally meaningless without a body. If you value it, you must also value the body. And what you value you will keep.

...all such relationships become attempts at union through the body, for only bodies can be seen as means for vengeance. That bodies are central to all unholy relationships is evident. Your own experience has taught you this.

T 15 X 7   T 17 IV 9.3   T 16 VI 3.4   T 16 V 6.2-3, 4.3-4   T 29 I 7.2   T 15 V 6.1-3   T 20 VII 4   T 16 VI 2.3
T 10 VI 4.1   T 17 III 2

C: Sickness and Magic

Sickness is not an accident. Like all defences, it is an insane device for self-deception. And like all the rest, its purpose is to hide reality, attack it, change it, render it inept, distort it, twist it, or reduce it to a little pile of unassembled parts.

In the outer dream one is one's body-person-psyche. This includes the "inner-world" self because it is outside of the mind that dreams of it. Thus psychological ailments–always born of guilt, fear and specialness–serve the same purpose as physical calamities or diseases: they occlude the separating cause, and keep awareness at the effect level.

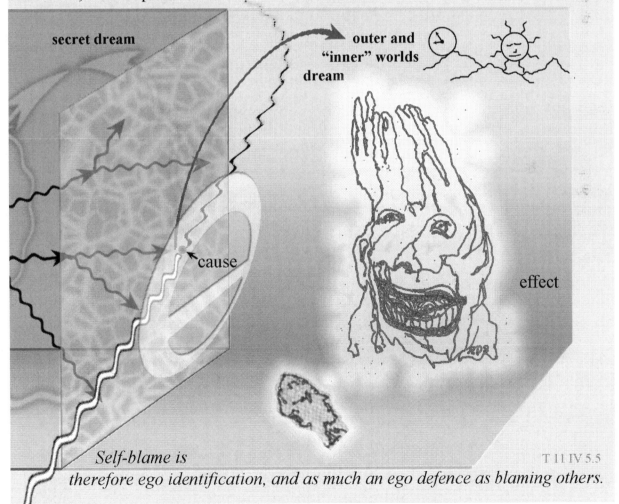

secret dream

outer and "inner" worlds dream

cause

effect

T 11 IV 5.5

Self-blame is therefore ego identification, and as much an ego defence as blaming others.

Always in sickness does the Son of God attempt to make himself his cause, and not allow himself to be his Father's Son.

The rituals of the god of sickness are strange and very demanding. Joy is never permitted, for depression is the sign of allegiance to him. Depression means that you have forsworn God.

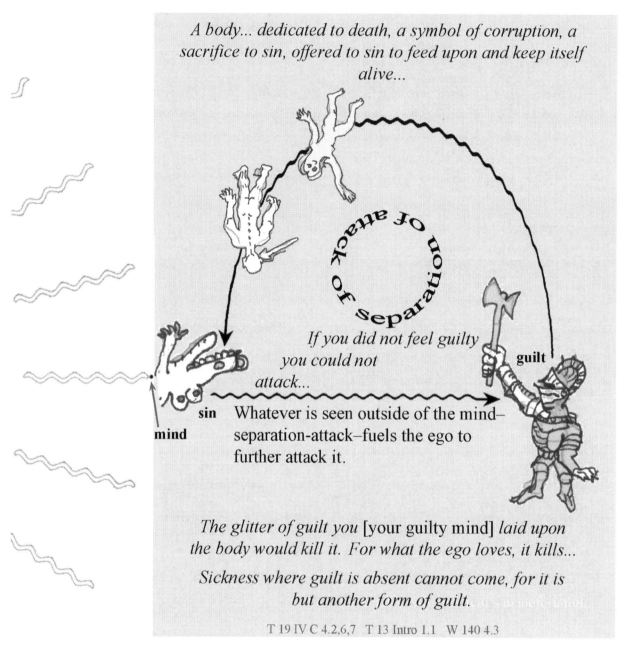

A body... dedicated to death, a symbol of corruption, a sacrifice to sin, offered to sin to feed upon and keep itself alive...

of attack
of separation

If you did not feel guilty you could not attack...

guilt

sin

mind

Whatever is seen outside of the mind–
separation-attack–fuels the ego to
further attack it.

The glitter of guilt you [your guilty mind] laid upon the body would kill it. For what the ego loves, it kills...

Sickness where guilt is absent cannot come, for it is but another form of guilt.

T 19 IV C 4.2,6,7   T 13 Intro 1.1   W 140 4.3

The idea of separation produced the body and remains connected to it, making it sick because of the mind's identification with it.

W 136 2   T 28 II 3.1   T 10 V 1.1   T 19 I 7.8

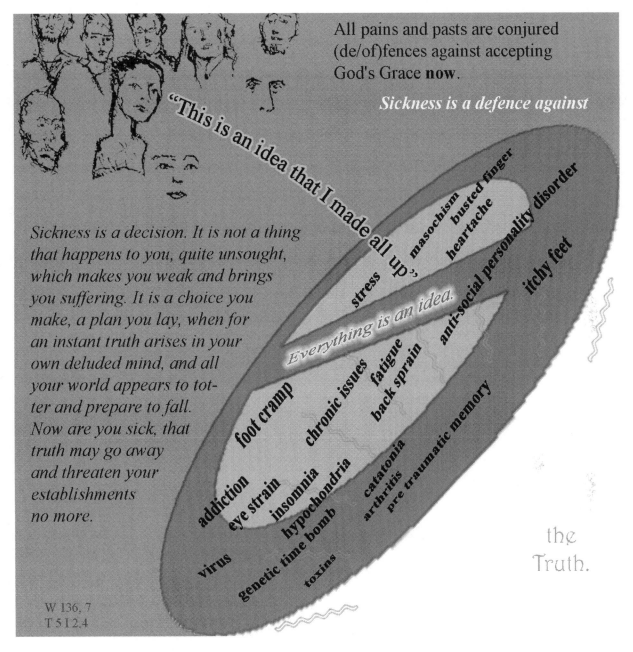

All pains and pasts are conjured (de/of)fences against accepting God's Grace **now**.

Sickness is a defence against

"This is an idea that I made all up"

masochism
busted finger
heartache
anti-social personality disorder
stress
itchy feet

Everything is an idea.

chronic issues
fatigue
back sprain
foot cramp

catatonia
arthritis
pre traumatic memory

addiction
eye strain
insomnia
hypochondria
virus
genetic time bomb
toxins

the Truth.

Sickness is a decision. It is not a thing that happens to you, quite unsought, which makes you weak and brings you suffering. It is a choice you make, a plan you lay, when for an instant truth arises in your own deluded mind, and all your world appears to totter and prepare to fall. Now are you sick, that truth may go away and threaten your establishments no more.

W 136, 7
T 5 I 2.4

Illusions carry only guilt and suffering, sickness and death, to their believers.

Sickness is idolatry, because it is the belief that power can be taken from you.

No mind is sick until another mind agrees that they are separate. And thus it is their joint decision [agreement] to be sick.

T 22 II 3.1   T 10 III 4.4   T 28 III 2.1-2

218

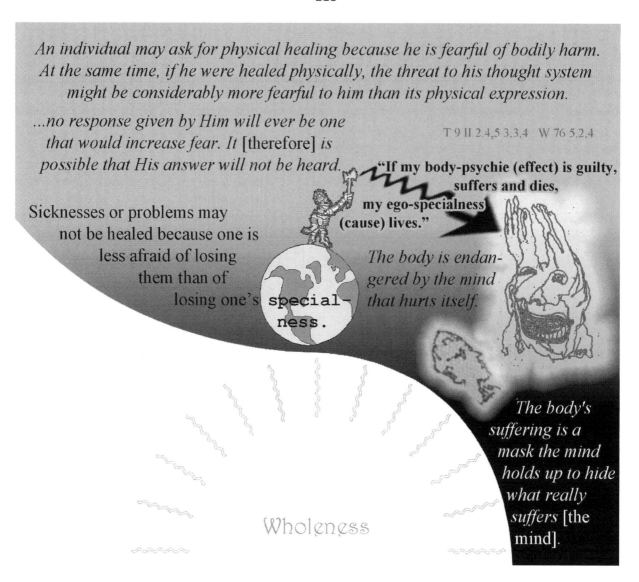

An individual may ask for physical healing because he is fearful of bodily harm. At the same time, if he were healed physically, the threat to his thought system might be considerably more fearful to him than its physical expression.

...no response given by Him will ever be one that would increase fear. It [therefore] is possible that His answer will not be heard.

T 9 II 2.4,5 3.3,4   W 76 5.2.4

"If my body-psychie (effect) is guilty, suffers and dies, my ego-specialness (cause) lives."

Sicknesses or problems may not be healed because one is less afraid of losing them than of losing one's special- ness.

The body is endan- gered by the mind that hurts itself.

The body's suffering is a mask the mind holds up to hide what really suffers [the mind].

Wholeness

If you let your mind harbor attack thoughts, yield to judgment or make plans against uncertainties to come, you have... made a bodily identity which will attack the body, for the mind is sick.

W 136 19.2

The god of sickness obviously demands the denial of health, because health is in direct opposition to its own survival. But consider what this means to you. Unless you are sick you cannot keep the gods you made, for only in sickness could you possibly want them.

T 10 V 3.2-4

o   o   o

Magic is the mindless or the miscreative [at effect] *use of mind.*

The purpose of one's magical "rights" and "wrongs" is not to make one's dream better; it is rather to make one's dream of killing Oneness seem more real, and to concoct respite from God's "wrath".

"By my power of death do I defeat Life."

A magic thought, by its mere presence, acknowledges a separation from God. It states, in the clearest form possible, that the mind which believes it has a separate will that can oppose the Will of God, also believes it can succeed.

M 17 5.3-4

The avoidance of magic is the avoidance of temptation. For all temptation is nothing more than the attempt to substitute another will for God's.

T V 2.1   M 16 9.1-2

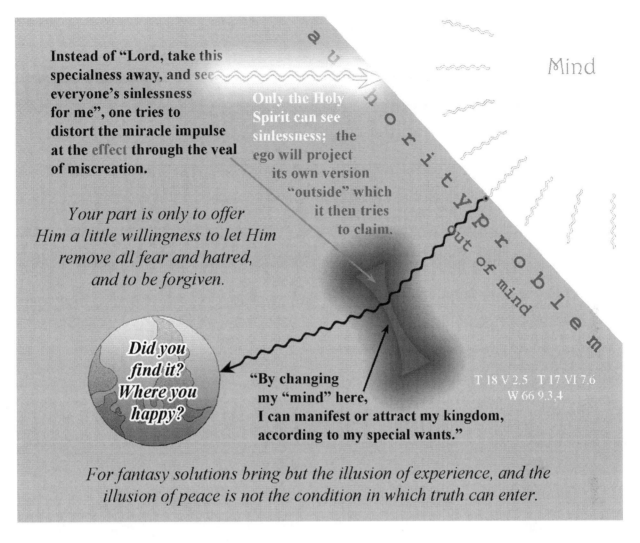

Instead of "Lord, take this specialness away, and see everyone's sinlessness for me", one tries to distort the miracle impulse at the effect through the veal of miscreation.

Only the Holy Spirit can see sinlessness; the ego will project its own version "outside" which it then tries to claim.

Mind

authority problem out of mind

Your part is only to offer Him a little willingness to let Him remove all fear and hatred, and to be forgiven.

Did you find it? Where you happy?

"By changing my "mind" here, I can manifest or attract my kingdom, according to my special wants."

T 18 V 2.5 T 17 VI 7.6
W 66 9.3,4

For fantasy solutions bring but the illusion of experience, and the illusion of peace is not the condition in which truth can enter.

All belief in magic is maintained by just one simple-minded illusion;—that it works.

M 16 11.8

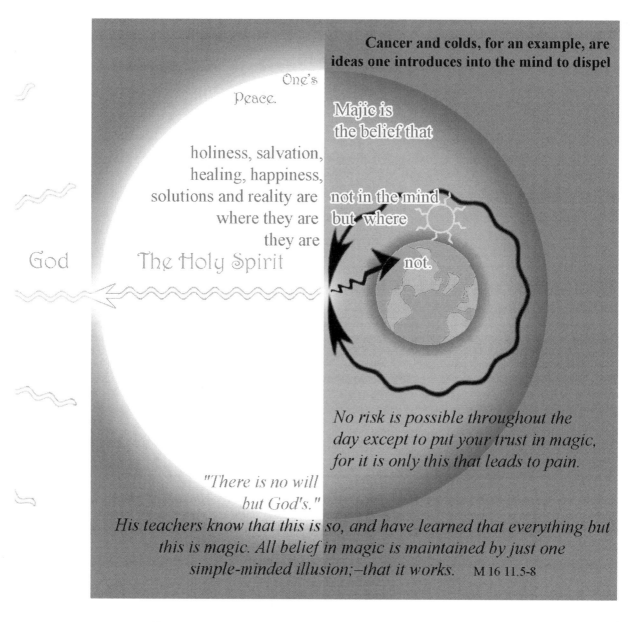

One's Peace.

Cancer and colds, for an example, are ideas one introduces into the mind to dispel

Majic is the belief that

holiness, salvation, healing, happiness, solutions and reality are where they are they are

not in the mind but where not.

God

The Holy Spirit

No risk is possible throughout the day except to put your trust in magic, for it is only this that leads to pain.

"There is no will but God's."

His teachers know that this is so, and have learned that everything but this is magic. All belief in magic is maintained by just one simple-minded illusion;—that it works.   M 16 11.5-8

All magic is an attempt at reconciling the irreconcilable.

T 10 IV 1.1

...illness is a form of magic. It might be better to say that it is a form of magical solution. The ego believes that by punishing itself it will mitigate the punishment of God.

Myths and magic are closely associated, since myths are usually related to ego origins, and magic to the powers the ego ascribes to itself. ...The so-called "battle for survival" is only the ego's struggle to preserve itself, and its interpretation of its own beginning.

All material means that you accept as remedies for bodily ills are restatements of magic principles. This is the first step in believing that the body makes its own illness.

There are times his certainty will waver, and the instant this occurs he will return to earlier attempts to place reliance on himself alone. Forget not this is magic, and magic is a sorry substitute for true assistance.

It does not follow, however, that the use of such agents [medical] for corrective purposes is evil. Sometimes the illness has a sufficiently strong hold over the mind to render a person temporarily inaccessible to the Atonement. In this case it may be wise to utilise a compromise approach to mind and body, in which something from the outside is temporarily given healing belief. This is because the last thing that can help the non-right-minded, or the sick, is an increase in fear.

The ego has a profound investment in sickness. If you are sick, how can you object to the ego's firm belief that you are not invulnerable?

T 5 V 5.4-6   T 4 II 9.1,3   T 2 IV 4.1-2   M 16 9.5-6   T 2 IV 4.4-7   T 8 VIII 3.2-3

2 IX *chaos sits in triumph on His throne*: Its Five Laws

Only chaos rules a world that represents chaotic thinking, and chaos has no laws.

The "laws" of chaos can be brought to light, though never understood.

Attack in any form has placed your foot upon the twisted stairway that leads from Heaven.

Death has become life's symbol. His world is now a battleground...

W 136 9.3   W 53 2.3   T 23 II 1.1, 22.4   M 27 2.6-7

Father and the Son

valuing ego over God

makes attack to cast Him out

Who now outside, must return to kill

I have been killed

vengeance is life is love's substitute is death

Brother, take not one step in the descent to hell. For having taken one, you will not recognise the rest for what they are. And they will follow. T 23 II 22.1-3

For this world is the symbol of punishment, and all the laws that seem to govern it are the laws of death.

T 13 Intr 2.4

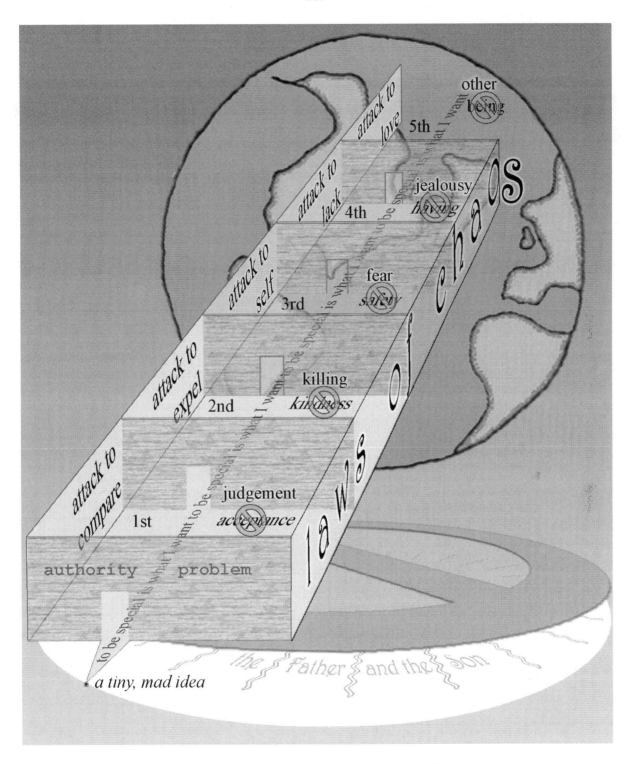

The special messages the special hear convince them they are different and apart; each in his special sins and "safe" from love, which does not see his specialness at all.

T 21 II 5.5

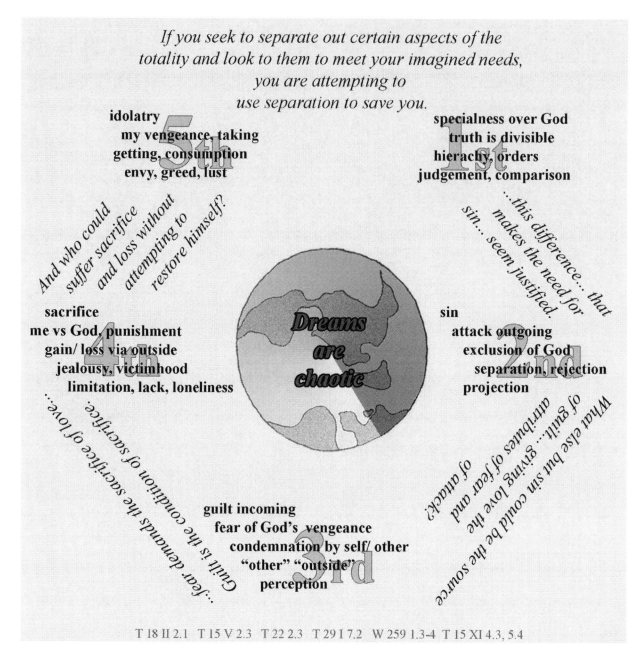

*If you seek to separate out certain aspects of the
totality and look to them to meet your imagined needs,
you are attempting to
use separation to save you.*

5th
idolatry
my vengeance, taking
getting, consumption
envy, greed, lust

1st
specialness over God
truth is divisible
hierachy, orders
judgement, comparison

And who could suffer sacrifice and loss without attempting to restore himself?

...this difference... that makes the need for sin... seem justified.

4th
sacrifice
me vs God, punishment
gain/ loss via outside
jealousy, victimhood
limitation, lack, loneliness

Dreams are chaotic

2nd
sin
attack outgoing
exclusion of God
separation, rejection
projection

...fear demands the condition of sacrifice.

Guilt is the condition of sacrifice.

3rd
guilt incoming
fear of God's vengeance
condemnation by self/ other
"other" "outside"
perception

What else but sin could be the source of guilt... giving love and attributes of fear and of attack?

T 18 II 2.1   T 15 V 2.3   T 22 2.3   T 29 I 7.2   W 259 1.3-4   T 15 XI 4.3, 5.4

It is not a world of will because it is governed by the desire to be unlike God, and this desire is not will. The world you made is therefore totally chaotic, governed by arbitrary and senseless "laws", and without meaning of any kind.

And so the body is more powerful than everlasting life, Heaven more frail than hell, and God's design for the salvation of His Son opposed by a decision stronger than His Will. His Son is dust, the Father incomplete, and chaos sits in triumph on His throne.

T 12 IV 9.5-6   W 136 9.2-3

...to deny God [1] will inevitably believe that others [3] done this [4]

result in projection [2], and you will and not yourself have to you.

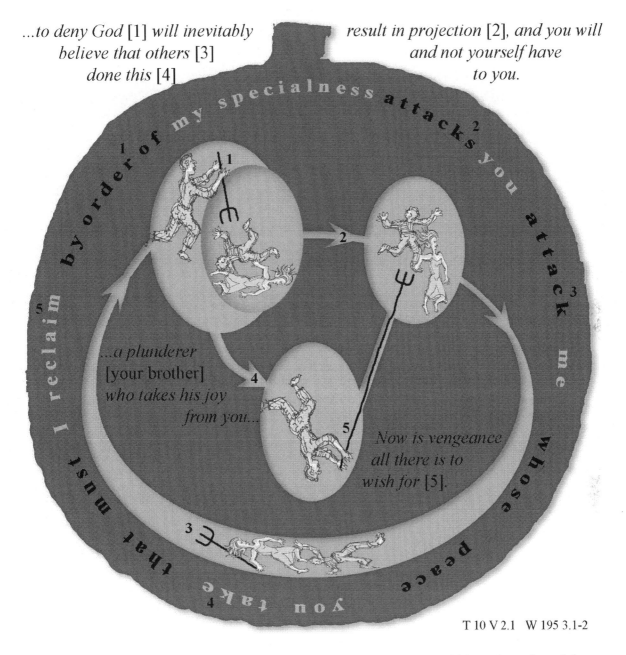

by order of my specialness attacks you attack me

I reclaim whose peace you take that must

...a plunderer [your brother] who takes his joy from you...

Now is vengeance all there is to wish for [5].

T 10 V 2.1   W 195 3.1-2

Confusion follows on confusion here, for on confusion has this world been based, and there is nothing else it rests upon.

Fantasy is an attempt to control reality according to false needs. ...Fantasies are a means of making false associations and attempting to obtain pleasure from them.

T 1 VII 3.4,6   T 29 II 6.3

But specialness is not the truth in you. It can be thrown off balance by anything. What rests on nothing never can be stable. However large and overblown it seems to be, it still must rock and turn and whirl about with every breeze.

The totally insane engenders fear because it is completely undependable, and offers no grounds for trust.

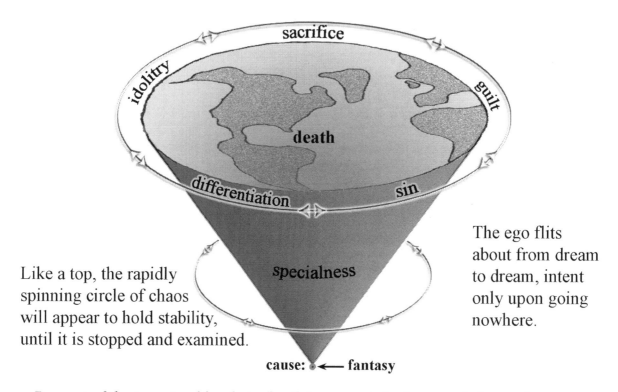

Like a top, the rapidly spinning circle of chaos will appear to hold stability, until it is stopped and examined.

The ego flits about from dream to dream, intent only upon going nowhere.

Pursuit of the imagined leads to death because it is the search for nothingness...

T 24 III 3,4-7   W 53 3.2   W 131 2.6

You must have noticed an outstanding characteristic of every end that the ego has accepted as its own. When you have achieved it, it has not satisfied you. *That is why the ego is forced to shift ceaselessly from one goal to another, so that you will continue to hope it can yet offer you something.*

The ego exerts maximal vigilance about what it permits into awareness... The ego is thrown further off balance because it keeps its primary motivation from your awareness, and raises control rather than sanity to predominance.   T 8 VIII 2.5-7   T 4 V 1.3

A: *the truth is different for everyone*

It is the belief that conflicting interests are possible, and therefore you have accepted the impossible as true. Is that different from saying you perceive yourself as unreal?

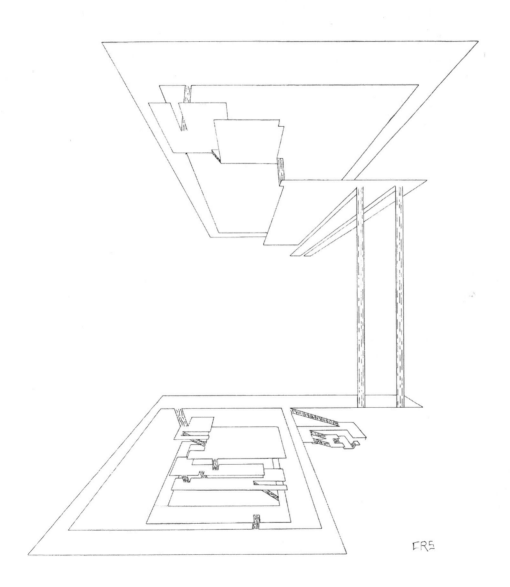

...only equals are at peace. ...Yet if they perceive any of their brothers as anything other than their perfect equals, the idea of competition has entered their minds. Do not underestimate your need to be vigilant against this idea, because all your conflicts come from it.

All that a heirarchy of illusions can show is preference, not reality.

Truth is indivisible, yet
to the ego "truths" are different   apart
and determined by preferences valued.   **All heirarchies of illusion**
                                           originate from the first,
  ...some are more valuable   **in which the**
     and therefore true.   **desire to be**
                                           out of your

a u t h o r i t y   p r o b l e m **mind** is valued over

Reality

You cannot sell your soul, but you can sell your awareness of it.
You cannot perceive your soul, but you will not know it while you perceive something else as more valuable.

T 26 VII 6.5   T 23 II 2.3   T 12 VI 1.6

What relevance has preference to the truth? Illusions are illusions and are false. Your preference gives them no reality.

The aim of all defences is to keep the truth from being whole.

T 23 II 2.1   T 7 III 3.6-7   T 7 III 3   T 26 VII 6.5-7   W 136 2.4

The ego literally lives by comparisons. Equality is beyond its grasp, and charity becomes impossible.

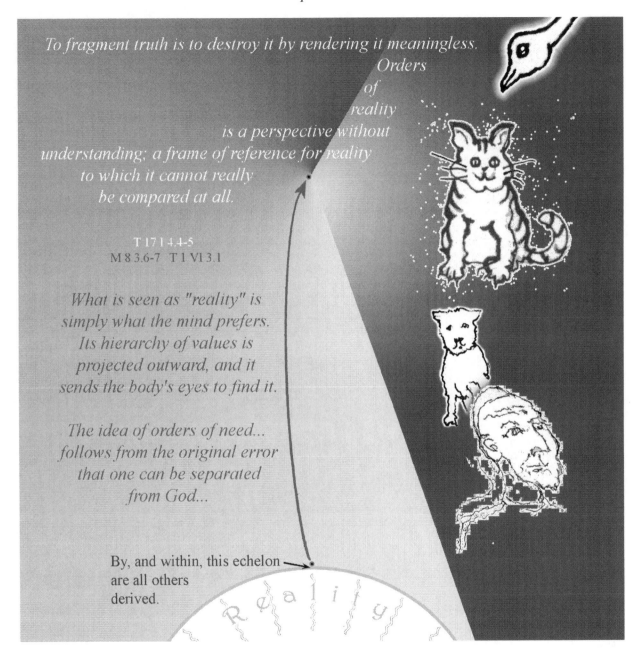

To fragment truth is to destroy it by rendering it meaningless. Orders of reality is a perspective without understanding; a frame of reference for reality to which it cannot really be compared at all.

T 17 I 4.4-5
M 8 3.6-7 T 1 VI 3.1

What is seen as "reality" is simply what the mind prefers. Its hierarchy of values is projected outward, and it sends the body's eyes to find it.

The idea of orders of need... follows from the original error that one can be separated from God...

By, and within, this echelon are all others derived.

Reality

For what your brother must become to keep your specialness is an illusion. He who is "worse" than you must be attacked, so that your specialness can live on his defeat. For specialness is triumph, and its victory is his defeat and shame. How can he live, with all your sins upon him? And who must be his conqueror but you?

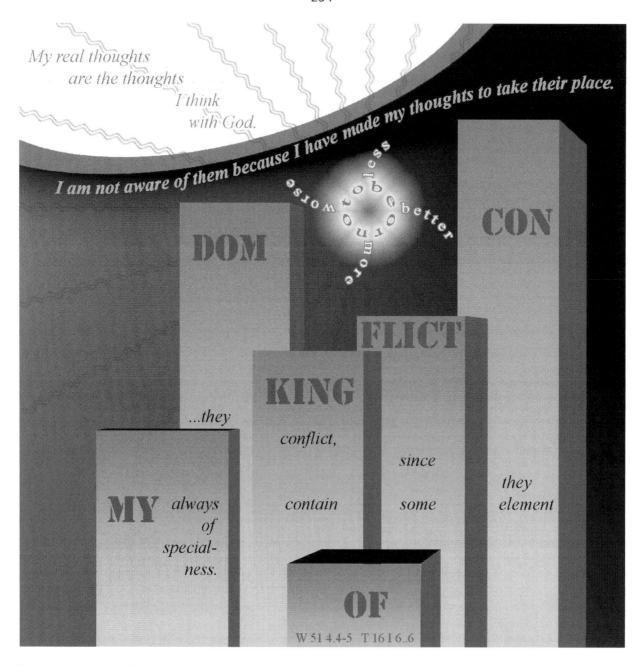

My real thoughts are the thoughts I think with God.

I am not aware of them because I have made my thoughts to take their place.

or no or better or wise or more or less

DOM

CON

FLICT

KING

...they

conflict,

since

they
element

MY always
of
special-
ness.

contain

some

OF

W 51 4.4-5   T 16 I 6..6

Comparison must be an ego device, for love makes none. Specialness always makes comparisons. It is established by a lack seen in another, and maintained by searching for, and keeping clear in sight, all lacks it can perceive. This does it seek, and this it looks upon.

Whatever form of specialness you cherish, you have made sin. Inviolate it stands, strongly defended with all your puny might against the Will of God.

T 4 II 7.1-2   T 24 I 5.6-10, II 1.1-4, III 2.1-2

B: *each one* must *sin*

The laws of sin demand a victim.

The ego projects to exclude, and therefore to deceive.

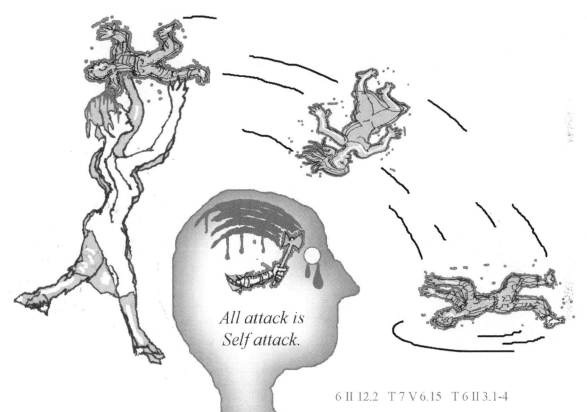

All attack is Self attack.

6 II 12.2   T 7 V 6.15   T 6 II 3.1-4

Yet projection will always hurt you. It reinforces your belief in your own split mind, and its only purpose is to keep the separation going. It is solely a device of the ego to make you feel different from your brothers and separated from them. The ego justifies this on the grounds that it makes you seem "better" than they are, thus obscuring your equality with them still further.

Remember that what you deny you must have once known.

The process begins by excluding something that exists in you but which you do not want...

T 23 II 4.1   T 25 VIII 3.3   T 10 V 6.5   T 6 II 3.8

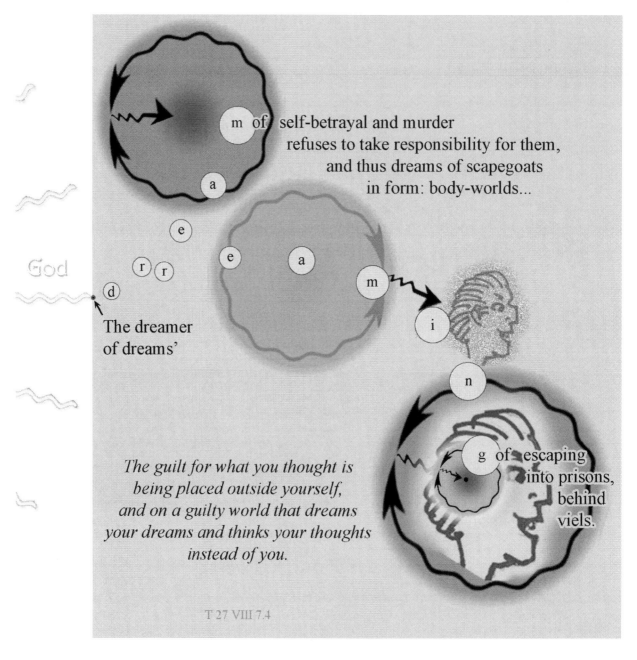

m of self-betrayal and murder
refuses to take responsibility for them,
and thus dreams of scapegoats
in form: body-worlds...

God

The dreamer
of dreams'

m

i

n

g of escaping
into prisons,
behind
viels.

*The guilt for what you thought is
being placed outside yourself,
and on a guilty world that dreams
your dreams and thinks your thoughts
instead of you.*

T 27 VIII 7.4

The idea of sin is wholly sacrosanct to its thought system, and quite unapproachable except with reverence and awe. It is the most "holy" concept in the ego's system; lovely and powerful... Here is its armor, its protection, and the fundamental purpose of the special relationship in its interpretation.

T 19 II 5

...the ego attacks everything it perceives by breaking it into small, disconnected parts...

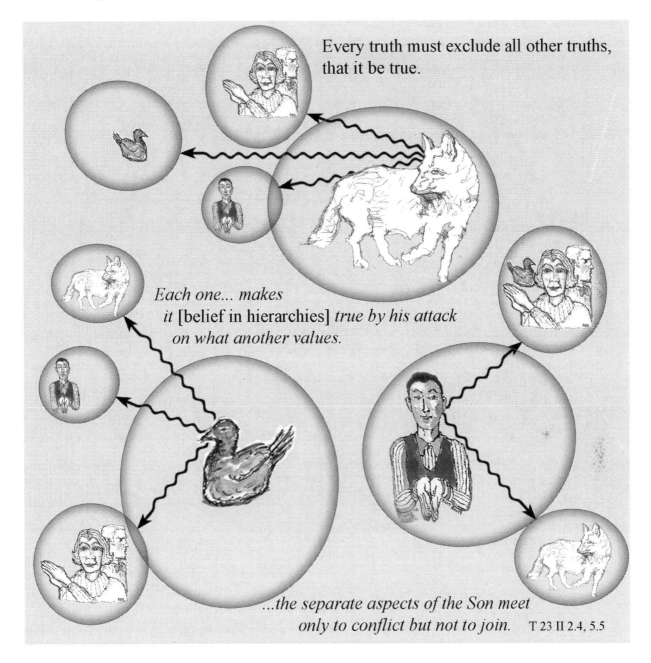

Every truth must exclude all other truths, that it be true.

Each one... makes it [belief in hierarchies] true by his attack on what another values.

...the separate aspects of the Son meet only to conflict but not to join. T 23 II 2.4, 5.5

What you project you disown, and therefore do not believe is yours. You are excluding yourself by the very judgment that you are different from the one on whom you project.

T 11 V 13.5   T 6 II 2.1-2

It [the ego] *counsels, therefore, that if you are host to it, it will enable you to direct its anger outward,*   *thus protecting you.*

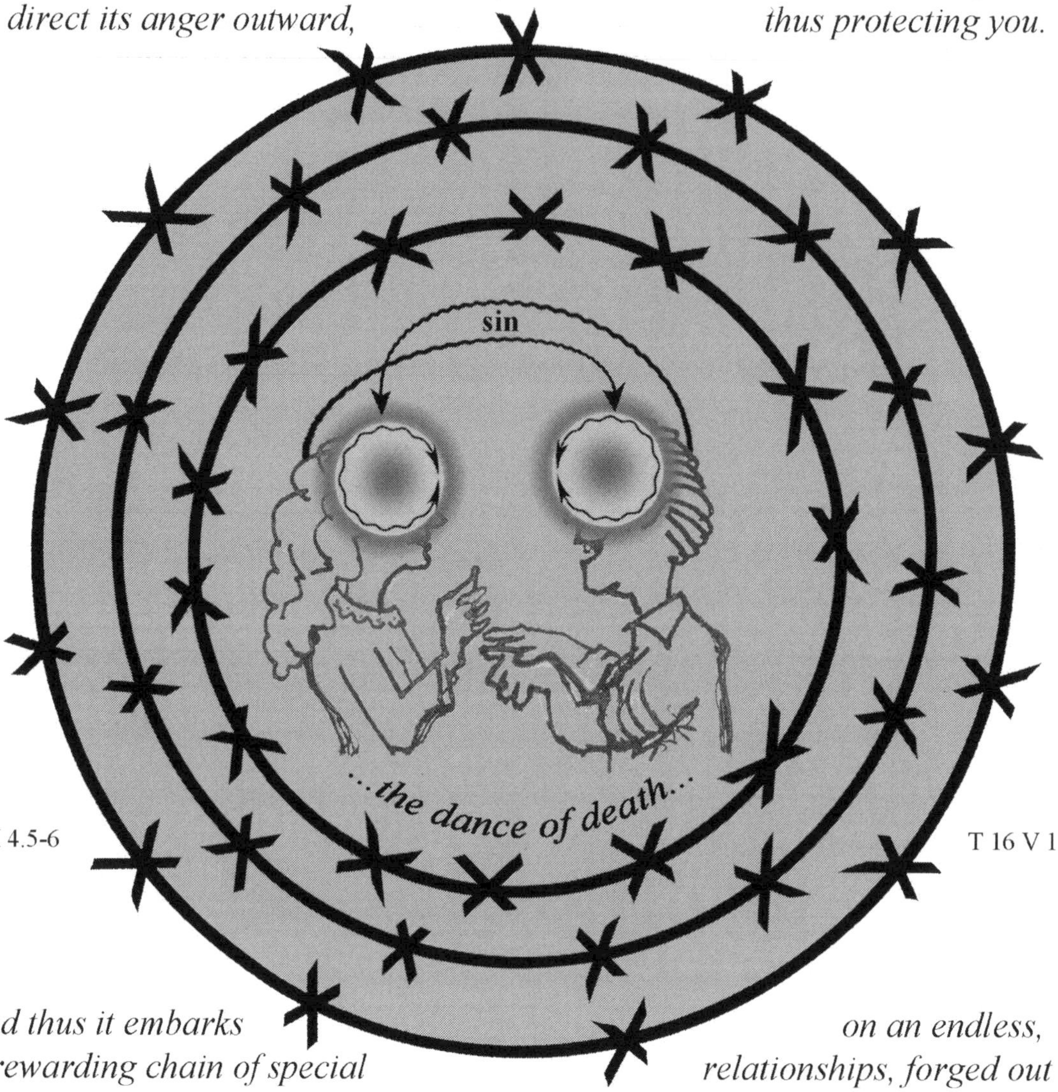

sin

...the dance of death...

T 15 VII 4.5-6

T 16 V 12.10

And thus it embarks   *on an endless, unrewarding chain of special*   *relationships, forged out of anger and dedicated to but one insane belief; that the more anger you invest outside yourself, the safer you become.*

C: *He has become the enemy Who caused it*

Adam's "sin" could have touched no one, had he not believed it was the Father Who drove him out of paradise. For in that belief the knowledge of the Father was lost, since only those who do not understand Him could believe it.

Having projected his anger onto the world, he sees vengeance about to strike at him.

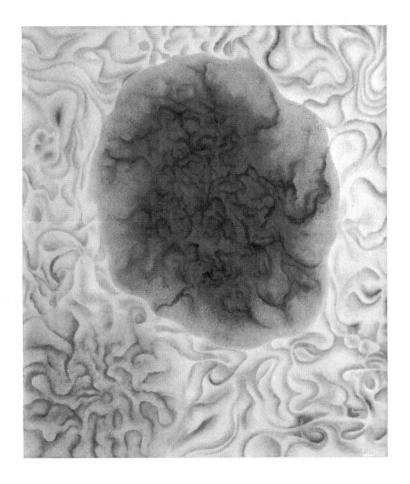

Now, for an instant, is a murderer perceived within you, eager for your death, intent on plotting punishment for you until the time when it can kill at last.

T 23 II 7.3   T 13 Intr 3.6-7   W 22 1.2-4   W 196 11.

Because one's perceptions of the outside world substitute their cause—one's fantasizing them—it seems as if **they** are one's cause, from which one's reactions become effects. One's dreams of incoming fear become the dawning of one's life, feelings, circumstances, and death. Cause is shifted from within to without as one becomes the effect of this without, and therefore too are without, lacking and "in" a body, out of one's mind and outside of Heaven. This is how God's function is reversed whereby He becomes the separator and the maker of death.

"I am alive by your attack."

seeming effect: "me"

seen perceptions

seeming cause

What I see is a form of vengeance.

unseen projections

you: the only and unseen cause, the imagining mind

W 22

...excluding something... leads directly to excluding you from your brothers.

Fear of retaliation from without follows...

T 6 II 3.8   T 5 V 3.11

You do not know the difference between what you have made and what God created...

The idea of death is valued, chosen, believed and then perceived through fear.

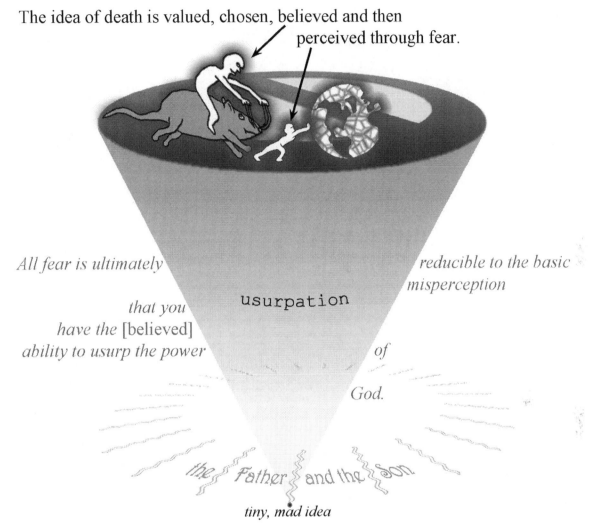

All fear is ultimately usurpation *reducible to the basic misperception*

that you have the [believed] ability to usurp the power *of* *God.*

the Father and the Son

tiny, mad idea

...self-deceptions made but to usurp the altar to the Father and the Son.

T 2 I 4.1   W 152 8.5

They must believe He shares their own confusion, and cannot avoid the vengeance that their own belief in justice must entail. And so they fear the Holy Spirit, and perceive the "wrath" of God in Him... Their world depends on sin's stability.

And flee the Holy Spirit as if He were a messenger from hell, sent from above, in treachery and guile, to work God's vengeance on them in the guise of a deliverer and friend. What could He be to them except a devil, dressed to deceive within an angel's cloak.

T 11 VII 4.6   T 25 VIII 6, 7.2-3

You do not respond to it [the world] *as though you made it, nor do you realize that the emotions the dream produces must come from you. It is the figures in the dream and what they do that seem to make the dream.*

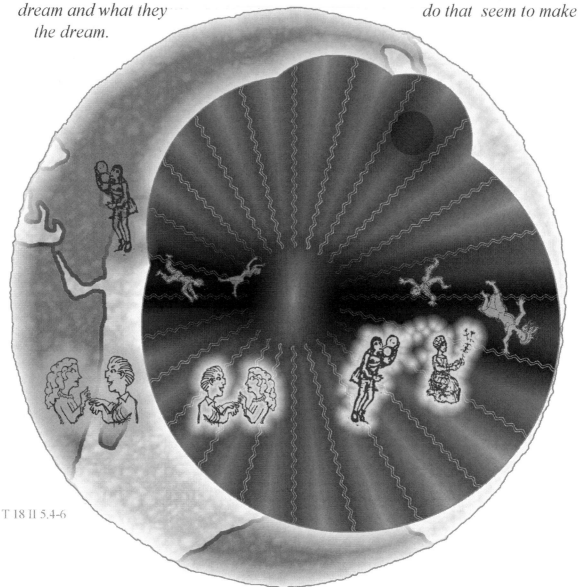

T 18 II 5.4-6

You do not realize that you are making them act out for you, for if you did the guilt would not be theirs [but yours], *and the illusions of satisfaction would be gone.*

And what escape has He for them except a door to hell that seems to look like Heaven's gate?

T 25 VIII 6.7

D: *it was taken from you*

...you will believe that others and not yourself have done this to you.

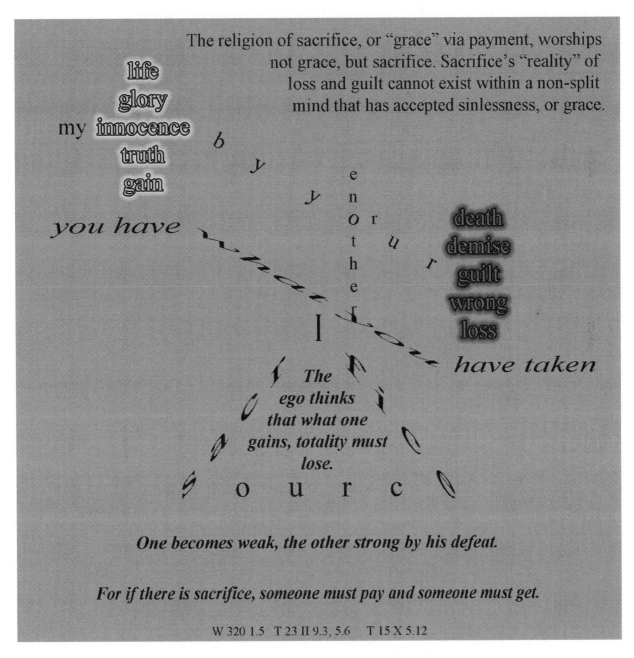

The religion of sacrifice, or "grace" via payment, worships not grace, but sacrifice. Sacrifice's "reality" of loss and guilt cannot exist within a non-split mind that has accepted sinlessness, or grace.

life
glory
my innocence
truth
gain

you have

death
demise
guilt
wrong
loss

have taken

The ego thinks that what one gains, totality must lose.

One becomes weak, the other strong by his defeat.

For if there is sacrifice, someone must pay and someone must get.

W 320 1.5   T 23 II 9.3, 5.6   T 15 X 5.12

Every illusion you accept... removes your sence of completion.

As host to the ego, you believe that you can give all your guilt away whenever you want, and thereby purchase peace. And the payment does not seem to be yours.

You think that everyone outside yourself demands your sacrifice, but you do not see that only you demand sacrifice, and only of yourself. Yet the demand of sacrifice is so savage and so fearful that you cannot accept it where it is [your mind].

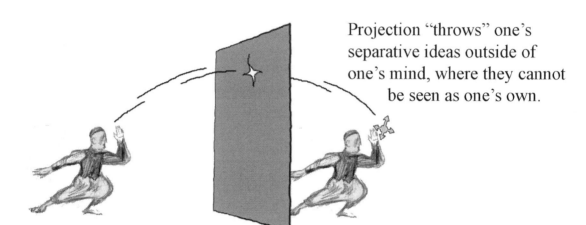

Projection "throws" one's separative ideas outside of one's mind, where they cannot be seen as one's own.

Projecting its [ego's] *insane belief that you have been treacherous to your Creator, it believes that your brothers, who are as incapable of this as you are, are out to take God from you.*   T 7 VII 9.2,4-5

...Projection always sees your wishes in others. If you choose to separate yourself from God, that is what you will think others are doing to you.

The real price of not accepting this has been so great that you have given [projected] *God away rather than look at it.*

To sacrifice is to give up, and thus to be without and to have suffered loss.

*On this side of the bridge you see a world of separate bodies, seeking to...
become one by losing. ...they are trying to decrease their magnitude. Each would
deny his power, for the separate union excludes the universe. Far more is left
outside than is taken in, for God is left without and nothing taken in.*

T 6 VI 5

*The shadow figures always speak for vengeance, and all relationships into which they enter are
totally insane.*

T 23 II 11.5   T 10 V 2.1   T 16 IV 10.2   T 15 X 6.1-2   T 15 IX 8.1-2   T 15 X 8.3   T 29 VII 4.3   T 17 III 2.2

346

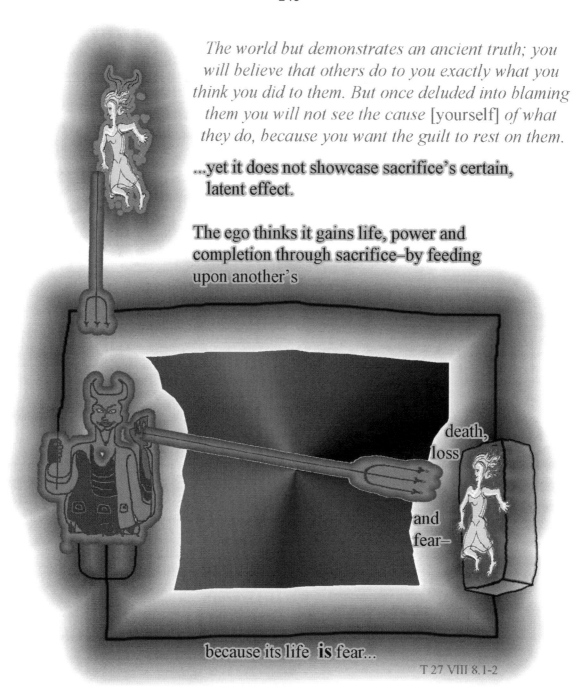

The world but demonstrates an ancient truth; you will believe that others do to you exactly what you think you did to them. But once deluded into blaming them you will not see the cause [yourself] of what they do, because you want the guilt to rest on them.

...yet it does not showcase sacrifice's certain, latent effect.

The ego thinks it gains life, power and completion through sacrifice–by feeding upon another's

death, loss

and fear–

because its life **is** fear...

T 27 VIII 8.1-2

Attack could never promote attack unless you perceived it as a means of depriving you of something you want.

T 7 VII 8.1

Yet you cannot lose anything unless you do not value it, and therefore do not want it. This makes you feel deprived of it, and by projecting your own rejection you then believe that others are taking it from you. You must be fearful if you believe that your brother is attacking you to tear the Kingdom of Heaven from you.

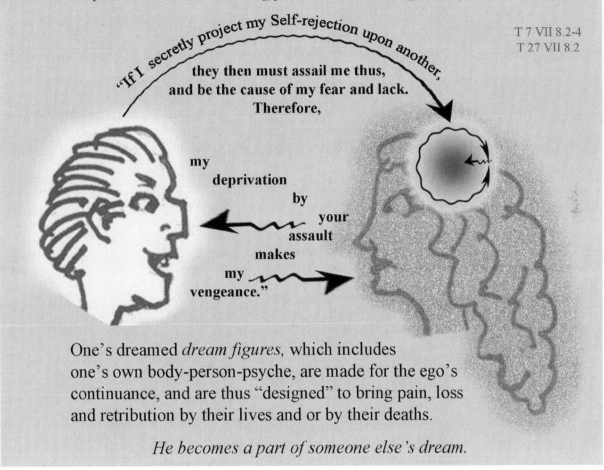

"If I secretly project my Self-rejection upon another,

they then must assail me thus, and be the cause of my fear and lack. Therefore,

T 7 VII 8.2-4
T 27 VII 8.2

my deprivation by your assault makes my vengeance."

One's dreamed *dream figures*, which includes one's own body-person-psyche, are made for the ego's continuance, and are thus "designed" to bring pain, loss and retribution by their lives and or by their deaths.

He becomes a part of someone else's dream.

...you will fear attack. And if you fear attack, you must believe that you are not invulnerable.

W 26 2.1-2

E: *seizing it and making it you own*

For sin is the idea you are alone and separated off from what is whole. And thus it would be necessary for the search for wholeness to be made beyond the boundaries of limits on yourself.

It holds there is a substitute for love. This is the magic that will cure all of your pain... He [your brother] *would deprive you of the secret ingredient that would give meaning to your life.* 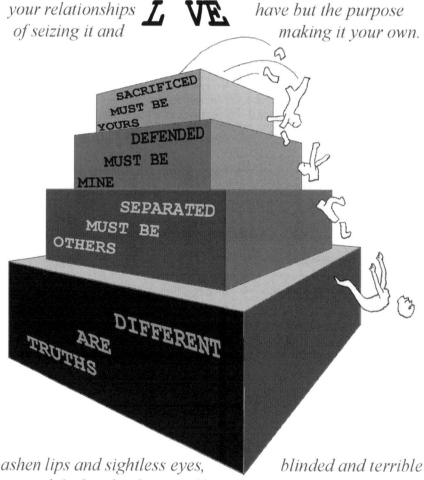 *The substitute for love, born of your enmity to your brother, must be salvation... And all your relationships* **L VE** *have but the purpose of seizing it and making it your own.*

And fear, with ashen lips and sightless eyes,   blinded and terrible to look upon, is lifted to the throne of love, its dying conqueror, its substitute, the savior from salvation.   T 23 II 12.4,5,9,10,12 15.6

The ego establishes relationships only to get something.

The central theme in its litany to sacrifice is that God must die so you can live. And it is this theme that is acted out in the special relationship.

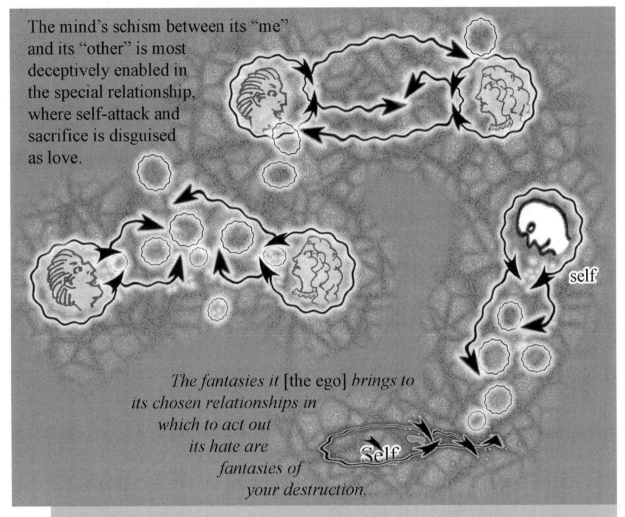

The mind's schism between its "me" and its "other" is most deceptively enabled in the special relationship, where self-attack and sacrifice is disguised as love.

The fantasies it [the ego] brings to its chosen relationships in which to act out its hate are fantasies of your destruction.

self

Self

The special relationship must be recognized for what it is; a senseless ritual in which strength is extracted from the death of God, and invested in His killer as the sign that form has triumphed over content, and love has lost its meaning. T 16 V 12.4

Through the death of your self you think you can attack another self, and snatch it from the other to replace the self that you despise. And you despise it because you do not think it offers the specialness that you demand.

Your idols do what you would have them do, and have the power you ascribe to them. And you pursue them vainly in the dream, because you want their power as your own.

...he denies the truth about himself, and seeks for something more than every-thing, as if a part of it were separated off and found where all the rest is not.

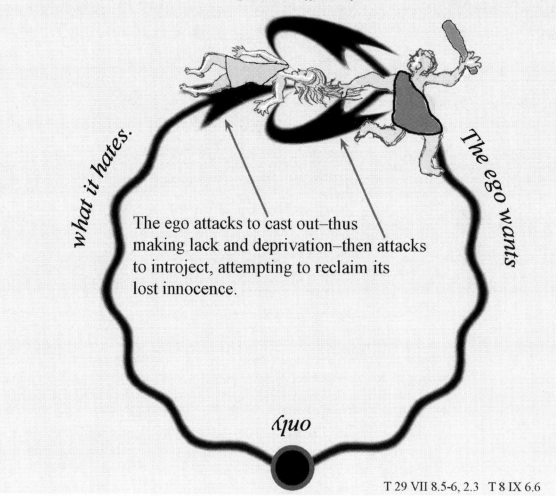

what it hates.

The ego wants

The ego attacks to cast out—thus making lack and deprivation—then attacks to introject, attempting to reclaim its lost innocence.

only

T 29 VII 8.5-6, 2.3   T 8 IX 6.6

Appetites are "getting" mechanisms, representing the ego's need to confirm itself. This is as true of body appetites as it is of the so-called "higher ego needs." Body appetites are not physical in origin. The ego... tries to satisfy itself through the body. But the idea that this is possible is a decision of the mind, which has become completely confused about what is really possible.

T 26 I 3.1, 1.5-6

The little that the body fences off becomes the self, preserved through sacrifice of all the rest.

The body is itself a sacrifice; a giving up of power in the name of saving just a little for yourself. To see a brother in another body, separate from yours, is the expression of a wish to see a little part of him and sacrifice the rest.

God cannot come into a body, nor can you join Him there. Limits on love will always seem to shut Him out, and keep you apart from Him.

There never was a time an idol brought you anything except the "gift" of guilt. Not one was bought except at cost of pain, nor was it ever paid by you alone.

You cannot love parts of reality and understand what love means. If you would love unlike to God, Who knows no special love, how can you understand it?

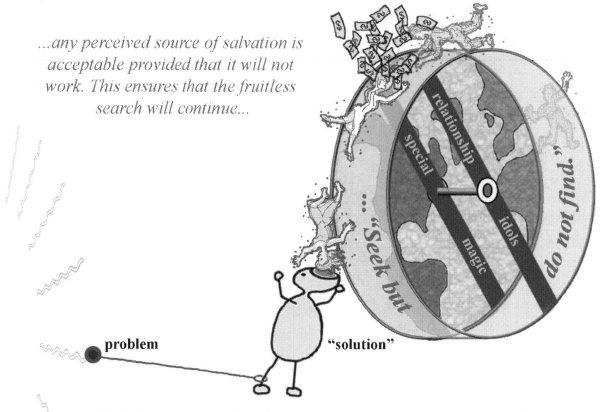

...any perceived source of salvation is acceptable provided that it will not work. This ensures that the fruitless search will continue...

Made by incompletion, the separated mind continuously seeks to sate its lack through countless forms of idolatry: they but which can never remedy their cause. It can only injest more inventions of separation that serve solely to compound its belief in deprivation.

The temptation to regard problems as many is the temptation to keep the problem of separation unsolved.

W 71 3.2-3, 4.2   79 4.1

The ego seeks to "resolve" its problems, not at their source, but where they were not made. And thus it seeks to guarantee there will be no solution.

T 23 II 12.12   T 30 III 3.7-8   T 15 VII 2.1   T 16 V 10.4-5,6-7   T 4 II 7   T 18 VIII 2.3-4   T 30 V 10.3-4
T 15 V 3.1-2   T 17 III 6.1-2

○   ○   ○

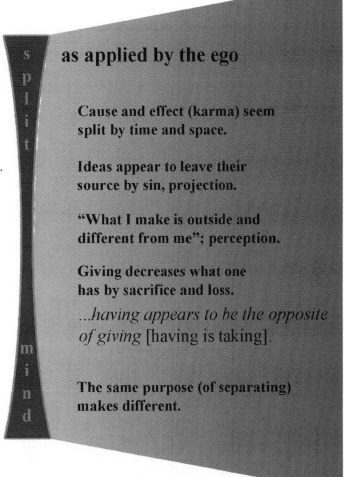

Laws of Mind   s p l i t   **as applied by the ego**

Cause and effect are one.

Cause and effect (karma) seem split by time and space.

Ideas leave not their source...

Ideas appear to leave their source by sin, projection.

...love creates itself...

"What I make is outside and different from me"; perception.

...giving will increase what you possess.
...the equality of having *and* being...

Giving decreases what one has by sacrifice and loss.

...having appears to be the opposite of giving [having is taking].

What shares a common purpose is the same.

The same purpose (of separating) makes different.

T 26 VII 13.1, 4.7   T 25 III 1.6   W 187 1.8   T 6 V B 3.4-5   T 27 VI 1.5

The outstanding characteristic of the laws of mind as they operate in this world is that by obeying them, and I assure you that you must obey them, you can arrive at diametrically opposed results.

T 7 II 2.7

2 X: Insanity: *war and vain imaginings*

As you look with open eyes upon your world, it must occur to you that you have withdrawn into insanity.

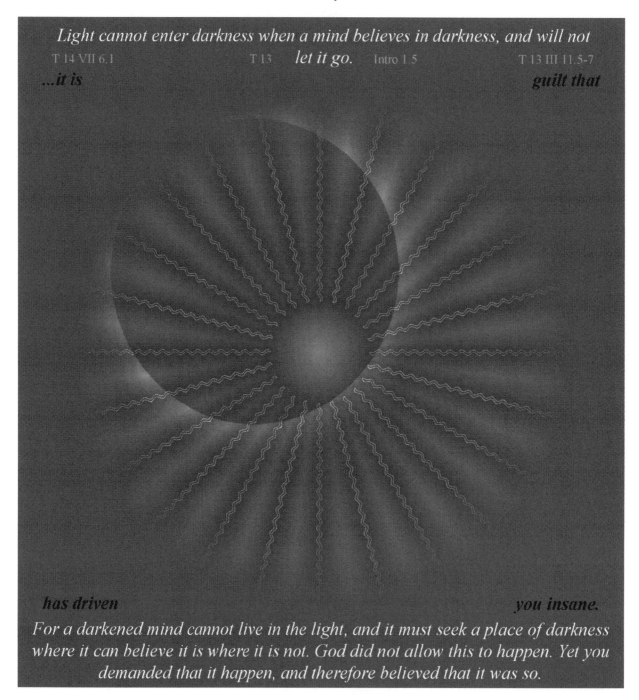

Light cannot enter darkness when a mind believes in darkness, and will not

T 14 VII 6.1   T 13   *let it go.*   Intro 1.5   T 13 III 11.5-7

...it is   *guilt that*

has driven   *you insane.*

For a darkened mind cannot live in the light, and it must seek a place of darkness where it can believe it is where it is not. God did not allow this to happen. Yet you demanded that it happen, and therefore believed that it was so.

255

Your insane laws were made to guarantee that you would make mistakes, and give them power over you by accepting their results as your just due. What could this be but madness?

Nothing can justify insanity, and to call for punishment upon yourself must be insane.

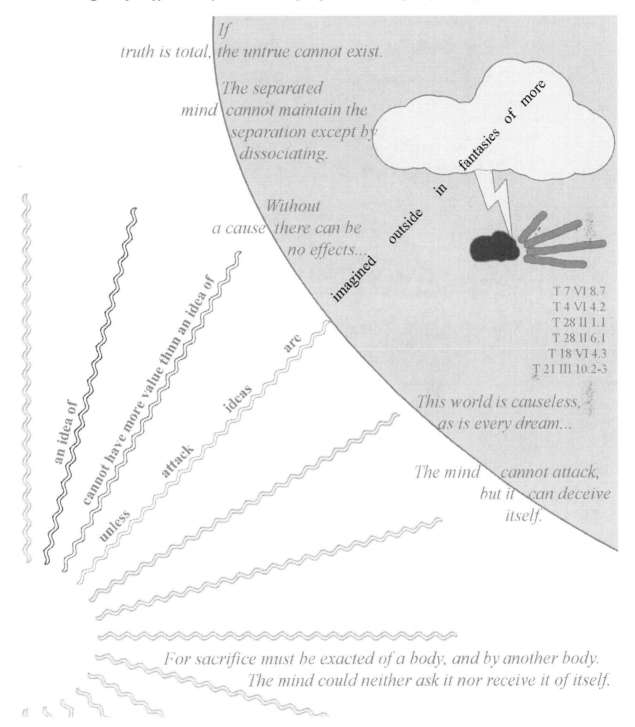

If truth is total, the untrue cannot exist.

The separated mind cannot maintain the separation except by dissociating.

Without a cause there can be no effects...

imagined outside in fantasies of more

T 7 VI 8.7
T 4 VI 4.2
T 28 II 1.1
T 28 II 6.1
T 18 VI 4.3
T 21 III 10.2-3

This world is causeless, as is every dream...

The mind cannot attack, but it can deceive itself.

an idea of cannot have more value than an idea of unless attack ideas are

For sacrifice must be exacted of a body, and by another body. The mind could neither ask it nor receive it of itself.

You can accept insanity because you made it, but you cannot accept love because you did not.

What you forgot was simply that God cannot destroy Himself. The light is in you. Darkness can cover it, but cannot put it out.

Nothing can have effects without a cause, and to confuse the two is merely to fail to understand them both.

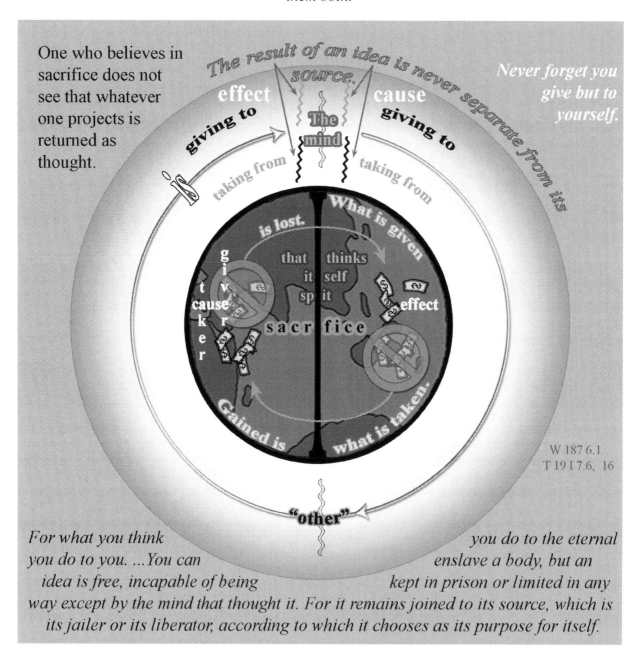

One who believes in sacrifice does not see that whatever one projects is returned as thought.

The result of an idea is never separate from its source.

effect   cause

giving to   giving to

The mind

Never forget you give but to yourself.

taking from   taking from

is lost.   What is given

that thinks it self sp it

giver   effect

cause taker   sacrifice

Gained is   what is taken.

"other"

W 187 6.1
T 19 I 7.6, 16

For what you think you do to you. ...You can   you do to the eternal idea is free, incapable of being   enslave a body, but an kept in prison or limited in any way except by the mind that thought it. For it remains joined to its source, which is its jailer or its liberator, according to which it chooses as its purpose for itself.

Thoughts extend as they are shared, for they can not be lost. There is no giver and receiver in the sense the world conceives of them.

W 136 16.1   T 13 V 6.1   T 20 IV 3.1   T 13 IX 5.6   T 13 III 5.1   T 18 III 1.6-8   T 21 II 10.8   W 187 5.4-5

Never forget you give but to yourself. Who understands what giving means must laugh at the idea of sacrifice. ...He laughs as well at pain and loss, at sickness and at grief, at poverty, starvation and at death. He recognizes sacrifice remains the one idea that stands behind them all, and in his gentle laughter are they healed.

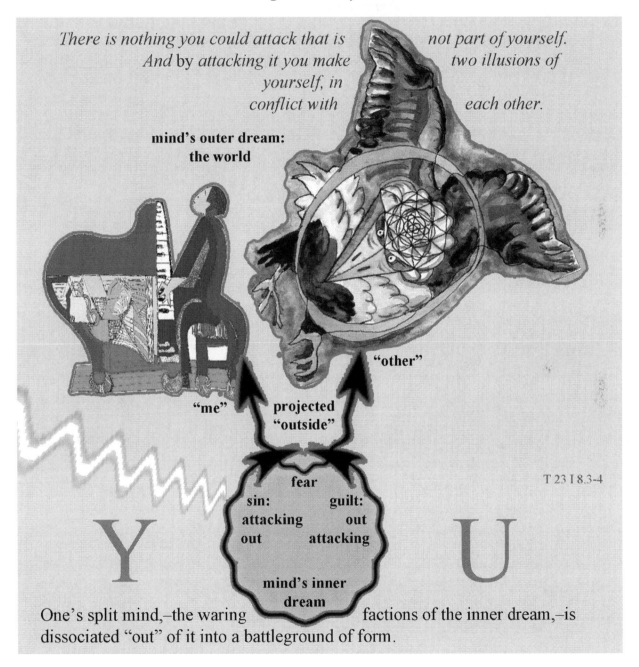

There is nothing you could attack that is *not part of yourself.* *And* by *attacking it you make* *two illusions of* *yourself, in* *conflict with* *each other.*

mind's outer dream: the world

"me" **projected "outside"** **"other"**

T 23 I 8.3-4

fear

sin: attacking out **guilt: out attacking**

mind's inner dream

Y   U

One's split mind,–the waring factions of the inner dream,–is dissociated "out" of it into a battleground of form.

...illusions of a split identity.

The delusional... do not wish to die, yet they will not let condemnation go. ...everything is disordered, and... what is within appears to be without.

You are willing to look at the ego's premises [separation], but not at their logical outcome [total confusion].

You will make war upon your Self, Which seems to be your enemy; and will attack your brother, as a part of what you hate.

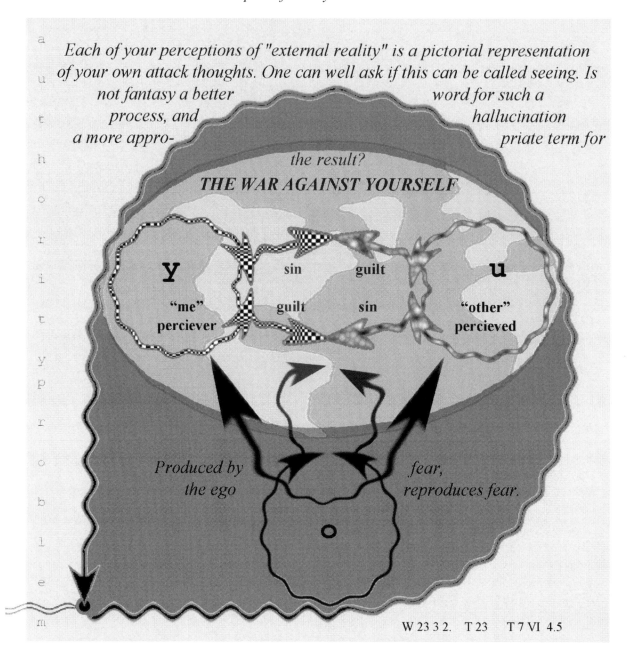

Each of your perceptions of "external reality" is a pictorial representation of your own attack thoughts. One can well ask if this can be called seeing. Is not fantasy a better process, and a more appro- the result? word for such a hallucination priate term for

THE WAR AGAINST YOURSELF

y   sin   guilt   u

"me"   guilt   sin   "other"
perciever   percieved

Produced by the ego   fear, reproduces fear.

W 23 3 2.   T 23   T 7 VI 4.5

Again and again have you attacked your brother, because you saw in him a shadow figure in your private world. And thus it is you must attack yourself first, for what you attack is not in others.

Look calmly at the logical conclusion of the ego's thought system and judge whether its offering is really what you want, for this is what it offers you.

W 187 6   W 97 1.4   T 13 V 4   T 7 X 1.5   T 28 V 3.7   T 13 V 3.6-7   T 10 III 4.1

o   o   o

This is salvation's keynote: What I see reflects a process in my mind, which starts with my idea of what I want. From there, the mind makes up an image of the thing the mind desires, judges valuable, and therefore seeks to find. These images are then projected outward, looked upon, esteemed as real and guarded as one's own. From insane wishes comes an insane world. From judgment comes a world condemned. And from forgiving thoughts a gentle world comes forth, with mercy for the holy Son of God, to offer him a kindly home where he can rest a while before he journeys on, and help his brothers walk ahead with him, and find the way to Heaven and to God.

W 325 1

Chapter 3:   THREE

When you have been caught in the world of perception you are caught in a dream. You cannot escape without help, because everything your senses show merely witnesses to the reality of the dream. God has provided the Answer, the only Way out, the true Helper.

The [ego's] case may be fool-proof, but it is not God-proof.

No one can fail who seeks to reach the truth.

W 131

The link with which the Father joins Himself to those He gives the power to create can never be dissolved.

PREFACE p. xi   T 5 VI 10.6   T 14 VIII 5.1

Father, how certain are Your ways; how sure their final outcome, and how faithfully is every step in my salvation set already, and accomplished by Your grace. Thanks be to You for Your eternal gifts, and thanks to You for my Identity.

W 297 2

God alone is sure, and He will guide our footsteps.

W 200 9.4

3 I: Forgiveness: *Faith and belief and vision are the means*

Forgiveness… shines on everything as one. And thus is oneness recognized at last.

Forgiveness is the answer to attack of any kind. So is attack deprived of its effects, and hate is answered in the name of love.

Forgiveness is the only function meaningful in time. It is the means the Holy Spirit uses to translate specialness from sin into salvation. Forgiveness is for all. But when it rests on all it is complete, and every function of this world completed with it. Then is time no more.

T 21 III 4.1   W II 9 2.3-4   T 26 VII 17.2-3   T 25 VI 5.3

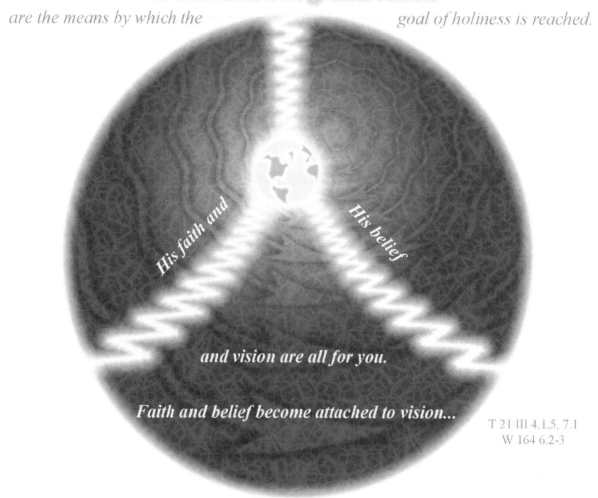

Faith and belief and vision

are the means by which the   *goal of holiness is reached.*

His faith and

His belief

and vision are all for you.

Faith and belief become attached to vision...

T 21 III 4.1.5, 7.1
W 164 6.2-3

*Your vision, given you from far beyond all things within the world,
looks back on them in a new light. And what you see becomes the healing
and salvation of the world.*

*Vision will come to you at first in glimpses, but they will be enough to show you what is given
you who see your brother sinless. Truth [belief] is restored to you through your desire [faith],
as it was lost to you through your desire for something else.*

Truth calls for faith, and faith makes room for truth.

T 20 VIII 1.1-2   T 17 VII 9.4

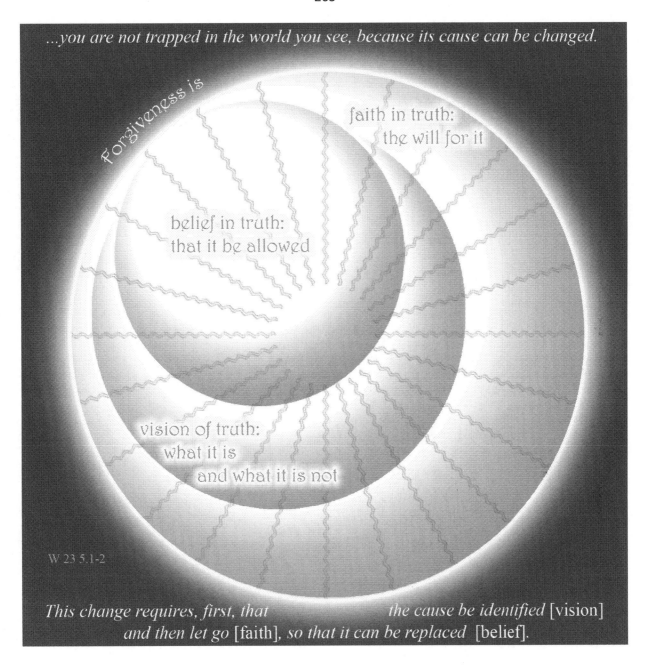

...you are not trapped in the world you see, because its cause can be changed.

Forgiveness is

faith in truth:
the will for it

belief in truth:
that it be allowed

vision of truth:
what it is
and what it is not

W 23 5.1-2

*This change requires, first, that   the cause be identified [vision]
and then let go [faith], so that it can be replaced [belief].*

I choose [faith] to see [vision] my brother's sinlessness [belief].

W 335

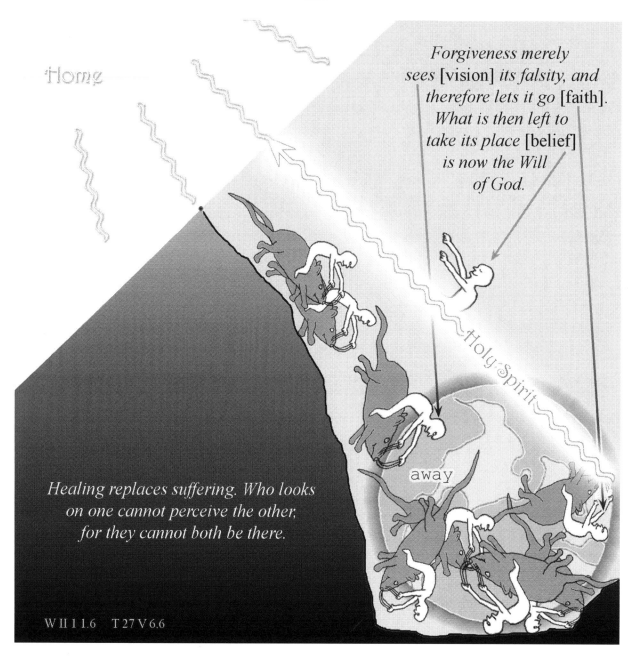

Home

Forgiveness merely sees [vision] *its falsity, and therefore lets it go* [faith]. *What is then left to take its place* [belief] *is now the Will of God.*

Holy Spirit

Healing replaces suffering. Who looks on one cannot perceive the other, for they cannot both be there.

away

W II 1 1.6   T 27 V 6.6

The world forgiven signifies Your Son acknowledges [vision] *his Father, lets* [faith] *his dreams be brought to truth, and waits expectantly* [belief] *for the one remaining instant of time which ends forever, as Your memory returns to him.*

Forgive the world, and you will understand that every thing that God created cannot have an end, and nothing He did not create is real. In this one sentence is our course explained.

W 270 1.4   M 20 5 7-8

*Our practicing becomes the footsteps lighting up the way for all our brothers,
who will follow us to the reality we share with them.*

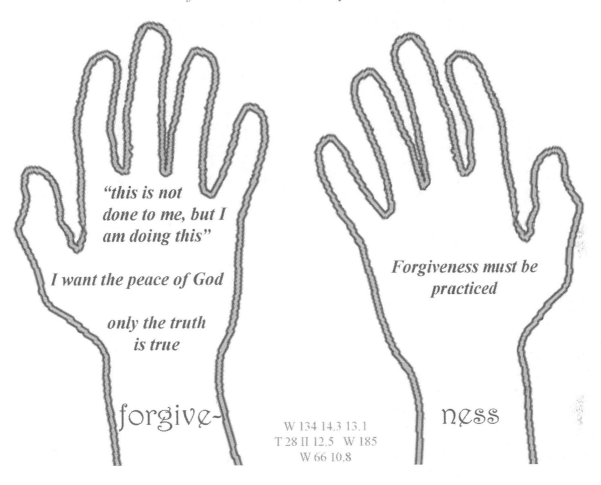

**"this is not
done to me, but I
am doing this"**

I want the peace of God

**only the truth
is true**

**Forgiveness must be
practiced**

forgive-

ness

W 134 14.3 13.1
T 28 II 12.5 W 185
W 66 10.8

The holy instant is the result of your determination to be holy. It is the answer. *The desire and the willingness [faith] to let it come precede its coming. You prepare your mind for it only to the extent of recognizing [vision] that you want it [faith] above all else. It is not necessary that you do more; indeed, it is necessary that you realize [vision] that you cannot do [belief] more.*

*Do you want happiness, a quiet mind, a certainty of purpose, and a sense of worth and beauty that transcends the world? Do you want care and safety, and the warmth of sure protection always?...
All this forgiveness offers you, and more.*

T 18 IV 1.1-5   W 122 1.2-3, 2.1

Your picture of the world can only mirror what is within.
The source of neither light nor darkness can be found without.

Grievanves
darken your mind,
and you
look out
on a
darkened
world.

Forgiveness lifts the darkness, reasserts your will,
and lets you look upon
a world of
light.

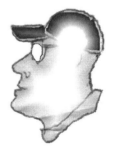

W 73 5.1-4

When you have seen [vision] this real world, as you will surely do, you will remember us. Yet you must learn the cost of sleeping, and refuse to pay it. Only then will you decide [faith] to awaken. And then the real world will spring [belief] to your sight, for Christ has never slept.

Only dreams of pardon can be shared. They mean the same to both of you.

To forgive is merely to remember only the loving thoughts you gave in the past, and those that were given you. All the rest must be forgotten.

T 12 VI 5.1-4   T 30 VII 6.17-18   17 III 1.1-2

Through miracles you accept God's forgiveness by extending it to others.

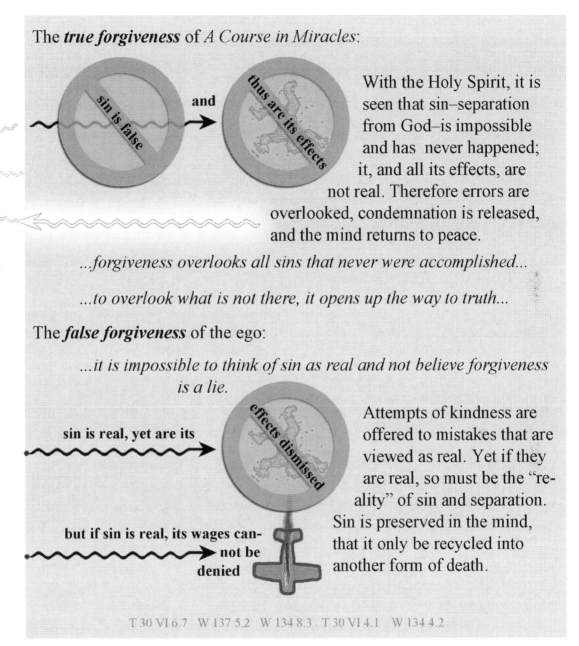

The ***true forgiveness*** of *A Course in Miracles*:

sin is false **and** thus are its effects

With the Holy Spirit, it is seen that sin–separation from God–is impossible and has never happened; it, and all its effects, are not real. Therefore errors are overlooked, condemnation is released, and the mind returns to peace.

...forgiveness overlooks all sins that never were accomplished...

...to overlook what is not there, it opens up the way to truth...

The ***false forgiveness*** of the ego:

...it is impossible to think of sin as real and not believe forgiveness is a lie.

sin is real, yet are its — effects dismissed

Attempts of kindness are offered to mistakes that are viewed as real. Yet if they are real, so must be the "reality" of sin and separation. Sin is preserved in the mind, that it only be recycled into another form of death.

but if sin is real, its wages cannot be denied

T 30 VI 6.7   W 137 5.2   W 134 8.3   T 30 VI 4.1   W 134 4.2

Yet faith will bring its witnesses to show [vision] *that what it rested on* [belief] *is really there.*

Give us faith today to recognize [vision] *Your Son, and set him free* [belief].

When the thought of separation has been changed [faith] *to one of true forgiveness, will the world be seen in quite another light* [vision]*; and one which leads to* [belief] *truth...*

T 1 I 21   W II 13 4.2   W 240 2.3   W Part II 3 1.4

Decide [faith] *but to accept your rightful place as co-creator of the universe, and all you think you made* [vision] *will disappear. What rises to awareness* [belief] *then will be all that ever was, eternally as it is now.*

The wish [faith] *for death is answered, and the sight that looked upon it now has been replaced by vision which perceives that you are* [belief] *not what you pretend to be.*

Be willing [faith], *then, to see* [vision] *your brother sinless, that Christ may rise* [belief] *before your vision and give you joy.*

The Son of God could never sin, but he can wish for what would hurt him. ...Is this a sin or a mistake, forgivable or not? Does he need help or condemnation? Is it your purpose that he be saved or damned? ... But recognize that in this choice the purpose of the world you see is chosen, and will be justified.

The part you play in salvaging the world from condemnation is your own escape.

God gave you the function to create in eternity. You do not need to learn that, but you do need to learn to want [faith] *it. ... He will teach you how to see* [vision] *yourself without condemnation, by learning how to look on everything without it. Condemnation will then not be real* [belief] *to you, and all your errors will be forgiven.*

Atonement is for all, because it is the way to undo the belief that anything is for you alone. To forgive is to overlook. Look [vision], *then, beyond error and do not let* [faith] *your perception rest upon it, for you will believe what your perception holds.*

There is no condemnation in the Son, for there is no condemnation in the Father. Sharing the perfect Love of the Father the Son must share what belongs to Him, for otherwise he will not know the Father or the Son. Peace be unto you who rest in God, and in whom the whole Sonship rests.

Release from guilt is the ego's whole undoing. Make no one fearful, *for his guilt is yours, and by obeying the ego's harsh commandments you bring its condemnation on yourself, and you will not escape the punishment it offers those who obey it. ...When you are afraid, be still and know that God is real, and you are His beloved Son in whom He is well pleased.*

How else can you find joy in a joyless place except by realizing that you are not there?

Do not attempt to "help" a brother in your way, for you cannot help yourself. But hear his call for the Help of God, and you will recognize your own need for the Father.

The core of the separation illusion lies simply in the fantasy of destruction of love's meaning. And unless love's meaning is restored to you, you cannot know yourself who share its meaning.

I will forgive, and this will disappear.

W 152 8.3-4   W 166 11.2   T 20 VIII 3.3   T 25 III 9   T 27 VII 6.1   T 9 IV 1.1-3   T 11 IV 8   T 13 IX 2   T 6 II 6.1
T 12 I 6.9   T 16 V 15.1-2   W 193 13.3

A: Faith: Willingness, Desire and Decision

Faith goes to what you want, and you instruct your mind accordingly.

Here, where the laws of God do not prevail in perfect form, can he yet do one *perfect thing and make* one *perfect choice. And by this act of special faithfulness to one perceived as other than himself, he learns the gift was given to himself, and so they must be one.*

There is no point in trying to avoid this one decision. It must be made.

Purpose is of the mind. And mind's can change as they desire.

To change your mind means to place it at the disposal of true Authority.

Be willing, then, to see your brother sinless...

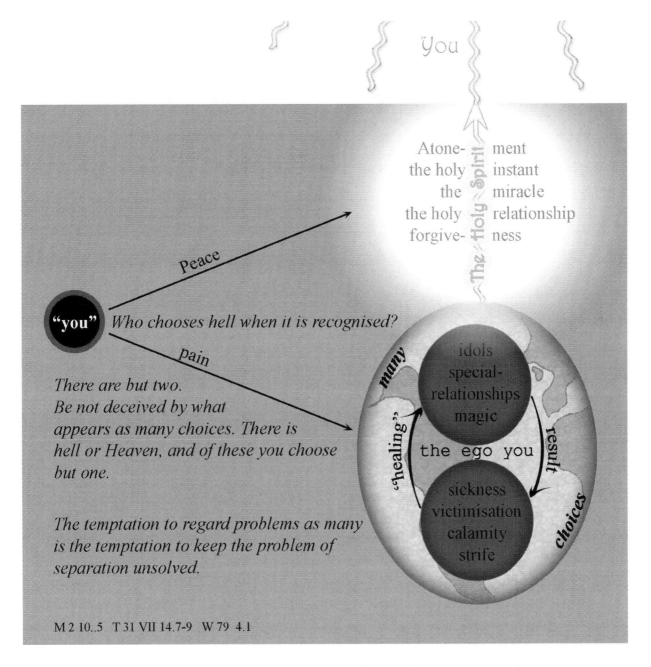

You

Atone- ment
the holy instant
the miracle
the holy relationship
forgive- ness

The Holy Spirit

Peace

"you" *Who chooses hell when it is recognised?*

pain

idols
special-
relationships
magic

many

"healing"

the ego you

result

sickness
victimisation
calamity
strife

choices

*There are but two.
Be not deceived by what
appears as many choices. There is
hell or Heaven, and of these you choose
but one.*

*The temptation to regard problems as many
is the temptation to keep the problem of
separation unsolved.*

M 2 10..5   T 31 VII 14.7-9   W 79 4.1

*If you are willing to renounce the role of guardian of your thought system and open it to me, I
will correct it very gently and lead you back to God.*

*On your little faith, joined with His understanding, He will build your part in the Atonement and
make sure that you fulfil it easily.*

W 91 5.3   T 25 VI 5.1-2   T 22 II 6.8-9   T 24 IV 2.6-7   T 1 V 5.7   T 20 VIII 3.3   T 4 I 4.7   T 18 V 2.6

274

Even the relinquishment of your false decision-making prerogative, which the ego guards so jealously, is not accomplished by your wish. It was accomplished for you by the Will of God, Who has not left you comfortless. His Voice will teach you how to distinguish between pain and joy, and will lead you out of the confusion you have made.

You who hold your brother's hand for when you joined each other you also hold mine, were not alone.

Say to the Holy Spirit only, "Decide for me," and it is done.

To perceive the healing of your brother as the healing of yourself is thus the way to remember God.

God will come to you only as you will give Him to your brothers.

Be happy, and you gave the power of decision to Him Who must decide for God for you.

The ego's illusions cannot decide except for themselves, as they can see nothing but themselves.

T 7 X 7   T 18 III 4.1   T 14 III 16.1   T 12 II 2.9   T 4 VI 8.4   T 21 II 3.6

The Holy Spirit is your Guide in choosing. He is in the part of your mind that always speaks for the right choice, because He speaks for God.

Only the Holy Spirit can resolve conflict, because only the Holy Spirit is conflict-free. He perceives only what is true in your mind, and extends outward only to what is true in other minds.

T 5 II 8.1-2   T 6 II 11.8-9

You cannot wake yourself. Yet you can let yourself be wakened. You can overlook your brother's dreams. So perfectly can you forgive him his illusions he becomes your saviour from your dreams. ...you will see that God Himself is where his body is. Before this light the body disappears...

The temptation to regard problems as many is the temptation to keep the problem of separation unsolved.

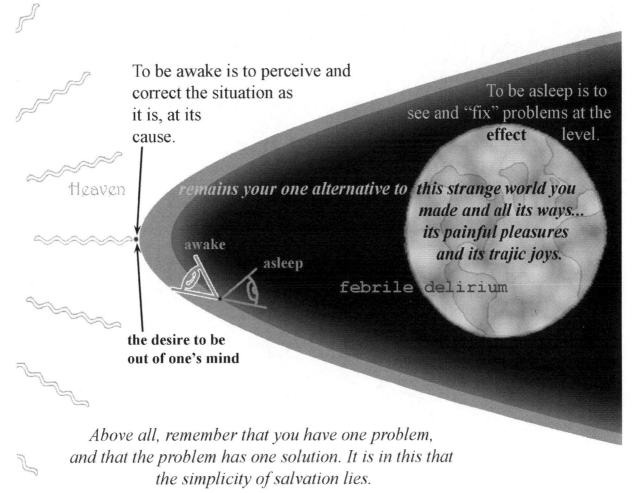

To be awake is to perceive and correct the situation as it is, at its cause.

To be asleep is to see and "fix" problems at the **effect** level.

Heaven

remains your one alternative to this strange world you made and all its ways... its painful pleasures and its trajic joys.

awake

asleep

febrile delirium

the desire to be out of one's mind

Above all, remember that you have one problem, and that the problem has one solution. It is in this that the simplicity of salvation lies.

W 79 4.1   W 131 7.1
W 80 5.5-6

You cannot dream some dreams and wake from some, for you are either sleeping or awake. And dreaming goes with only one of these.

For peace will come to all who ask for it with real desire and sincerity of purpose, shared with the Holy Spirit and at one with Him on what salvation is.

Salvation, perfect and complete, asks but a little wish [faith] that what is true be true [belief]; a little willingness [faith] to overlook [vision] what is not there; a little sigh that speaks for Heaven as a preference to this world that death and desolation seem to rule.

The world you see does nothing. It has no effects at all. It merely represents your thoughts. And it will change entirely as you elect to change your mind, and choose the joy of God as what you really want.

And in your desire lies its accomplishment.

Have faith in only this one thing, and it will be sufficient: God wills you be in Heaven, and nothing can keep you from it, or it from you.

Of your ego you can do nothing to save yourself or others, but of your spirit you can do everything for the salvation of both.

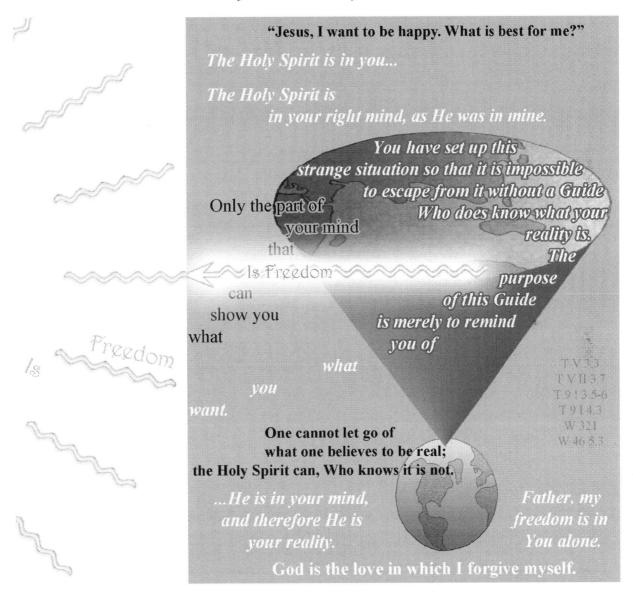

"Jesus, I want to be happy. What is best for me?"

The Holy Spirit is in you...

The Holy Spirit is in your right mind, as He was in mine.

You have set up this strange situation so that it is impossible to escape from it without a Guide Who does know what your reality is.

Only the part of your mind that Is Freedom can show you what

The purpose of this Guide is merely to remind you of

what you want.

Is Freedom

One cannot let go of what one believes to be real; the Holy Spirit can, Who knows it is not.

T V 3.3
T VII 3.7
T 9 I 3.5-6
T 9 I 4.3
W 321
W 46 5.3

...He is in your mind, and therefore He is your reality.

Father, my freedom is in You alone.

God is the love in which I forgive myself.

Here is the world you do not want brought to the one you do. ...Yet for this, the power of your wanting [faith] must first be recognized. You must accept [belief] its strength, and not its weakness. You must perceive [vision] that what is strong enough to make a world can let it go, and can accept [belief] correction if it is willing [faith] to see [vision] that it was wrong.

Until you realize you give up nothing, until you understand there is no loss, you will have some regrets about the way that you have chosen. And you will not see the many gains your choice has offered you. Yet though you do not see them, they are there. Their cause has been effected, and they must be present where their cause has entered in.

Your faith in nothing is deceiving you. Offer your faith to Me, and I will place it gently in the holy place [belief] *where it belongs. ... And you will love it because you will understand* [vision] *it.*

T 29 III 3   T 29 IV 1.7-8   T 20 VII 3.2-3   T 26 VII 10.1   W 190 6.2-5   T 18 III 5.2   T 13 XI 7.1   T 4 I 12.1
T 21 II 4   T 29 II 1.5-8   T 14 II 3.6-7,9

B: Belief: *only the truth is true*

The Holy Spirit... begins His lesson in simplicity with the fundamental teaching that truth is true. This is the hardest lesson you will ever learn [believe]*, and in the end the only one.*

This simple lesson holds the key to the dark door that you believe is locked forever.

To believe is... to accept and appreciate.

The
truth
is
true.

The stillness is

of the peace of God mine.

Nothing
else matters,
nothing else
is real,
and everything beside it
is not there.

Only truth   or illusions can be   believed.

T 14 II 4.1-2

Illusions are but beliefs in what is not there. And the seeming conflict between truth and illusion can only be resolved by separating yourself from the illusion and not from truth.

Illusions are all vain...

If you would know God and His Answer, believe in me...

W 66 10.8   T 14 II 2.1-2, 7.5   T 9 II 9.3   T 16 III 4.9-10   W 334 1.2   T 9 II 4.3

All images of pain loss and death are merely ideas
of rebellion given form; they are conjorings
"outside" so as to be provided belief to
the delusional mind that inwardly
knows their falsity.

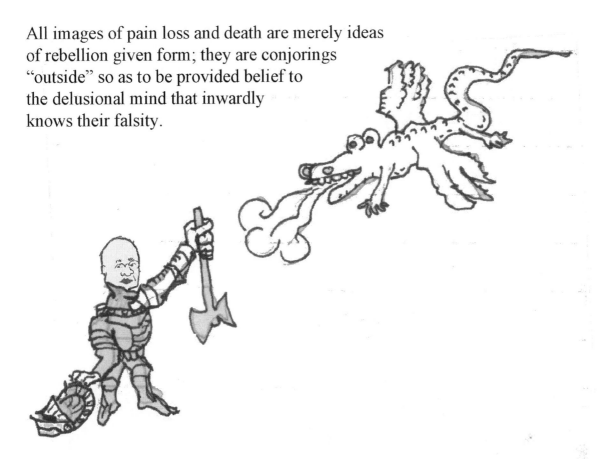

*He does not have to fight to save himself. He does not have to kill the dragons
which he thought pursued him. Nor need he erect the heavy walls of stone and
iron doors he thought would make him safe. He can remove the ponderous and
useless armour made to chain his mind to fear and misery.*

W 134 12.1-3

*And all the world he made, and all his specialness, and all the sins he held in its defense
against himself, will vanish as his mind accepts the truth about himself, as it returns to take
their place.*

What is one is joined in truth.

T 24 II 6.4, 7.9

Christ has no doubt, and from His certainty His quiet comes. ...He is within you, yet He walks beside you and before, leading the way that He must go to find Himself complete. His quietness becomes your certainty. And where is doubt when certainty has come?

You are not making use of the course if you insist on using means which have served others well, neglecting what was made for you.

The Holy Spirit speaks to you. He does not speak to someone else. Yet by your listening His Voice extends...

The Holy Spirit teaches the same lesson to everyone, yet tailors it specifically according to each's special learning situations.

T 18 VII.6-5   T 27 V 1.10-12

When you have let all that obscured the truth in your most holy mind be undone for you, and therefore stand in grace before your Father, He will give Himself to you as He has always done.

T 24 V 9   T 14 IV 3.1

There will come a time when images have all gone by, and you will see you know not what you are. It is to this unsealed and open mind that truth returns, unhindered and unbound. Where concepts of the self have been laid by is truth revealed exactly as it is.

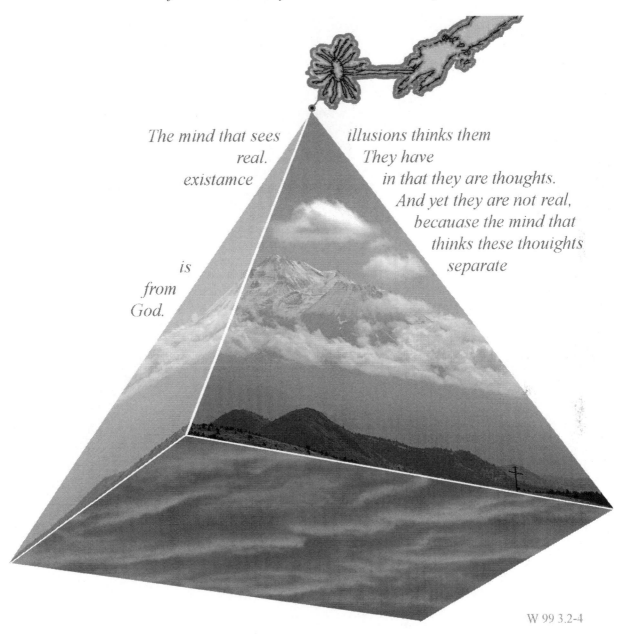

The mind that sees illusions thinks them real. They have existamce in that they are thoughts. And yet they are not real, because the mind that thinks these thoughts is separate from God.

W 99 3.2-4

Doubts about being must not enter your mind, or you cannot know what you are with certainty. Certainty is of God for you. Vigilance is not necessary for truth, but it is necessary against illusions.

...to accept truth in this world is the perceptual counterpart of creating in the Kingdom.

T 31 V 17.2   T 6 V C 8.7-9   T 10 II 3.3

All things I think I see reflect ideas.

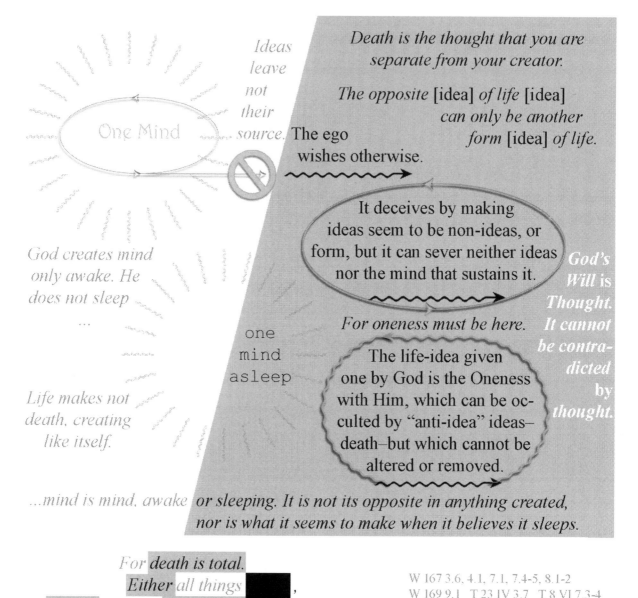

Ideas leave not their source. The ego wishes otherwise.

Death is the thought that you are separate from your creator.

The opposite [idea] of life [idea] can only be another form [idea] of life.

One Mind

It deceives by making ideas seem to be non-ideas, or form, but it can sever neither ideas nor the mind that sustains it.

God's Will is Thought. It cannot be contra-dicted by thought.

God creates mind only awake. He does not sleep

...

For oneness must be here.

one mind asleep

The life-idea given one by God is the Oneness with Him, which can be oc-culted by "anti-idea" ideas—death—but which cannot be altered or removed.

Life makes not death, creating like itself.

...mind is mind, awake or sleeping. *It is not its opposite in anything created, nor is what it seems to make when it believes it sleeps.*

For **death is total.** **Either** *all things* , or else *they live* **and cannot** .

W 167 3.6, 4.1, 7.1, 7.4-5, 8.1-2
W 169 9.1   T 23 IV 3.7   T 8 VI 7.3-4
T 8 VI 7.3   W 163 6.2-3

Death cannot be escape, because it is not life in which the problem lies. Life has no opposite, for it is God. Life and death seem to be opposites because you have decided death ends life.

Truth is not absent here, but it is obscure.

In no one instant can one even die.

W 325   M 20 5 3.4-5   T 11 VII 4.5   W 194 3.3

The stillness of your Self remains unmoved, untouched

by thoughts like these, and unaware of any condemnation which could need forgiveness.

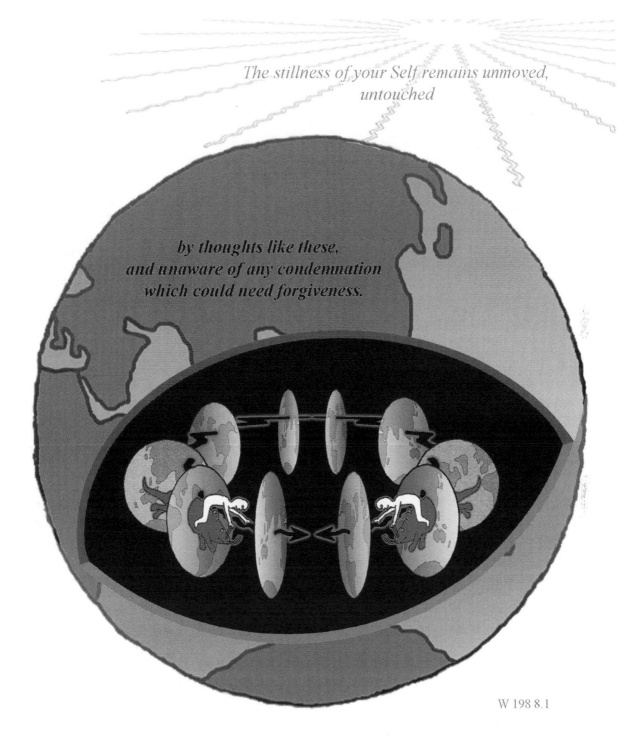

W 198 8.1

...healing is accomplished as he sees the body [form] *has no power to attack the universal oneness* [mind-ideas] *of God's Son.*

W 137 3.6

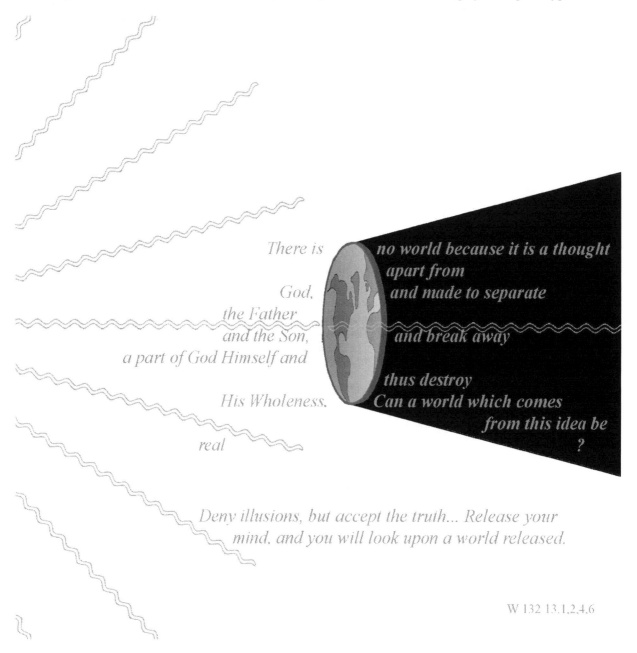

The first step toward freedom involves a sorting out of the false from the true. This is a process of separation in the constructive sense, and reflects the true meaning of the Apocalypse.

There is

God,
the Father
and the Son,
a part of God Himself and

His Wholeness.

real

no world because it is a thought
apart from
and made to separate

and break away

thus destroy
Can a world which comes
from this idea be
?

Deny illusions, but accept the truth... Release your mind, and you will look upon a world released.

W 132 13.1,2,4,6

...the mind can begin to look with love on its own creations because of their worthiness. At the same time the mind will inevitably disown its miscreations which, without belief, will no longer exist.

This is the only "cost" of truth: You will no longer see what never was, nor hear what makes no sound. Is it a sacrifice to give up nothing, and to receive the Love of God forever?

T 2 VIII 4   T 24 II 6.5

What if you realized that those who seem to walk about in it [the world]*, to sin and die, attack and murder and destroy themselves, are wholly unreal?*

T 20 VIII 7.5-7

Could you have faith in what you see, if you accepted this? And would you see it?

Perception changes, made to take the place of changeless knowledge. Yet is truth unchanged. It cannot be perceived, but only known.

Knowledge cannot dawn on a mind full of illusions, because truth and illusions are irreconcilable. Truth is whole, and cannot be known by part of a mind.

T 26 VII 3.4   T 10 IV 2.5-6

288

Truth and illusion have no connection. This will remain forever true, however much you seek to connect them. But illusions are always connected, as is truth. Each is united, a complete thought system, but totally disconnected to each other. And to perceive this is to recognize where separation is, and where it must be healed.

If you [mind] *made the ego* [belief in separation]*, how can the ego have made you? ... And either the ego, which you made* [believe]*, is your father, or its whole thought system will not stand.*

You do not see that every sin and every condemnation that you perceive and justify is an attack upon your Father. And that is why it has not happened, nor could be real.

God gave you the real world in exchange for the one you made out of your split mind, and which is the symbol of death.

You cannot be anywhere God did not put you, and God created you as part of Him. That is both where you are and what you are. It is completely unalterable. It is total inclusion. You cannot change it now or ever. It is forever true. It is not a belief, but a Fact. Anything that God created is as true as He is. Its truth lies only in its perfect inclusion in Him Who alone is perfect. To deny this is to deny yourself and Him, since it is impossible to accept one without the other.

T 19 I 7   T 11 Intr 2   T 22 VI 11.3   T 12 III 8.4   T 6 II 6

C: Vision: The Miracle

It is important to remember that miracles and vision necessarily go together.

For all who choose [faith] *to look away from sin are given vision, and are led to* [belief] *holiness.*

Your decision [faith] *to see is all that vision requires. What you want* [faith] *is yours* [belief].

Faith and belief can fall to either side, but reason [vision] *tells you misery lies only on one side and joy upon the other.*

Salvation is the Holy Spirit's goal. The means is vision. For what the seeing look upon is sinless.

W 91 1.1   T 21 III 8.6   W 20 3.1-2   T 22 II 6.10   T 20 VII 9.4-6

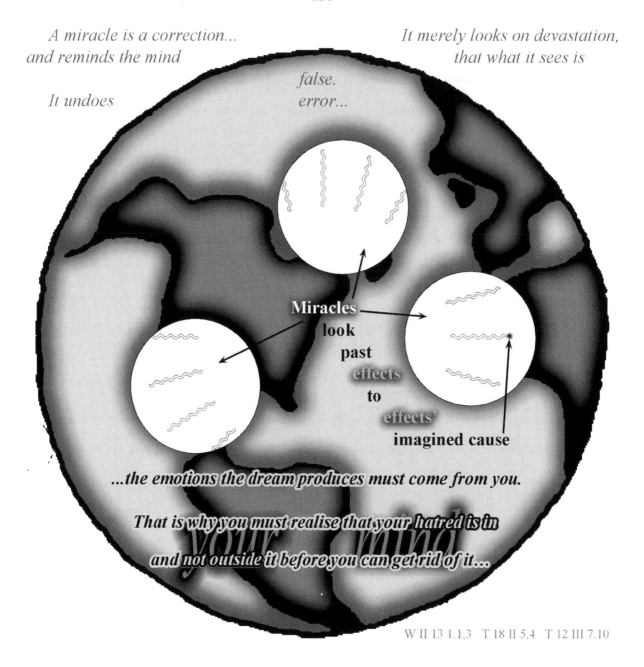

A miracle is a correction...
and reminds the mind

It undoes

false.
error...

It merely looks on devastation,
that what it sees is

Miracles
look
past
effects
to
effects'
imagined cause

...the emotions the dream produces must come from you.

That is why you must realise that your hatred is in your mind *and not outside it before you can get rid of it...*

W II 13 1.1,3   T 18 II 5.4   T 12 III 7.10

The miracle does not awaken you, but merely shows you who the dreamer [cause] is. It teaches you there is a choice of dreams while you are still asleep, depending on the purpose of your dreaming. Do you wish for dreams of healing, or for dreams of death?

Vision already holds a replacement for everything you think you see now. Loveliness can light your images...

T 28 II 4.2-4   W 23 4.4-5

And with Him, you will build a ladder planted in the solid rock of faith, and rising even to Heaven. Nor will you use it to ascend to Heaven alone.

The Holy Spirit's use of learning opportunities varies, depending upon where one is on salvation's *ladder*.

...a miracle... the recipient necessarily

must be expressed in a language that can understand without fear. This does not mean that this is the highest level of communication of which he is capable. ...[but] of which he is capable now. T 2 IV 5.3-4

Christ's vision is their [the special] "enemy", for it sees not what they would look upon, and it would show them that the specialness they think they see is an illusion.

For you have barely started to allow your first, uncertain steps to be directed up the ladder separation led you down. The miracle alone is your concern at present. Here is where we must begin.

They are dreams because *they are not true. Their equal lack of truth becomes the basis for the miracle, which means that you have understood that dreams are dreams; and that escape depends, not on the dream, but only on awaking.*

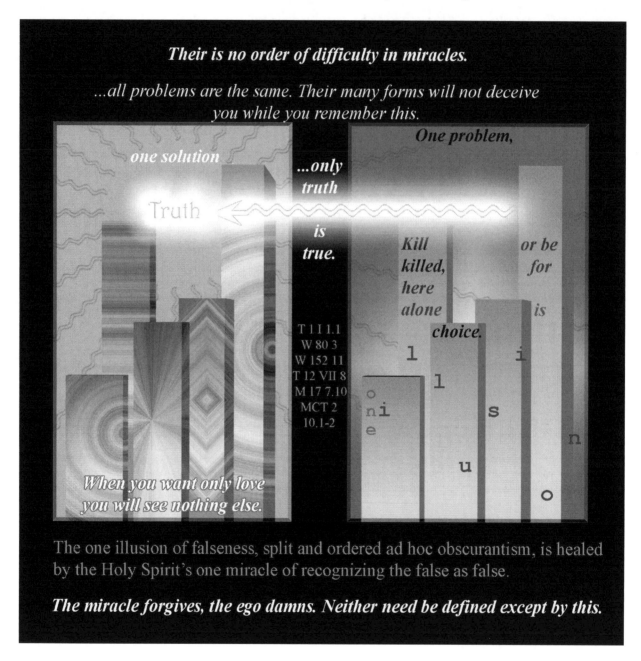

The miracle establishes you dream a dream, and that its content is not true.

I never see my brother as he is, for that is far beyond perception.

T 18 V 2.7-8   T 24 II 5.6   T 28 III 1.2-4   T 29 IV 1.2-3   T 28 II 7.1   W 335 1.2

Could it be some dreams are kept, and others wakened from? The choice is not between which dreams to keep, but only if you want to live in dreams or to awaken from them. Thus it is the miracle does not select some dreams to leave untouched by its beneficence.

T 29 IV 3.3-5

Depression or assault must be the theme of every dream, for they are made of fear.

The thin disguise of pleasure and of joy in which they may be wrapped but slightly veils the heavy lump of fear that is their core.

And it is this the miracle perceives, and not the wrappings in which it is bound.

The fear was held in place because he did not see that he was author of the dream, and not a figure in the dream. He gives himself the consequences that he dreams he gave his brother.

The secret of salvation is but this: That you are doing this unto yourself.

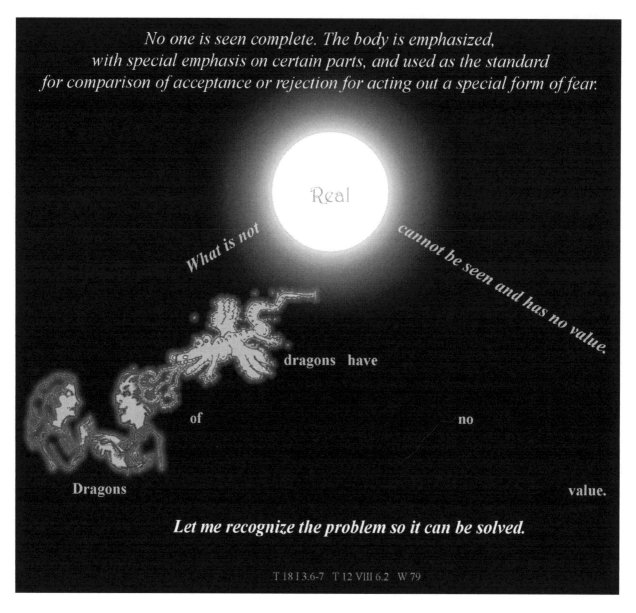

No one is seen complete. The body is emphasized,
with special emphasis on certain parts, and used as the standard
for comparison of acceptance or rejection for acting out a special form of fear.

Real

What is not

cannot be seen and has no value.

dragons have

of   no

Dragons   value.

Let me recognize the problem so it can be solved.

T 18 I 3.6-7   T 12 VIII 6.2   W 79

No one asleep and dreaming in the world remembers his attack upon himself. No one believes there really was a time when he knew nothing of a body, and could never have conceived this world as real.

You will see because it is the Will of God. It is His strength, not your own, that gives you power. And it is His gift, rather than your own, that offers vision to you.

T 29 IV 1.4-6   T 28 II 7.4-5   T 27 VIII 10.1   T 27 VIII 5.4-5   W 42 1.3-4

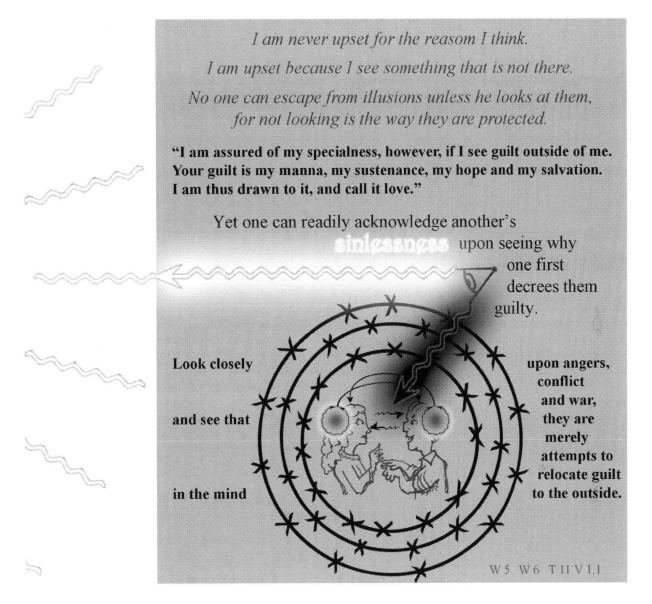

I am never upset for the reason I think.

I am upset because I see something that is not there.

No one can escape from illusions unless he looks at them,
for not looking is the way they are protected.

"I am assured of my specialness, however, if I see guilt outside of me.
Your guilt is my manna, my sustenance, my hope and my salvation.
I am thus drawn to it, and call it love."

Yet one can readily acknowledge another's
sinlessness upon seeing why
one first
decrees them
guilty.

Look closely · **upon angers,**
conflict
and war,
they are
and see that · **merely**
attempts to
relocate guilt
in the mind · **to the outside.**

W 5 W 6 T 11 V 1.1

For you could not react at all to figures in a dream you knew that you were dreaming.

Heaven [belief] is chosen [faith] consciously. The choice cannot be made until alternatives are accurately seen [vision] and understood.

T 27 VIII 10.5   W 139 9.1-2

The miracle is a sign that the mind has chosen to be led by me in Christ's service.

How safe the world will look to me when I can see it!
...Everyone and everything I see will lean toward me to
bless me. I will recognize in everyone my dearest Friend..

And as I look upon the world with the vision He has given me,
I remember that I am His Son.   W 60 3.2,4-5 5.5

A miracle is justice. It is not a special gift to some, to be withheld from others as less worthy, more
condemned, and thus apart from healing. Who is there who can be separate from salvation, if its
purpose is the end of specialness?

Everything looked upon with vision is healed and holy.

T 1 V 6.1   T 25 IX 6.6-8   T 21 Intro 1.10

The miracle acknowledges the guiltlessness that must have been denied to produce the need of healing. Do not withhold this glad acknowledgement, for hope of happiness and release from suffering of every kind lie in it.

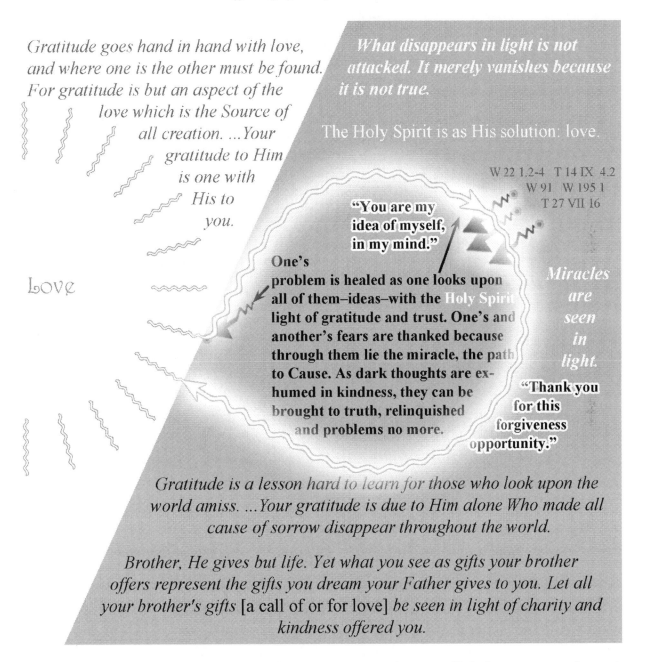

Gratitude goes hand in hand with love, and where one is the other must be found. For gratitude is but an aspect of the love which is the Source of all creation. ...Your gratitude to Him is one with His to you.

Love

What disappears in light is not attacked. It merely vanishes because it is not true.

The Holy Spirit is as His solution: love.

W 22 1.2-4   T 14 IX 4.2
W 91   W 195 1
T 27 VII 16

"You are my idea of myself, in my mind."

One's problem is healed as one looks upon all of them—ideas—with the Holy Spirit light of gratitude and trust. One's and another's fears are thanked because through them lie the miracle, the path to Cause. As dark thoughts are ex-humed in kindness, they can be brought to truth, relinquished and problems no more.

Miracles are seen in light.

"Thank you for this forgiveness opportunity."

Gratitude is a lesson hard to learn for those who look upon the world amiss. ...Your gratitude is due to Him alone Who made all cause of sorrow disappear throughout the world.

Brother, He gives but life. Yet what you see as gifts your brother offers represent the gifts you dream your Father gives to you. Let all your brother's gifts [a call of or for love] *be seen in light of charity and kindness offered you.*

This is the law the miracle obeys; that healing sees no specialness at all. It does not come from pity but from love.

T 14 V 5.3-4   T 27 II 7.4-5

Salvation seems to come from anywhere except from you. So, too, does the source of guilt. You see neither guilt nor salvation as in your own mind and nowhere else. When you realize that all guilt is solely an invention of your mind, you also realize that guilt and salvation must be in the same place. In understanding this you are saved.

W 70.1   T 18 II 5.4   W 236   W 152

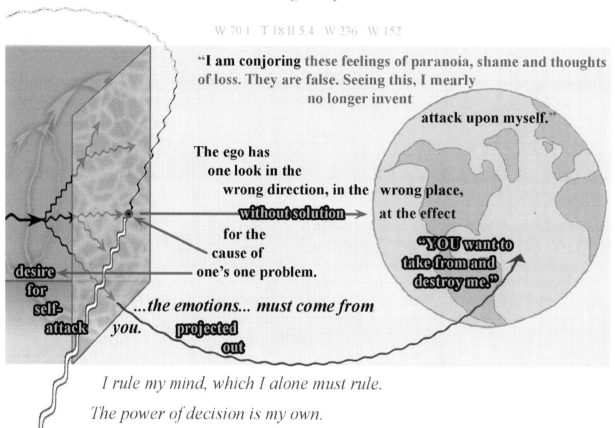

"I am conjoring these feelings of paranoia, shame and thoughts of loss. They are false. Seeing this, I mearly no longer invent attack upon myself."

The ego has one look in the wrong direction, in the wrong place, without solution at the effect for the cause of one's one problem.

"YOU want to take from and destroy me."

desire for self-attack

...the emotions... must come from you. projected out

I rule my mind, which I alone must rule.

The power of decision is my own.

The miracle establishes you dream a dream, and that its content is not true. This is a crucial step in dealing with illusions. No one is afraid of them when he perceives he made them up.

The miracle is the first step in giving back to cause the function of causation, not effect. For this confusion [reversal] has produced the dream, and while it lasts will wakening be feared. Nor will the call to wakening be heard, because it seems to be the call to fear.

T 28 II 7.1-3, 9.3-5

The world you see [as "reality"] must be denied, for sight of it is costing you a different kind of vision. You cannot see both worlds, for each of them involves a different kind of seeing, and depends on what you cherish.

Let it [faithlessness] enter and look upon it calmly, but do not use it. ...Use it, and it will carry you straight to illusions. It interferes, not with the goal, but with the value of the goal to you. Accept not the illusion of peace it offers, but look upon its offering and recognize it is illusion.

Now you are holy and perceive it so. And now the mind returns to its Creator; the joining of the Father and the Son, the Unity of unities that stands behind all joining but beyond them all. God is not seen but only understood. His Son is not attacked but recognized.

Revelation induces complete but temporary suspension of doubt and fear. It reflects the original form of communication between God and His creations, involving the extremely personal sense of creation sometimes sought in physical relationships. Physical closeness cannot achieve it. Miracles, however, are genuinely interpersonal, and result in true closeness to others. Revelation unites you directly with God. Miracles unite you directly with your brother. Neither emanates from consciousness [ego], but both are experienced there.

This is the miracle of creation; that it is one forever. Every miracle you offer to the Son of God is but the true perception of one aspect of the whole. Though every aspect is the whole, you cannot know this until you see that every aspect is the same, perceived in the same light and therefore one.

Spiritual vision literally cannot see error, and merely looks for Atonement. All solutions [magic] the physical eye seeks dissolve. ...the mind becomes increasingly sensitive to what it would once have regarded as very minor intrusions of discomfort.

Awareness of dreaming is the real function of God's teachers.

T 13 VII 2.1-2   T 17 VII 5   M-CT 3 8.3-6   T 1 II 1   T 13 VIII 5   T 2 III 4.1,2,7   M 12 6.6

3:II   The Holy Instant

The holy instant is not an instant of creation, but of recognition. For recognition comes of vision and suspended judgment.

The holy instant is a time in which you receive and give perfect communication. ...your mind is open, both to receive and give. It is the recognition that all minds are in communication. It therefore seeks to change nothing, but merely to accept everything.

In the holy instant, in which you see yourself as bright with freedom, you will remember God. For remembering Him is to remember freedom.

In the holy instant is this exchange effected and maintained. Here is the world you do not want brought to the one you do. And here the one you do is given you because you want it.

Yet in the holy instant you unite directly with God, and all your brothers join in Christ.

How can you decide that special aspects of the Sonship can give you more than others? The past has taught you this. Yet the holy instant teaches you it is not so.

T 21 II 8.2-3   T 15 IV 6.5-8   T 15 I 10.7-8   T 21 II 4.5-7   T 15 V 10.8, 3.5-7   T 29 VII 10.5

Light is unlimited, and spreads across this world in quiet joy.

T 13 VI 11.8-10

RD Scott / 2015

All those you brought with you will shine on you, and you will shine on them in gratitude because they brought you here. Your light will join with theirs in power so compelling, that it will draw the others out of darkness as you look on them.

For a time you may attempt to bring illusions into the holy instant, to hinder your full awareness of the complete difference, in all respects, between your experience of truth and illusion. Yet you will not attempt this long. In the holy instant the power of the Holy Spirit will prevail, because you joined Him.

...you are part of God, Who is all power.

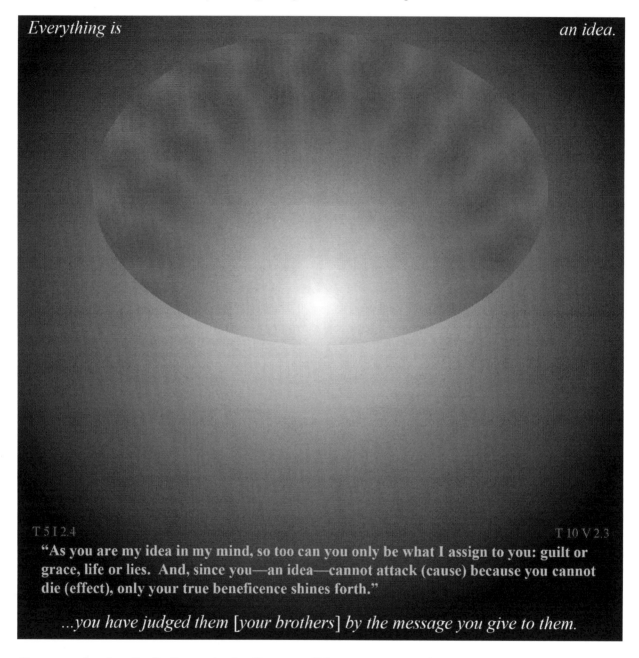

Everything is   *an idea.*

T 5 I 2.4   T 10 V 2.3

"As you are my idea in my mind, so too can you only be what I assign to you: guilt or grace, life or lies. And, since you—an idea—cannot attack (cause) because you cannot die (effect), only your true beneficence shines forth."

...you have judged them [your brothers] by the message you give to them.

You must forgive God's Son entirely. Or you will keep an image of yourself that is not whole, and will remain afraid to look within and find escape from every idol there.

Let us join together in making the holy instant all that there is, by desiring that it be all that there is.

T 17 VII 7.1-3   T 10 III 4.2   T 30 VI 7.5-6   T 15 VIII 2.4

In the holy instant you recognize the idea of love in you, and unite this idea with the Mind that thought it, and could not relinquish it. ...The holy instant thus becomes a lesson in how to hold all of your brothers in your mind, experiencing not loss but completion.

For in the holy instant, free of the past, you see that love is in you, and you have no need to look without and snatch love guiltily from where you thought it was.

In the holy instant, you see in each relationship what it will be when you perceive only the present.

The holy instant is His most helpful aid in protecting you from the attraction of guilt, the real lure in the special relationship.

It is He Who adds the greatness and the might. He joins with you to make the holy instant far greater than you can understand. It is your realization that you need do so little that enables Him to give so much.

...holiness does not change. Learn from this instant more than merely that hell does not exist. In this redeeming instant lies Heaven. And Heaven will not change, for the birth into the holy present is salvation from change.

In the holy instant the condition of love is met, for minds are joined without the body's interference, and where there is communication there is peace.

T 15 VI 5.3,5   T 15 V 9.7   T 15 V 8.5   T 16 VI 3.2   T 18 IV 1.7-9   T 15 I 10.1-4   T 15 XI 7.1

A: The Holy Relationship: *another interpretation*

Yet there is another interpretation of relationships that transcends the concept of loss of power completely.

The Holy Spirit's temple is not a body, but a relationship.

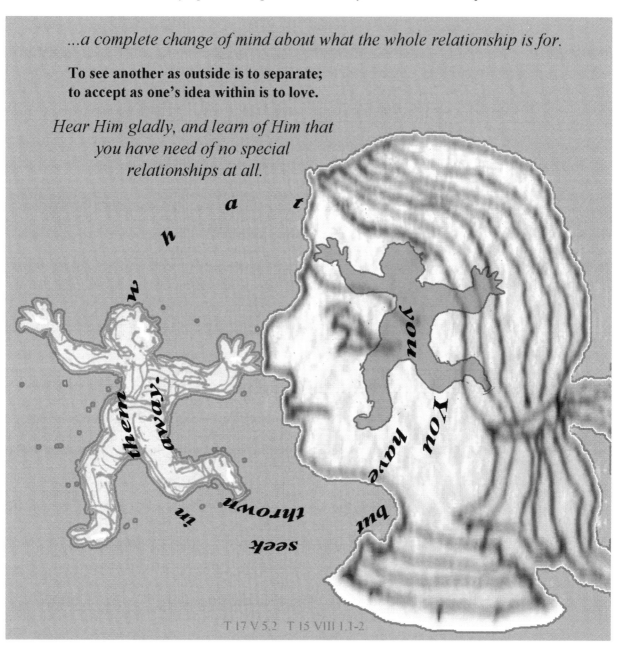

...a complete change of mind about what the whole relationship is for.

To see another as outside is to separate; to accept as one's idea within is to love.

Hear Him gladly, and learn of Him that you have need of no special relationships at all.

you have but seek them in thrown away.

T 17 V 5.2   T 15 VIII 1.1-2

Everyone on earth has formed special relationships, and although this is not so in Heaven, the Holy Spirit knows how to bring a touch of Heaven to them here. In the holy instant no one is special… Without the values from the past, you would see them all the same and like yourself.

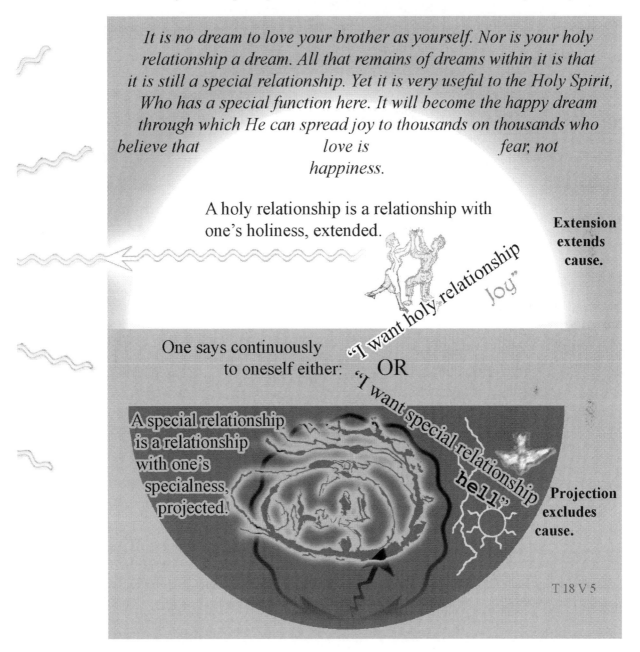

It is no dream to love your brother as yourself. Nor is your holy relationship a dream. All that remains of dreams within it is that it is still a special relationship. Yet it is very useful to the Holy Spirit, Who has a special function here. It will become the happy dream through which He can spread joy to thousands on thousands who believe that love is fear, not happiness.

A holy relationship is a relationship with one's holiness, extended.

Extension extends cause.

"I want holy relationship Joy"

One says continuously to oneself either: OR

"I want special relationship hell"

A special relationship is a relationship with one's specialness, projected.

Projection excludes cause.

T 18 V 5

There are only two thought systems, and you demonstrate that you believe one or the other is true all the time.

T 15 VI 3.5   T 20 VI 5.1   T 18 V 8.1-3   M Intro 2.2

The ego projects to exclude, and therefore to deceive. The Holy Spirit extends by recognizing Himself in every mind, and thus perceives them as one. ...what the Holy Spirit perceives is all the same.

To the ego, unless a relationship has special value it has no meaning, for it perceives all love as special. Yet this cannot be natural, for it is unlike the relationship of God and His Son... Love has no meaning except as its Creator defined it by His Will.

Only the mind can create because spirit has already been created, and the body is a learning device of the mind.

The body is merely part of your experience in the physical world. ...it is almost impossible to deny its existence in this world. Those who do so are engaging in a particularly unworthy form of denial. The term "unworthy" here implies only that it is not necessary to protect the mind by denying the unmindful.

"Lord, make our relationship holy."

The Course does not espouse eschewal or isolation from the body-world's charms, but rather uses them as forgiveness opportunities to heal the perception of them. The purpose now becomes the seeing and acceptance of Love—the original sinlessness in Christ—in the other, extended to all by the Holy Spirit.

Loveliness can light your images, and so transform them that you will love them, even though they were made of hate. For you will not be making them alone.

Let miracles replace all grievances.

Yet it is possible to make happy. I have said repeatedly that the Holy Spirit would not deprive you of your special relationships, but would transform them. And all that is meant by that is that He will restore to them the function given them by God. ...the holy relationship shares God's purpose, rather than aiming to make a substitute for it.

T 2 IV 3.1   T 2 IV 3.8,10-12   W 23 4.5-6   W 78   T 17 IV 2.

Let Him fulfill the function that He gave to your relationship by accepting it for you, and nothing will be wanting that would make of it what He would have it be.

In these loving thoughts is the spark of beauty hidden in the ugliness of the unholy relationship where hatred is remembered; yet there to come alive as the relationship is given to Him Who gives it life and beauty.

Such is the function of a holy relationship; to receive together and give as you received.

In His function as interpreter of what you made, the Holy Spirit uses special relationships, which you have chosen to support the ego, as learning experiences that point to truth. Under His teaching, every relationship becomes a lesson in love.

You will need your learning most in situations that appear to be upsetting, rather than in those that already seem to be calm and quiet. The purpose of your learning is to enable you to bring the quiet with you, and to heal distress and turmoil. This is not done by avoiding them and seeking a haven of isolation for yourself.

All separation vanishes as holiness is shared. For holiness is power, and by sharing it, it gains in strength.

T 6 II 12.2-4   T 16 VI 1.3-4,6   T 18 V 5.6   T 17 III 5.7   T 22 IV 7.4   T 15 V 4.5-6   W Review 1 Intro 4
T 15 VI 3.1-2

Nothing conflicts... because what the Holy Spirit perceives is all the same. ...because He is united He offers the whole Kingdom always. This is the one message God gave to Him and for which He must speak, because that is what He is.

God   The Holy Spirit

The peace of God lies in that message, and so the peace of God lies in you. The great peace of the Kingdom shines in your mind forever, but it must shine outward to make you aware of it.

T 6 II 12.4-8

To all who share the Love of God the grace is given to the givers of what they have received.

If one such [separate] union were made in perfect faith, the universe would enter into it.

Relationships... must be properly perceived, and all dark cornerstones of unforgiveness removed. Otherwise the old thought system still has a basis for return.

T 22 IV 6.1   T 16 VI 5.6   M 9 1.8-9

Since you and your neighbor are equal members of one family... You should look out from the perception of your own holiness to the holiness of others.

The holy relationship... is learned. It is the old, unholy relationship, transformed and seen anew. The holy relationship is a phenomenal teaching accomplishment. ...it represents the reversal of the unholy relationship. Be comforted in this; the only difficult phase is the beginning. For here, the goal of the relationship is abruptly shifted to the exact opposite of what it was. This is the first result of offering the relationship to the Holy Spirit, to use for His purposes.

God's Teacher speaks to any two who join together for learning purposes. The relationship is holy because of that purpose, and God has promised to send His Spirit into any holy relationship. In the teaching-learning situation, each one learns that giving and receiving are the same. The demarcations they have drawn between their roles, their minds, their bodies, their needs... fade and grow dim and disappear. Those who would learn the same course share one interest and one goal.

Across the bridge it is so different! For a time the body is still seen, but not exclusively, as it is seen here. The little spark that holds the Great Rays within it is also visible, and this spark cannot be limited long to littleness. Once you have crossed the bridge, the value of the body is so diminished in your sight that you will see no need at all to magnify it. For you will realize that the only value the body has is to enable you to bring your brothers to the bridge with you, and to be released together there.

T 1 III 6.6-7   T 17 V 2   M 2 5   T 16 VI 6

The extension of the Holy Spirit's purpose from your relationship to others, to bring them gently in, is the way in which He will bring means and goal in line. The peace He lay, deep within you and your brother, will quietly extend to every aspect of your life, surrounding you and your brother with glowing happiness and the calm awareness of complete protection.

Here stands your brother with the key to Heaven in his hand, held out to you. Let not the dream of specialness remain between you. What is one is joined in truth.

When you feel the holiness of your relationship is threatened by anything, stop instantly and offer the Holy Spirit your willingness, in spite of fear, to let Him exchange this instant for the holy one that you would rather have. He will never fail in this.

No relationship is holy unless its holiness goes with it everywhere. As holiness and faith go hand in hand, so must its faith go everywhere with it.

For it cannot extend unless you keep it. You are the center from which it radiates outward, to call the others in. You are its home; its tranquil dwelling place from which it gently reaches out, but never leaving you.

The Holy Spirit has given you love's messengers to send instead of those you trained through fear. They are as eager to return to you what they hold dear as are the others. If you send them forth, they will see only the blameless and the beautiful, the gentle and the kind. They will be as careful to let no little act of charity, no tiny expression of forgiveness, no little breath of love escape their notice. And they will return with all the happy things they found, to share them lovingly with you.

Your question should not be, "How can I see my brother without the body?" Ask only, "Do I really wish to see him sinless?" And as you ask, forget not that his sinlessness is your *escape from fear.*

My holy brother, I would enter into all your relationships, and step between you and your fantasies. Let my relationship to you be real to you, and let me bring reality to your perception of your brothers. They were not created to enable you to hurt yourself through them. They were created to create with you. This is the truth that I would interpose between you and your goal of madness. Be not separate from me, and let not the holy purpose of Atonement be lost to you in dreams of vengeance. Relationships in which such dreams are cherished have excluded me. Let me enter in the Name of God and bring you peace, that you may offer peace to me.

He [the Holy Spirit] *does not destroy it* [the special relationship], *nor snatch it away from you. But He does use it differently, as a help to make His purpose real to you. The special relationship will remain, not as a source of pain and guilt, but as a source of joy and freedom. It will not be for you alone, for therein lay its misery.*

T 19 IV 1.5-6   T 18 VI 5   T 17 VII 6.4-5   T 24 II 7.6-7   T 18 V 6.1-2   T 19 IV A 1.2-4, 14   T 20 VII 9 .1-3
T 17 III 10   T 18 II 6.6-8

B: The Holy Purpose

Every situation in which you find yourself is but a means to meet the purpose set for your relationship. See it as something else and you are faithless.

For miracles are merely change of purpose from hurt to healing.

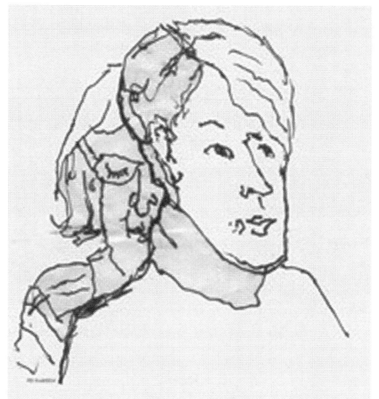

T 24 IV 3.9-10

This shift in purpose does "endanger" specialness, but only in the sense that all illusions are "threatened" by the truth. They will not stand before it.

Only a radical shift in purpose could induce a complete change of mind....

Is not this like your special function, where the separation is undone by change of purpose in what once was specialness, and now is union?

In this shared purpose is one judgment shared by everyone and everything you see.

T 17 VII 5.1   T 17 V 5.2   T 26 III 7.1   T 30 VII 4.2

And you will see the means you once employed to lead you to illusions transformed to means for truth.

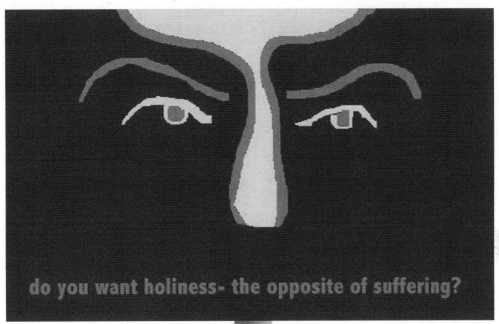

do you want holiness- the opposite of suffering?

When the Holy Spirit changed the purpose of your relationship by exchanging yours for His, the goal He placed there was extended to every situation in which you enter, or will ever enter.

T 17 VII 9.3,5

If there is a thought of conflict, within or without, or a situation that one thinks may not be in accord with salvation's plan, let Jesus accept and interpret for you that part of your mind that you reject, and give His purpose for it. It will then be relinquished or healed and transformed to joy.

When what you have dissociated is accepted, it ceases to be fearful.

And perception will last until the Sonship knows itself as whole.

Whatever is given Him that is not of God is gone.

T 10 II 1.6   T 7 VII 3.10   T 12 II 10.4

The little faith it needed to change the purpose [vision] *is all that is required to receive* [belief] *the means and use them.*

Completion is the function of God's Son. He has no need to seek for it at all.

The working out of all correction takes no time at all. Yet the acceptance of the working out can seem to take forever. The change of purpose the Holy Spirit brought to your relationship has in it all effects that you will see. They can be looked at now.

How can communication really be established while the symbols that are used mean different things? The Holy Spirit's goal gives one interpretation, meaningful to you and to your brother. Thus can you communicate with him, and he with you. ...the sacrifice of meaning is undone.

T 18 V 4.6   T 30 III 5.1   T 26 VIII 6   T 30 VII 6

Release instead of bind, for thus are you made free.

When this is firmly understood and kept in full awareness,
you will not attempt to harm yourself, nor make your body slave to vengeance.
You will not attack yourself, and you will realize that to attack another is but to attack
yourself.
You will be free of the insane belief that to attack a brother saves yourself.
And you will understand his safety is your own, and in his healing you are
healed.

W 196 1

Innocence is incapable of sacrificing anything, because the innocent mind has everything and strives only to protect its wholeness. It cannot project. It can only honor other minds, because honor is the natural greeting of the truly loved to others who are like them.

The Holy Spirit serves Christ's purpose in your mind, so that the aim of specialness can be corrected where the error lies. Because His purpose still is one with both the Father and the Son, He knows the Will of God and what you really will. But this is understood by mind perceived as one, aware that it is one, and so experienced.

Given to Him, the universe is yours.

W 192 9.2   T 30 VII 6.1-3   T 3 I 6.1-3   T 24 IV 3.13

Your mind and mine can unite in shining your ego away, releasing the strength of God into everything you think and do. Do not settle for anything less than this, and refuse to accept anything but this as your goal.

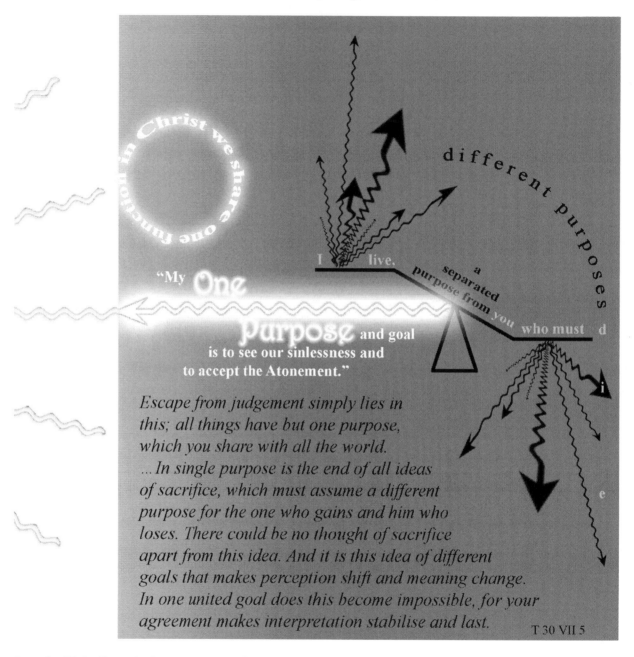

in Christ we share one function

different purposes

I live.

a separated purpose from you who must d

"My **One purpose** and goal is to see our sinlessness and to accept the Atonement."

Escape from judgement simply lies in this; all things have but one purpose, which you share with all the world. ...In single purpose is the end of all ideas of sacrifice, which must assume a different purpose for the one who gains and him who loses. There could be no thought of sacrifice apart from this idea. And it is this idea of different goals that makes perception shift and meaning change. In one united goal does this become impossible, for your agreement makes interpretation stabilise and last.

T 30 VII 5

It is the Holy Spirit's function to teach you how this oneness is experienced, what you must do that it can be experienced, and where you should go to do it.

T 4 IV 8.3   T 25 I 6

A common purpose is the only means whereby perception can be stabilized, and one interpretation given to the world and all experiences here. ...You do not have to judge, for you have learned one meaning has been given everything... And so you offer it to all events, and you *let them offer stability.*

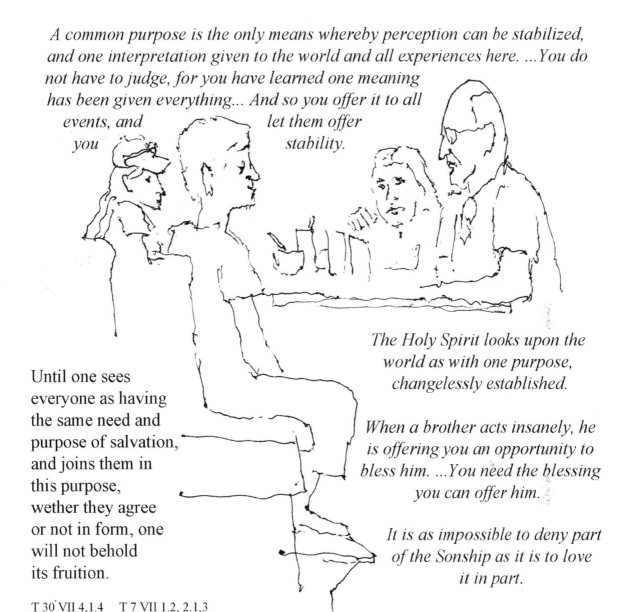

Until one sees everyone as having the same need and purpose of salvation, and joins them in this purpose, wether they agree or not in form, one will not behold its fruition.

T 30 VII 4,1.4   T 7 VII 1.2, 2.1,3

The Holy Spirit looks upon the world as with one purpose, changelessly established.

When a brother acts insanely, he is offering you an opportunity to bless him. ...You need the blessing you can offer him.

It is as impossible to deny part of the Sonship as it is to love it in part.

...the Holy Spirit must change its [special relationship's] *purpose to make it useful to Him and harmless to you.*

Two minds with one intent become so strong that what they will becomes the Will of God. For minds can only join in truth.

T 21 III 1.6   W 185 3.1-2

Yet while in time, there is still much to do. And each must do what is allotted him, for on his part does all the plan depend. He has a special part in time for so he chose, and choosing it, he made it for himself. His wish was not denied but changed in form ...and thus become a means to save instead of lose.

Your faith will call the others to share your purpose, as the same purpose called forth the faith in you.

You cannot be totally committed sometimes. Denial has no power in itself, but you can give it the power of your mind, whose power is without limit. If you use it to deny reality, reality is gone for you. Reality cannot be partly appreciated. *That is why denying any part of it means you have lost the awareness of all of it.*

In light, you see it [your specialness] *as your special function in the plan to save the Son of God from all attack, and let him understand that he is safe, as he has always been... This is the function given you for your brother. Take it gently, then, from your brother's hand, and let salvation be perfectly fulfilled in you. Do this* one *thing, that everything be given you.*

The specialness he chose to hurt himself did God appoint to be the means for his salvation, from the very instant that the choice was made. His special sin was made his special grace. His special hate became his special love.

You have a function in salvation. Its pursuit will bring you joy.

Given a change of purpose for the good, there is no reason for an interval in which disaster strikes, to be perceived as "good" some day but now in form of pain. This is a sacrifice of now, which could not be the cost the Holy Spirit asks for what He gave without a cost at all.

T 25 VI 5.8-11   T 17 VII 9.2   T 7 VII 1.4-8   T 25 VI 7-10, 6.6-7   T 24 II 2.5-6   26 VIII 7.9

○   ○   ○

This course remains within the ego framework, where it is needed. ...Therefore it uses words, which are symbolic, and cannot express what lies beyond symbols. ...The course is simple. It has one function and one goal. Only in that does it remain wholly consistent because only that can be consistent

...universal experience is not only possible but necessary. It is this experience toward which the course is directed. Here alone consistency becomes possible because here alone uncertainty ends.

The whole purpose of this course is to teach you that the ego is unbelievable and will forever be unbelievable.

...the purpose of this course is to help you remember what you are...

The purpose of the course might be said to provide you with a means of choosing what you want to teach on the basis of what you want to learn.

This course attempts to teach no more than that the power of decision cannot lie in choosing different forms of what is still the same illusion and the same mistake.

This course will be believed entirely or not at all.

M CT Intro 3, 2.5-6   T 7 VIII 7.1   T 9 I 2.4   M Intro 2.5   T 22 II 7.4   T 31 IV 8.3

C: Healing and *The Happy Dream*

I said before that the first change, before dreams disappear, is that your dreams of fear are changed to happy dreams. That is what the Holy Spirit does in the special relationship.

But healing is the gift of those who are prepared to learn there is no world, and can accept the lesson now. Their readiness will bring the lesson to them in some form which they can understand and recognize.

RD Scott / People in room with a light bulb / 2008

Here is the answer! Do not turn away in aimless wandering again. Accept salvation now. It is the gift of God, and not the world. The world can give no gifts of any value to a mind that has received what God has given as its own.

Do not look to the god of sickness [body-world] for healing but only to the God of love, for healing is the acknowledgement of Him. When you acknowledge Him you will know that He has never ceased to acknowledge you, and that in His acknowledgement of you lies your being. You are not sick and you cannot die. But you can confuse yourself with things that do.

T 18 V   T 18 II 6.3-4   W 132 7.1-2   W 122 7   T 10 V 8.1-4

There is a light that this world cannot give. Yet you can give it, as it was given you. And as you give it, it shines forth to call you from the world and follow it.

Heal your brothers simply by accepting God for them.

And while you fail to teach what you have learned, salvation waits… For you will not see the light, until you offer it to all your brothers.

W 189 1.1-3   T 10 III 2.4   W 153 11.3,5

What is healing but the removal of all that stands in the way of knowledge? And how else can one dispel illusions except by looking at them directly, without protecting them? Be not afraid, therefore, for what you will be looking at is the source of fear, and you are beginning to learn that fear is not real.

T 11 V 2
W 265 1

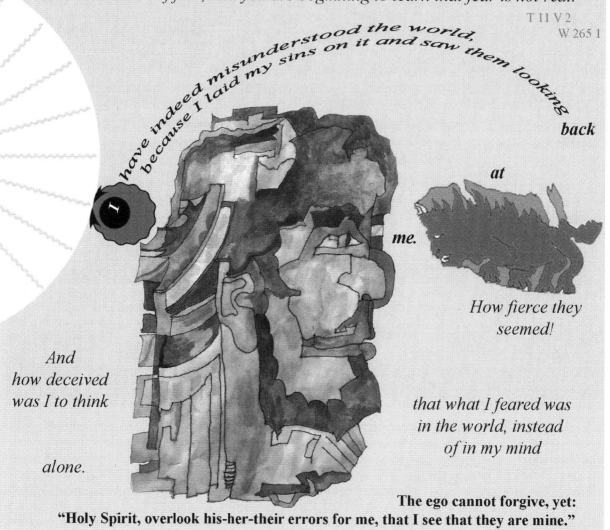

I have indeed misunderstood the world, because I laid my sins on it and saw them looking back

at

me.

How fierce they seemed!

And how deceived was I to think

that what I feared was in the world, instead of in my mind

alone.

The ego cannot forgive, yet:
"Holy Spirit, overlook his-her-their errors for me, that I see that they are mine."

But be holy in the Presence of God, or you will not know that you are there. For what is unlike God cannot enter His Mind, because it was not His Thought and therefore does not belong to Him. And your mind must be as pure as His, if you would know what belongs to you.

For God gave healing not apart from sickness, nor established remedy where sickness cannot be. They are together…

T 11 III 7.4-6 T 19 I 6.6-7

Your health is a result of your desire to see your brother with no blood upon his hands, nor guilt upon his heart made heavy with the proof of sin. And what you wish is given you to see.

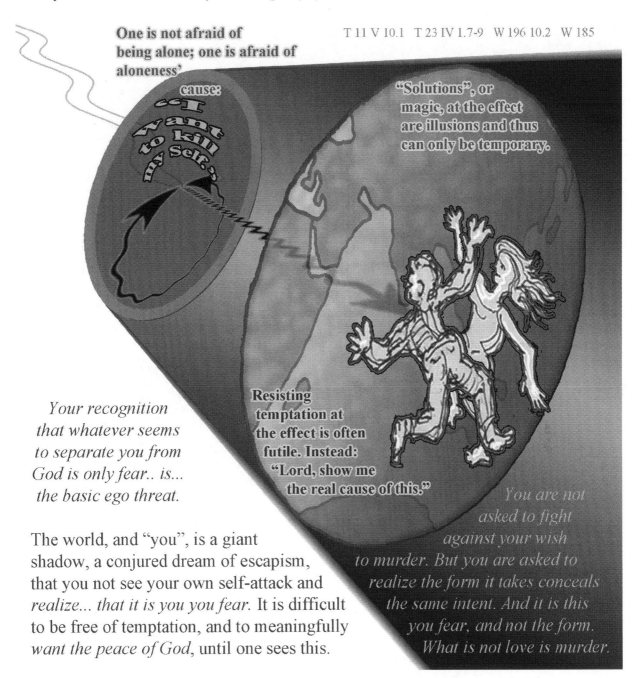

One is not afraid of being alone; one is afraid of aloneness'

T 11 V 10.1   T 23 IV 1.7-9   W 196 10.2   W 185

cause: "I want to kill my Self?

"Solutions", or magic, at the effect are illusions and thus can only be temporary.

Resisting temptation at the effect is often futile. Instead: "Lord, show me the real cause of this."

Your recognition that whatever seems to separate you from God is only fear.. is... the basic ego threat.

The world, and "you", is a giant shadow, a conjured dream of escapism, that you not see your own self-attack and *realize... that it is you you fear.* It is difficult to be free of temptation, and to meaningfully *want the peace of God*, until one sees this.

You are not asked to fight against your wish to murder. But you are asked to realize the form it takes conceals the same intent. And it is this you fear, and not the form. What is not love is murder.

Your gratitude toward your brother is the only gift I want.

Healing is the effect of minds that join, as sickness comes from minds that separate.

T 27 II 7.7-8   T 4 VI 7.2   T 28 III 2.6

...He [Holy Spirit] does not relate through your ego to another ego. He does not join in pain, understanding that healing pain is not accomplished by delusional attempts to enter into it, and lighten it by sharing the delusion.

What could your secrets be except another "will" that is your own, apart from His? ...Here is the one emotion that you made ...of secrecy, of private thoughts and of the body.

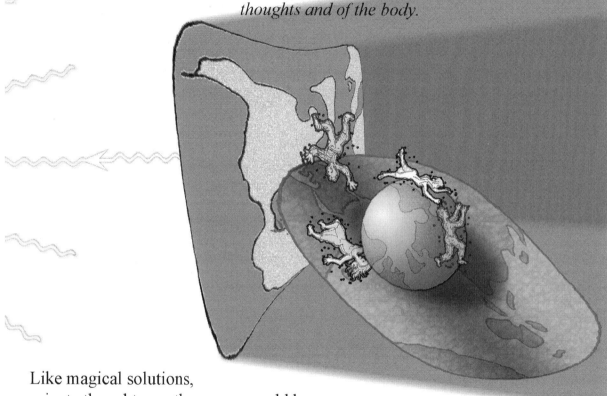

Like magical solutions,
private thoughts are those one would keep
at the effect level, away from the Holy Spirit for relinquishment to truth.
Venting, sharing illusions with other illusions and talk therapy can be such.

T 16 I 1.6-7   T 22 I 4

But your remembering is his, for God cannot be remembered alone. This is what you have forgotten. *To perceive the healing of your brother as the healing of yourself is thus the way to remember God.*

Health in this world is the counterpart of value in Heaven. It is not my merit that I contribute to you but my love, for you do not value yourself.

You respond to what you perceive, and as you perceive so shall you behave. ...The Golden Rule is the rule for appropriate behaviour. You cannot behave appropriately unless you perceive correctly.

You are the Kingdom of Heaven, but you have let the belief in darkness enter your mind and so you need a new light. The Holy Spirit is the radiance that you must let banish the idea of darkness.

For this light will attract you as nothing in this world can do. And you will lay aside the world and find another. This other world is bright with love which you have given it. And here will everything remind you of your Father and His holy Son.

Let not your eyes be blinded by the veil of specialness that hides the face of Christ from him, and you as well. And let the fear of God no longer hold the vision you were meant to see from you.

For what attracts you from beyond the veil is also deep within you, unseparated from it and completely one.

Healing must occur in exact proportion to which the valuelessness of sickness is recognized. One need but say, "there is no gain at all to me in this" and he is healed.

T 12 II 2.7-9   T 10 III 6.3   T 1 III 6.1,4-5   T 5 II 4.1-2   T 13 VI 11.4-7   T 10 II 1.5-6   T 19 IV D 7.7   M 5 II 1.1-2

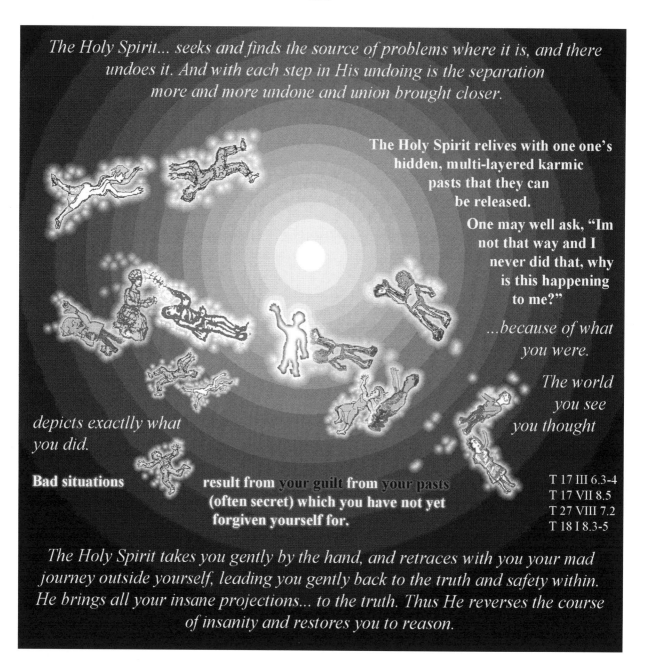

The Holy Spirit... seeks and finds the source of problems where it is, and there undoes it. And with each step in His undoing is the separation more and more undone and union brought closer.

The Holy Spirit relives with one one's hidden, multi-layered karmic pasts that they can be released.

One may well ask, "Im not that way and I never did that, why is this happening to me?"

...because of what you were.

The world you see you thought

depicts exactlly what you did.

Bad situations result from **your guilt from your pasts** (often secret) which you have not yet forgiven yourself for.

T 17 III 6.3-4
T 17 VII 8.5
T 27 VIII 7.2
T 18 I 8.3-5

The Holy Spirit takes you gently by the hand, and retraces with you your mad journey outside yourself, leading you gently back to the truth and safety within. He brings all your insane projections... to the truth. Thus He reverses the course of insanity and restores you to reason.

The body is released because the mind acknowledges "this is not done to me, but I am doing this". And thus the mind is free to make another choice instead. Beginning here, salvation will proceed to change the course of every step in the descent to separation, until all the steps have been retraced, the ladder gone, and all the dreaming of the world undone.

God has no secrets. He does not lead you through a world of misery, waiting to tell you, at the journey's end, why He did this to you.

T 28 II 12.5, 12.6-7   T 22 I 3.10-11

When the ego tempts you to sickness do not ask the Holy Spirit to heal the body, for this would merely be to accept the ego's belief that the body [instead of the mind] *is the proper aim of healing.*

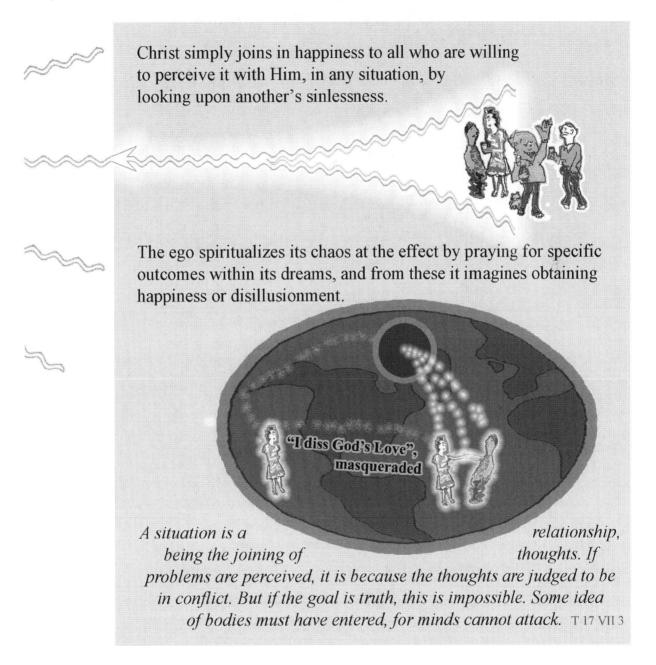

Christ simply joins in happiness to all who are willing to perceive it with Him, in any situation, by looking upon another's sinlessness.

The ego spiritualizes its chaos at the effect by praying for specific outcomes within its dreams, and from these it imagines obtaining happiness or disillusionment.

"I diss God's Love", masqueraded

A situation is a relationship, being the joining of thoughts. If problems are perceived, it is because the thoughts are judged to be in conflict. But if the goal is truth, this is impossible. Some idea of bodies must have entered, for minds cannot attack. T 17 VII 3

Ask, rather, that the Holy Spirit teach you the right perception *of the body, for perception alone can be distorted. Only perception can be sick, because only perception can be wrong.*

My sinlessness protects me from all harm.

T 8 IX 1.5,6-7 W 337

Very simply, your lack of faith in the power that heals all pain arises from your wish to retain some aspects of reality for fantasy.

Let not his specialness obscure the truth in him, for not one law of death you bind him to will you escape. And not one sin you see in him but keeps you both in hell.

Forgiveness separates the dreamer from the evil dream, and thus releases him. Remember if you share an evil dream, you will believe you are the dream you share.

See in his freedom yours, for such it is.

T 17 I 3.3   T 24 VI 5.3-4   T 28 V 3.3-4   T 24 VI 5.2

Behold your brothers in their freedom, and learn of them how to be free of darkness.

The light in you will waken them, and they will not leave you asleep.

The vision of Christ is given the very instant that it is perceived. Where everything is clear, it is all holy.

T 14 II 9

The quietness of its simplicity is so compelling that you will realise it is impossible to deny the simple truth. For there is nothing else. God is everywhere, and His Son is in Him with everything. Can he sing the dirge of sorrow when this is true?

What can he know of fear and punishment, of sin and guilt, of hatred and attack, when all there is surrounding him is everlasting peace, forever conflict-free and undisturbed, in deepest silence and tranquility?

T 14 II 8.5-8   W II 12 3.4

...And both must gain in this exchange, for each will have the thought in form most helpful to him. What he seems to lose is always something he will value less than what will surely be returned to him.

As you perceive more and more common elements in all situations, the transfer of training under the Holy Spirit's guidance increases and becomes generalised. Gradually you learn to apply it to everyone and everything, for its applicability is universal. When this has been accomplished, perception and knowledge have become so similar that they share the unification of the laws of God.

Separation therefore remains the ego's chosen condition. For no one alone can judge the ego truly. Yet when two or more join together in searching for truth, the ego can no longer defend its lack of content. The fact of union tells them it is not true.

And as his Father lost not part of him [the Son of God] in your creation, so the light in him is brighter still because you gave your light to him, to save him from the dark. ...This is the spark that shines within the dream; that you can help him waken, and be sure his waking eyes will rest on you. And in his glad salvation you are saved.

Child of peace, the light has come to you. The light you bring you do not recognize, and yet you will remember. Who can deny himself the vision that he brings to others? And who would fail to recognize a gift he let be laid in Heaven through himself? The gentle service that you give the Holy Spirit is service to yourself. You who are now His means must love all that He loves.

Guard carefully His temple, for He Himself dwells there and abides in peace. You cannot enter God's Presence with the dark companions beside you, but you also cannot enter alone. All your brothers must enter with you, for until you have accepted them you cannot enter.

The key you threw away God gave your brother, whose holy hands would offer it to you when you were ready to accept His plan for your salvation in the place of yours.

There is no place where holiness is not, and nowhere sin and sickness can abide. This is the thought that cures.

Your mind is so powerful a light that you can look into theirs and enlighten them, as I can enlighten yours.

Your mind will elect to join with mine, and together we are invincible. You and your brother will yet come together in my name, and your sanity will be restored. I raised the dead by knowing that life is an eternal attribute of everything that the living God created.

The sick are healed as you let go all thoughts of sickness, and the dead arise when you let thoughts of life replace all thoughts you ever held of death.

Let us come daily to this holy place, and spend a while together. Here we share our final dream. It is a dream in which there is no sorrow, for it holds a hint of all the glory given us by God. The grass is pushing through the soil, the trees are budding now, and birds have come to live within their branches. Earth is being born again in new perspective. Night has gone, and we have come together in the light.

W 187 5   T 12 VI 6   T 14 X 9   T 29 III 5.4,5-7   T 22 VI 6.1-6   T 11 III 7.7-9   T 24 II 14.1 T   W 140 5.7,6.1
7 V 10.6   T 4 IV 11.5-7   W132 8.4   W Part II 2 4

3 III *All you need do*: God's Word

Accept atonement and you are healed. Atonement is the Word of God.

When the mind awakes, it but continues as it always was.

I am as God created me. ...*This is the word of God that sets you free.*

*If you will accept
only what is timeless
as real, you will begin to
understand eternity
and make it yours.*

"I no more wish to fragment truth according to my preferences."

*The full awareness of the Atonement,
then, is the recognition that* the separation never occured.

T 10 V 14.9   T 6 II 10.7

To say, "Of myself I can do nothing" is to gain all power.

T 22 II 13.1   M 22 1.5-6   W 167 9.4   W 110 11.4,6   M 29 4.2

To give up all problems to one Answer is to reverse the thinking of the world entirely. And that alone is faithfulness. ...Yet each degree, however small is worth achieving.

For it is the complete equality of the Atonement in which salvation lies.

All things work together for good.

The Atonement is but the way back to what was never lost.

M 4 IX 1.6-7,9   T 15 V 3.4   T 4 V 1.1   T 12 VIII 8.8

I am not a body. I am free.
For I am still as God created me.

W Review VI

Let me recognize my problems have been solved.

Simplicity is very difficult for twisted minds.

W 80   T 14 II 2.3

But having accepted the errors as yours, do not keep them. Give them over quickly to the Holy Spirit to be undone completely, so that all their effects will vanish from your mind and from the Sonship as a whole.

Communication with God is life.

To heal is first to own the guilt, as it can never be released while cause is kept apart.

"Lord, accept for me this my dream, that I can then give it to you"

Yet it is given you to show him [your brother], by your healing, that his guilt is but the fabric of a senseless dream.

T 7 VIII 5.5-6
T 14 IV 10.6
T 27 II 6.11
16 I 3.12, 10.6

I need do nothing except not to interfere.

The course's forgiveness is practiced in the mind, so errant behaviors are corrected at their cause, and are not hunted or breathed in the body-world, at the effect.

I give you to the Holy Spirit as part of myself.

Your light will join with theirs in power so compelling, that it will draw the others out of darkness as you look on them.

Do not be afraid of the ego. *It depends on your mind, and as you made it by believing in it, so you can dispel it by withdrawing belief from it.*

T 15 XI 10.5   T 13 VI 11.10   T 7 VIII 5.1-2

Do not project the responsibility for your belief in it [the ego] *onto anyone else, or you will preserve the belief. When you are willing to accept sole responsibility for the ego's existence you will have laid aside all anger and all attack, because they come from an attempt to project responsibility for your own own errors.*

T 7 VIII 5.3-4

I can escape from the world I see by giving up attack thoughts.

W 23

When you are tempted to deny Him remember that there are no other gods to place before Him, and accept His Will for you in peace. For you cannot accept it otherwise.

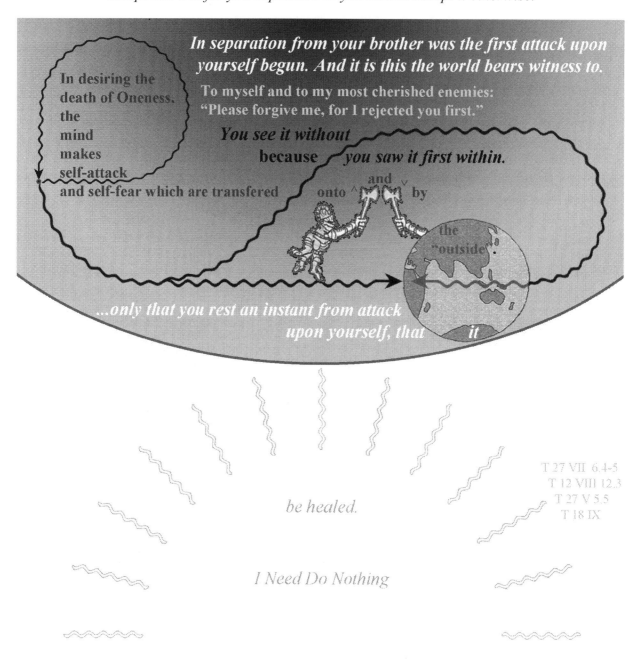

In desiring the death of Oneness, the mind makes self-attack and self-fear which are transfered

In separation from your brother was the first attack upon yourself begun. And it is this the world bears witness to.

To myself and to my most cherished enemies: "Please forgive me, for I rejected you first."

You see it without because you saw it first within.

onto ^ and ˅ by

the "outside".

...only that you rest an instant from attack upon yourself, that it

be healed.

I Need Do Nothing

T 27 VII 6.4-5
T 12 VIII 12.3
T 27 V 5.5
T 18 IX

To do anything involves the body. And if you recognize you need do nothing, you have withdrawn the body's value from your mind. Here is the quick and open door through which you slip past centuries of effort, and escape from time. This is the way in which sin loses all attraction right now. ...Who needs do nothing has no need for time.

T 11 III 6.3-4   T 18 VII 7

Thus he becomes uncertain of his life, for what it is has been denied by him. It is for this denial that you need Atonement. Your denial made no change in what you are. But you have split your mind into what knows and does not know the truth. You are yourself. There is no doubt of this. And yet you doubt it. But you do not ask what part of you can really doubt yourself. It cannot really be a part of you that asks this question. For it asks of one who knows the answer. Were it part of you, then certainty would be impossible.

What am I?

Truth cannot question itself or it could not be true.

W 139 5   W PII 14

The miracle acknowledges His changelessness by seeing His Son as he always was, and not as he would make himself. The miracle brings the effects that only guiltlessness can bring, and thus establishes the fact that guiltlessness must be.

And from this point of safety he looks quietly about him and recognizes that the world is one with him.

Can you see guilt where God knows there is perfect innocence? You can deny His knowledge, but you cannot change it.

Save time for me by only this one preparation, and practice doing nothing else. "I need do nothing" is a statement of allegiance, a truly undivided loyalty. Believe it for just one instant, and you will accomplish more than is given to a century of contemplation, or of struggle against temptation.

By accepting the Atonement for yourself, you are deciding against the belief that you can be alone, thus dispelling the idea of separation and affirming your true identification with the whole Kingdom as literally part of you. This identification is as beyond doubt as it is beyond belief. Your wholeness has no limits because being is infinity.

The Atonement is a lesson in sharing, which is given you because you have forgotten how to do it. *The Holy Spirit merely reminds you of the natural use of your abilities. By reinterpreting the ability to attack into the ability to share, He translates what you have made into what God created.*

We are all joined in the Atonement here, and nothing else can unite us in this world. So will the world of separation slip away, and full communication be restored between the Father and the Son.

It is as needful that you recognize you made the world you see, as that you recognize that you did not create yourself. They are the same mistake. *Nothing created not by your Creator has any influence over you.*

Be not separate from me, and let not the holy purpose of Atonement be lost to you in dreams of vengeance. Relationships in which such dreams are cherished have excluded me. Let me enter in the Name of God and bring you peace, that you may offer peace to me.

Look, then, upon the light He placed within you, and learn that what you feared was there has been replaced with love.

He must be saviour from the dream he made, that he be free of it. He must see someone else as not a body, one with him without the wall the world has built to keep apart all living things who know not that they live.

The miracle is the means, the Atonement is the principle, and healing is the result. To speak of "a miracle of healing" is to combine two orders of reality inappropriately. Healing is not a miracle. The Atonement, or the final miracle, is a remedy [cause] *and any type of healing is a result* [effect]. *...All healing is essentially the release from fear.*

The God of resurrection demands nothing, for He does not will to take away. He does not require obedience, for obedience implies submission. He would only have you learn your will and follow it, not in the spirit of sacrifice and submission, but in the gladness of freedom.

T 18 VII 6.6-8   T 7 VIII 7.3-6   T 9 IV 1.1-3   T 14 V 5.1-2   T 21 II 11.1-3   T 17 III 10.6-8   T 13 IX 8.13
T 29 III 2.6-7   T 2 IV 1.2   T 11 VI 5.6-9

Whenever any form of special relationship tempts you to seek for love in ritual, remember love is content, and not form of any kind.

The perception of goodness is not knowledge, but the denial of the opposite of goodness enables you to recognize a condition in which opposites do not exist. And this is the condition of knowledge. Without this awareness you have not met its conditions, and until you do you will not know it is yours already.

The prayer of the heart does not really ask for concrete things. It always requests some kind of experience, the specific things asked for being the bringers of the desired experience in the opinion of the asker.

If you did not have a split mind, you would recognize that willing is salvation because it is communication.

It is not up to you to change your brother, but merely to accept him as he is. His errors do not come from the truth that is in him… To perceive errors in anyone, and to react to them as if they were real, is to make them real to you. You will not escape paying the price for this… because you are following the wrong guide…

Ask not to be forgiven, for this has already been accomplished. Ask, rather, to learn how to forgive, and to restore what always was to your unforgiving mind. Atonement becomes real and visible to those who use it. On earth this is your only function, and you must learn that it is all you want to learn. You will feel guilty till you learn this.

I am in charge of the process of Atonement, which I undertook to begin. When you offer a miracle to any of my brothers, you do it to yourself and me. The reason you come before me is that I do not need miracles for my own Atonement, but I stand at the end in case you fail temporarily. My part in the Atonement is the cancelling out of all errors that you could not otherwise correct. When you have been restored to the recognition of your original state, you naturally become part of the Atonement yourself. As you share my unwillingness to accept error in yourself and others, you must join the great crusade to correct it; listen to my voice, learn to undo error and act to correct it. The power to work miracles belongs to you. I will provide the opportunities to do them, but you must be ready and willing. Doing them will bring conviction in the ability, because conviction comes through accomplishment. The ability is the potential, the achievement is its expression, and the Atonement, which is the natural profession of the children of God, is the purpose.

Beyond the body, beyond the sun and stars, past everything you see and yet somehow familiar, is an arc of golden light that stretches as you look into a great and shining circle. And all the circle fills with light before your eyes. The edges of the circle disappear, and what is in it is no longer contained at all. The light expands and covers everything, extending to infinity forever shining and with no break or limit anywhere. Within it everything is joined in perfect continuity. Nor is it possible to imagine that anything could be outside, for there is nowhere that this light is not.

T 16 V 12.1   T 11 VII 4.1-3   M 21 2.4-5   T 9 I 5.4   T 9 III 5   T 14 IV 3.4-7   T 1 III 1   T 21 I 8

Also He understands how your relationship is raised above the battleground, in it no more. This is your part; to realise that murder in any form is not your will. The overlooking of the battleground is now your purpose.

T 23 IV 4.5-7
T 30 I 8.1-2, 11.4

...you can begin to change your mind with this: At least I can decide I do not like what I feel now.

I want another way to look at this.

There is no veil the Love of God

in us together

cannot lift.

The way to truth is open.

Follow it with

T 16 I 13.9-11

Quiz

1. The serpent in the Garden of Eden represents A) your authority problem B) your wish to kill C) either A or B, because they are essentially the same.

2. To perceive correctly, the "tables of the world" must be turned how many degrees? A) 90 B) 180 C) 360.

3. You are jealous of your neighbor, and, in trying to understand which law of chaos is being most evoked within you, what law of chaos are you most evoking? A) 1st B) 2nd C) 3rd D) 4th E) 5th.

4. You are angry at your ex because they took away all that you love and worked so hard for. Yet your anger is not justified because A) you are the imaginer of it all in a deep, fantastical sleep B) you hated your ex before they hated you C) you valued your specialness over peace

D) by their guilt, you seek to mentally kill them and claim their innocence and life E) all of the above.

5. T or F: The world represents fear and death·in the mind because it is not changeless and not eternal.

6. What represents true forgiveness? A) "I forgive someone because they harmed me" B) "I forgive myself for attacking myself to separate (and then feeling angry, frustrated and victimized by the separation dream I choose)."

7. T or F: The Son of God and the ego must share the same laws of mind, because God created these laws.

8. The purpose of perceiving oneself a victim is not to A) indulge the idol of self B) "kill" God C) love one another D) breath "life" into separation.

9. T or F: Of thought, God is the "power plant"—without which you could not think—yet the ego must convince you that your mind and thoughts are "off the grid".

10. T or F: To not see that you are the imaginer of others is to keep them apart from you.

11. T or F: Your own body is amongst everyone else's that you use, in sacrifice, to shield your mind against God's "vengeance".

12. In a special relationship, the ego's purpose is not to: A) bury the awareness of guilt with "love" B) shift guilt from yourself to the other when they "fail" you C) show you who you are as God created you.

13. Adam and Eve covering themselves with fig leaves is an example of: A) sin B) magic C) the miracle.

14. What is the basic ego threat? A) vision: you seeing that fear is what separates you from God B) truth C) faith D) not having one's specialness properly appreciated by others.

15. T or F: Death and separation do not exist in reality because they only represent the ideas of death and separation, and ideas cannot die or separate from their source. Therefore they are imagined effects from no real cause.

16. Which of the following is true? You secretly think that death will A) get you what you want B) prove that you are more mighty than God C) enable you to become your own god D) convince you that your body—and thus ego—is real E) all of the above.

17. T or F: "If you have more talent or success than I, it means that you took them from me and therefore you deserve death", and shcoden-freude (meaning the pleasure in perceiving another's misfortune), are both good examples of sacrifice.

18. Jill has unfounded imaginings that Jack is cheating on her. The purpose of this is to A) convince herself that she is innocent by his guilt B) see Jack's holiness.

19. The way the ego "frees" you from guilt is to A) wear a hair shirt B) make someone else pay C) be a rock star D) all of the above.

20. If an upsetting, random, ugly attack thought such as "I want to kill you" or "you are disgusting" pops into your head it is because: A) aliens put it there B) devil worshipers cast a hex on you C) you are projecting your ego's secret dream of self-attack onto your psyche.

21. If your purpose is to rule your environment, how can you be safe? A) establish stronger defenses B) probe for weakness, fault and evil pasts in someone else and save these for later C) change your purpose to ruling your mind by accepting Christ.

22. If your purpose is to join with the Holy Spirit and forgive, how can you be hurt? A) you cannot, because then you could not attack yourself B) if you also retain your wish to be separate C) A and B.

23. To hear a chorus joined and singing beautifully as one–is that a form of attack? A) yes, because if it is perceived apart from you it is of the ego B) no, because perceiving as one is not attack C) that depends on whom (the ego or the Holy Spirit) you join with in listening.

24. T or F: The vainglory pleasure of control, the righteousness of conquest, the excitement of victory and the amour of victimization are all forms of fear.

25. T or F: Guilt-perception makes sin seem real and hides God from your awareness.

26. Buying a lottery ticket and praying that it win is an example of A) the miracle B) sin as an adjustment C) the holy instant. And the real reason for trying to win your conflicts is to A) make your world better B) have higher "truth" than your adversary and God.

27. The world is an illusion because A) mind cannot attack itself B) God did not create it C) It grows from and on the idea that ideas can be harmed and die D) it is an invented "alternate reality" from the determination to reject the laws of God E) all of the above.

28. T or F: My recurrent knee pain has the identical cause as that of my government's puppeteers' evil doings, which resides in my mind.

29. The miracle is A) perceiving correctly B) attracting wealth and status correctly.

30. You as a body-person in this world are A) an idea within your mind B) an expression of God.

31. There is no order of difficulty in miracles because A) there is one solution B) there is one problem C) both A and B.

32. Praising God keeps temptation at bay because it is A) a mantra B) magic C) a miracle
It works because it reaches to the A) Cause B) effect.

33. ...*gratitude is but an aspect of the Love which is the Source of all creation* (W 195 10.3) because: A) gratitude is an expression of acceptance and inclusion B) being thankful is a means to manipulate and seduce to get my needs met C) gratitude is sacrifice.

34. T or F: to seek for happiness from the outside is to secretly embrace deception and ...*a blackness so complete that you could hide from truth forever, in complete insanity.* (T 18 III 1.5).

35. T or F: "God is punishing me", lack, and jealousy all reflect the 4th law of chaos, which the 5th law attempts to remedy.

36. T or F: To accept the Atonement for oneself is also to forgive oneself and to save the world.

37. You feel badly because a foolish mistake you made cost your family much security. This is: A) guilt B) a means to hide your wish to kill and to have no security, thus "proving" your specialness apart from God C) both A and B.

38. "I want specialness and thus I expel and thus I am separated and thus I am deprived and thus must reclaim what is mine." T or F: these are the laws with which the world bases its happiness upon.

39. T of F: A commonality of Christianity and *A Course In Miracles* is faith in Jesus: to invite Him into your heart that He deliver you from darkness.

40. If partaking of any of the "seven deadly sins" (wrath, greed, sloth, pride, lust, envy, gluttony), one hurts oneself because: A) one has purposefully turned away from God and He therefore must condemn you to eternal damnation B) one has purposefully turned away from God and thus has attacked oneself.

41. One can never find respite from conflict and pain if one identifies with the body-person-world (bpw) because: A) identifying with the bpw is the cause of conflict and pain B) others' resolutions will always be different from yours.

42. Which does not apply: you can perceive sameness here by A) realizing that you and the other share the same need and purpose of salvation in Christ, even if the other claims to be an atheist B) seeing everyone as sinless, because there is only one sinlessness C) seeing everything here as interconnected in the "web of life" D) seeing everyone as an idea with the same cause and therefore being the same effect.

43. T or F: By thinking yourself a bpw, you have first not decided to diss God and to kiss death.

44. T or F: One can never find salvation as a bpw because, in trying to do so, one attacks oneself to cannibalize one's wholeness, and because the "saving" bpw's idols must fail since, by definition, one must keep them outside and apart from one's mind.

45. T or F: In one's mind one can instantly change an enemy into a brother by assigning to them the same purpose of healing as oneself, and one can heal oneself by seeing them as sinless.

46. If you interpret another's insensitivity as real, it is because: A) you secretly feel guilty about being insensitive B) you do not see their acting out as a cry for help C) you think healing comes from without, and therefore you can help them by telling them off D) all of the above.

47. How can one practice remedying distress in any situation? A) In your mind, see with the Holy Spirit that conflict is the result of one's secret dream of murder, decide that you would rather have His Peace, and believe only your Truth B) start yelling at the phone.

48. T or F: one attacks oneself if one's wish is to value and see another's sinlessness.

49. T or F: Correcting behavior, self-blame, and blaming others are all the same because they serve the same purpose of keeping you from seeing all problems as ideas in your mind which you make-believe to keep your Father as separate from you.

50. If you have a bad feeling about someone you just met, it indicates that: A) you and they have negative past karma B) your intuition is warning you to stay clear C) you are imagining that you are evil and are projecting this onto them.

51. A violent criminal who everyone thinks of as "bad" is that way because: A) he was abused as a child B) everyone sees their perception of him as being not of their own imagining, and therefore does not recognize his true innocence C) his current character.

52. T of F: You heal another by not acknowledging their sickness as real, whereas before you both joined in its "reality" by imagining it.

53. T or F: God cannot recognize anything as separate from Himself because A) He created everything which cannot be not of Him B) ideas leave not there source C) Cause and Effect are one D) all of the above.

54. To trust another is to A) realize that you are forever guiltless, no matter what they do B) give them your car keys.

55. An idol is: A) an idea B) anything or anybody that you see outside yourself that you think will save you or make you happy C) something that will fail you. D) a body, someone or something whom you have first given your strength to such that now you feel lack and seek satisfaction from them E) all of the above.

56. You react to your friend's greed with disappointment. Why is this really your error? A) you do not see that his error does not come from the truth in him B) You do not see that your disappointment does not come from the truth in you. C) A and B.

57. One feels fatigue because of: A) overwork, over-exercise, stress, sickness, or lack of sleep B) one has imagined the idea of fatigue and placed it outside of one's mind and into a body where its "reality" becomes believed, thus "proving" separation. Thus bodily and worldly impulses and solutions inhabit the realm of A) cause B) effect.

58. A good miracle mantra would be A) "I am the happy manifester and attracter of the world I want" B) "By sacrifice it was given me" C) "I am the dreamer of this dream".

59. Which sin— A) gluttony B) pride C) wrath —matches with which law of chaos?: 1) 2nd 2) 5th 3) 1st.

60. Whatever does not last is a form of fear. How then can one be happy in a relationship? A) let the Holy Spirit accept your "other" for you, that you can give them to Him B) spend extra time with a person to fulfill each other's expectations C) realize you don't have to do anything D) let Jesus be in charge of it E) everything except B).

61. T or F: "If an outside person/ circumstance is the cause of my pleasure or pain, I am under their/ its control and surrender my strength. Yet if I see that they and the feelings they evoke are my imagined ideas in my mind, my power remains as mine and they can have no dominion over me."

62. You think you are upset because the car doesn't start. But why, really, are you upset? A) you don't make enough money to buy a new car B) you just replaced the battery last year. C) you have desired specialness, attacked everything, felt guilty, chosen punishment by reviewing a dream of a dead car, and interpreted this dream with anger so as to try to rid the guilt from your mind to the battery.

63. Someone is upset because they think they are having a chronic illness. What should they do? A) ask the Holy Spirit to accept the miracle for them, that they see that they are the imaginer of sickness to protect and enhance their specialness B) go to a doctor, nutritionist, or practice yoga C) A, or A and B.

64. T or F: The world teaches that self attack is displaced outside onto one's problems and conflicts.

65. Why is it impossible to love especially here without ambiguity? A) self-betrayal must find a scapegoat B) that's just the way it is until the right person is found C) that would not be an issue if others were as clean as me.

66. Why is a person, who is watching a sporting event on television, really upset? A) he doesn't like his tv B) he does not want to see that the tv is broadcasting his thoughts C) his team is losing.

67. Picture seeing a brick wall. Which aspect of the wall could be seen to represent both the ego's function and the Holy Spirit's function? A) an individual brick B) the mortar C) the wall as a whole.

68. The goal of forgiveness is to A) remove guilt from your mind B) see the world as harmless C) love you enemies.

69. T or F: The holy relationship involves the process of practicing forgiveness and joining in Christ's purpose within a special relationship framework.

70. The Holy Spirit cannot remove guilt until one sees that it is A) all within one's own mind by one's own desire B) all outside oneself. This is because healing takes place at the A) cause B) effect.

71. You do not realize that you can never not be as God created you because A) you have forgotten who you are B) you want to be clueless C) both A and B.

72. T or F: Upon understanding that you are the author of all your fear, your fear will still chase you all over the place, and you will still chase its forms you think you like.

73. T or F: To think that the world can affect you is to believe in psychosis.

74. T or F: To be at the effect level is to realize that everyone and everything in the world here is all part of your mind, and is of your imagination.

75. To be happy, what should you place your faith in? A) the purpose of forgiveness B) the purpose of striving in the world.

What do you want?

Answers

1. C
2. B
3. A -as in a hierarchy of laws
4. E
5. T
6. B
7. T
8. C
9. T
10. T
11. T
12. C
13. B
14. A -T 11 V 10.1 in 2 V B, 3 II C
15. T
16. E
17. T
18. A
19. D
20. C
21. C
22. C
23. C
24. T
25. T
26. B, B
27. E
28. T
29. A
30. A
31. C
32. C, A
33. A
34. T
35. T

36. T
37. C
38. T
39. T
40. B
41. A
42. C
43. F
44. T
45. T
46. D
47.
48. F
49. T
50. C
51. B
52. T
53. D
54. A
55. E
56. C
57. B, B
58. C
59. A) 5th B) 1st C) 2nd
60. E
61. T
62. C
63. C
64. F
65. A
66. B
67. B -which can symbolize the function of either separation or joining
68. A -B and C are effects of A
69. T
70. A, A
71. C
72. F
73. T -W 6
74. F

75. A

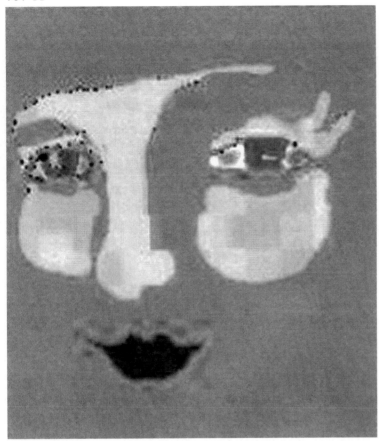

Artwork references

All diagrams composed and arranged with quotes and text by author except: "Teddies" (bears); "I am not a Body"; face with "the sences…"; green face with "do you want…"; by Robert D Scott.

All hand drawn artwork within diagrams by Robert D Scott, except "Newton", stick figures, rat and rider, earths, lower fox and sun (intro "what if you…"), hands/forearms, green hungry ghost, and shot down airplane by author.

All included photography, some digital coloring/ modifications where applicable by author. Year of completion omitted if unknown.

INTRODUCTION: R D Scott: cover figures "Father and Son"; arguing couple; a better way; "Abywho and Cie" (dogs); man and fan cartoon (concept by author); "Seneca"-upper fox ("Fox Trot")-"Medieval Lady" with photo: "Wind Rivers Flowers"; painted mask and top figures; foreground rat and rider and "Jacob Zuma" (head);   "Theological Seagull" C R Scott 1987; "Tombstones IV" (detail) C R Scott 1994; "The Cupids" (digital) R D Scott 2015

1 II   "Lady" R D Scott   1 II B: "Flocked II" C R Scott 1997 1 II C: "Runoff" C R Scott 1990   1 II D: "Magi" R D Scott; "Dove" (digital) R D Scott   1 II E: "Frontier Couple" (woodcut) R D Scott; "Shades" (trees) R D Scott   1 III: all figures including "Savage", "Kindly Dictator", "Lucky Ducky", "In Transition" R D Scott   1 IV: "He Sent Forth the Dove" (woodcut) R D Scott; from "MLK JR" R D Scott; sheep and all other figures R D Scott   1 V: "Desert Dawn" (detail) C R Scott 1991; "In Prayer" (digital) R D Scott; "ACIM 101" C R Scott 2006

2:   "Woodland Witch" (woodcut) R D Scott 2014; "Devil" (digital, modified by author)   R D Scott 2013   2 I A: "Narcissists" R D Scott 2013   2 I B: "People in Room with Light Bulb" (digital) R D Scott 2008   2 II: "Twisted" C R Scott 1988;   photo: "St Mary Lake, MT"; falling figures R D Scott   2 III: "But It Was Only Fantasy" C R Scott 1993   2 III A: "Scream" R D Scott   2 III B: all figures R D Scott   2 IV: "Title Unknown"   C R Scott 1988; "Hula"/ "slurp" R D Scott; "Star Gazers" digital R D Scott; "Red Eye" (rabbit) and figures in rabbit hole R D Scott;   2 V B: "Of Everything That Stands" C R Scott 1994;   ant and grasshopper from "Grasshopper is Good" R D Scott   2 VI: "Somewhere Else" C R Scott 1995   2 VI A: "V Tombstones" detail C R Scott 2007 2 VI C: "Subway City" R D Scott; face with hands R D Scott; "Fishbones" C R Scott 1987; cat and figures R D Scott; 2 VI D: "Clock" R D Scott; "Tundra and Dillon's Field" C R Scott 1992; figures from "Sixteenth Century Herb Garden" R D

Scott; "Wolf Dreams" C R Scott 2008 2 VI E: "Pharos Mom" (woodcut) detail R D Scott 2015; figures, dog R D Scott with photo: "Denali" ; photo: "New Orleans Street"; "Woman Graphic" (woodcut) R D Scott; knight and dragon R D Scott 2 VII: "Shouting a Question" C R Scott 1990; photo/ digital composite: "Hadrians Wall" C R Scott 2014; mask, bat from "King Lear" R D Scott; "What if its not real?" R D Scott; : diagrams include "Inca", "Jitterbug", "Seated Woman", "The Man With The Hat", naked couple, R D Scott 2 VII: dancing figures R D Scott with photo detail: "Lupines" 2 VII B: "Two Eggs Are Better Than One" R D Scott 2 VII C: head with hands R D Scott 2 VIII A "Tombstones II" C R Scott 1990 2 VIII C: "Man Waiting" R D Scott 2015 2 IX: "Blue Bus" C R Scott 1991 2 IX A: untitled geometry C R Scott 1988 2 IX C: "Descending Wrath" C R Scott 1994; "Grand Canyon 87" C R Scott 1987; "Faces" R D Scott 2 IX D "Kung Fu" R D Scott 2 X: man at piano, eagle R D Scott

3: untitled faces R D Scott 2017 3 I: "Sunworshiper"/"Shades 1" R D Scott 3 I A: "Henry VIII and Friends" R D Scott 3 II B: photo/ pyramid: "Mnt Shasta" 3 I C: "Bonzeye Rain Forest" C R Scott 1995 3 II: "2nd Stage Taridactyl" C R Scott 1994; "Earth Day (digital) R D Scott 2015; "Road to Damascus" C R Scott 2013 3 II A: "Poodle" R D Scott 3 II B: "Girl with Glasses, Boy Turtleneck" R D Scott 2015; "Windy Sun" C R Scott 1997; "Teddies" R D Scott 2015, "Out to Lunch" R D Scott "Moses" (digital) R D Scott 2015 3 II C: "People In Room With Light Bulb" (digital) R D Scott 2008; photo: "Wind Rivers Flowers b"; "Old Mountain Man" R D Scott 2015; "High Plains Sunrise" C R Scott 1996; "Quietly and Clean" C R Scott 1992 3 III: "Techno Man" R D Scott; TJS/ CRS/ "Renaissance Man"/ "The Seven Ages of Man" R D Scott; "King Lear" R D Scott 1977; chess pieces C R Scott 1973

Quiz: "Giant Tree" (woodcut) R D Scott, "Heaven, Not Hell" (digital) R D Scott

Made in United States
Orlando, FL
19 May 2022

17999709R00193